LIMITS

of the

KNOWN

LIMITS

of the

KNOWN

David Roberts

W. W. NORTON & COMPANY

INDEPENDENT PUBLISHERS SINCE 1923

NEW YORK | LONDON

For information about permission to reproduce selections from this book, write to
Permissions, W. W. Norton & Company, Inc., 500 Fifth Avenue, New York, NY 10110

For information about special discounts for bulk purchases, please contact
W. W. Norton Special Sales at specialsales@wwnorton.com or 800-233-4830

Manufacturing by LSC Harrisonburg
Book design by Daniel Lagin
Production manager: Beth Steidle

Library of Congress Cataloging-in-Publication Data

Names: Roberts, David, 1943– author.
Title: Limits of the known / David Roberts.
Description: First edition. | New York : W. W. Norton & Company, 2018. |
Includes bibliographical references.
Identifiers: LCCN 2017048507 | ISBN 9780393609868 (hardcover)
Subjects: LCSH: Roberts, David, 1943– | Mountaineering—History. | Adventure and
adventurers—History. | Mountaineers—United States—Biography. | Adventure
and adventurers—United States—Biography.
Classification: LCC GV199.92.R624 A3 2018 | DDC 796.522092 [B]—dc23
LC record available at https://lccn.loc.gov/2017048507

ISBN 978-0-393-35659-5 pbk.

W. W. Norton & Company, Inc.
500 Fifth Avenue, New York, N.Y. 10110
www.wwnorton.com

W. W. Norton & Company Ltd.
15 Carlisle Street, London W1D 3BS

1 2 3 4 5 6 7 8 9 0

For Sharon—
Then, now, and forever

Contents

Prologue

In June 2015, Matt Hale and I spent nine days in Alaska. We were anxious about our mission: if our visit failed to generate the kind of enthusiasm we hoped for, we'd return to our homes in Virginia and Massachusetts humbled and depressed.

It was our plan to give slide shows in Anchorage and Talkeetna celebrating the fiftieth anniversary of our first ascent of the west face of Mount Huntington. That climb had been in many respects the cardinal achievement of our careers as mountaineers. Now I was seventy-two, Matt seventy-one. We'd be reliving the exploit we had performed at twenty-two and twenty-one. But what if nobody cared about some long-ago climb? What if only sparse gatherings showed up in the auditoriums we had rented? What if a trickle of polite applause for our antiquarian adventure was all we might wring from those jaded attendees?

We had reason to hope otherwise. Back in 1965, as we set our eyes on the soaring wall on one of the most beautiful mountains in the world, we told ourselves that if we got up the route, we could claim bragging rights to "the hardest thing yet done in Alaska." Huntington had been climbed only once by any route, just the year before, when eight crack Frenchmen led by the legendary Lionel Terray—Matt's and my hero for his expeditions all over the world, from Annapurna to Fitz Roy—had struggled for a month before taming the northwest ridge.

Young though we were, the four of us felt that we had enough experience under our belts to prepare us for a challenge as daunting as the west face. Don Jensen and I were the veterans of two previous Alaskan expeditions, one of which had made the first direct ascent of the Wickersham Wall, Mount McKinley's north face, at 14,000 feet from base to summit the tallest precipice in the Western Hemisphere. And though Matt and Ed Bernd had never before been on an expedition, they had proved their mettle on trips to the Colorado Rockies in winter, the ice gullies of Mount Washington's Huntington Ravine, and crags such as Cannon and Cathedral in New Hampshire. It was the Harvard Mountaineering Club that had brought us together, and in the early 1960s the HMC was the leading collegiate climbing organization in the country.

We spent forty days in July and August 1965 on the Tokositna Glacier and the west face. During the first twenty-five days, plagued by horrendous weather and nightmarish logistics, we got almost nowhere. Our morale plunged in the teeth of Huntington's stern demands, and we began to think that after all we weren't good enough for such a route. But slowly we inched our way upward, toward the near-vertical headwall where the serious climbing began. And then, seizing a stretch of five days of perfect weather, we blitzed our way to the top, all four roped together. We stood on the summit at 3:30 AM on July 30, the thirty-second day of the expedition.

During the next few years, our Huntington climb acquired a certain cachet. I wrote my first book, *The Mountain of My Fear*, about the expedition, and gradually that narrative gained the status of a minor adventure classic. Other climbers tipped their caps to our feat. As late as 2009, one of them, Doug Robinson, wrote, "I'll say it was the state-of-the-art alpine climb in the world [to that date]."

By 2015, Matt and I had been for more than four decades the only surviving members of our team. Only twenty hours after we stood on top, Ed Bernd was killed when his rappel anchor failed and he plunged, without a word, 4,000 feet to his death. And in 1973 Don Jensen died when he was hit by a truck while bicycling to work at a university in Scotland.

In Talkeetna and Anchorage, Matt's and my fears that no one would care about our ancient deed proved gloriously unfounded. The auditoriums were packed. Raucous attendees hooted at the photos of our period gear (goldline ropes, Kelty packs), but cheered our moves on the golden granite of the upper wall. The applause at the end was long, and folks came up to chat; some even sought our autographs. We both signed copies of *The Mountain of My Fear*, still in print forty-seven years after Vanguard Press rescued it from the slush pile.

The whole return to Alaska was halcyon. We greeted old cronies we hadn't seen in years, and downed beers with some of the best young climbers who live in the Far North today. We gossiped about unclimbed prizes off in the hinterlands as if we still imagined that we might do battle with them.

Matt and I hoped to fly around Huntington. I'd made two trips by small plane past the scene of our triumph in later years, but Matt hadn't seen the west face in half a century. Alas, the Alaska Range stayed socked in during the span of our visit, just as the storms had seemed to doom our chances in 1965. We never got to fly.

As we walked the dirt streets of Talkeetna, marveling at the gift shops and restaurants that had turned the town into a tourist mecca, we stopped in at the only landmarks that had been there fifty years before—the Fairview Inn, the Roadhouse (famed for its gargantuan breakfasts), and the B & K Trading Post, whose candy counter the two great bush pilots of the day, Don Sheldon and Cliff Hudson, had shattered in an epic fistfight. The arts center where Matt and I gave our slideshow had been converted from Sheldon's hangar, inside which the four of us had camped as we waited for the skies to clear so that the pilot could fly us in to the Tokositna.

Yet our rambles through the streets of Talkeetna had a melancholy tinge. The old dirt runway Sheldon used for takeoffs and landings, overgrown with weeds, conjured up the bursting ambitions we had nursed in 1965, when all of Alaska gleamed with peaks and routes no one had attempted. Knowing that we would never again set forth so boldly into the unknown, Matt and I now heard the mournful echo of the siren song that had sounded so keen in our youthful ears.

And Talkeetna was redolent with memories of the glum aftermath of our Huntington expedition, when the three of had slowly packed our gear, while the hours ticked off until I faced the dreadful duty that had hung over us since midnight on July 30—the phone call to Ed's parents in Pennsylvania, when I would have to tell them what had happened to their son.

———

On our second day in Talkeetna, as we sat in our motel room planning the day's activities, I noticed a small lump on the right side of my neck. I wondered if it was located on a lymph node, or only nearby. I asked Matt to look at it. He'd had a cyst on the back of his neck the year before, much larger than my incipient lump. Though it became annoying, after he had the cyst lanced and took a course of antibiotics, it cleared up completely.

Matt's guess was that my lump was also a cyst. Through the rest of our Alaska trip, I didn't worry about it. But on the long plane flight home, I noticed that the lump had grown a little. It was hard to the touch, but not at all painful.

Back in Boston, I went to my general practitioner. He didn't think the lump was a cyst. To be safe, he ordered, in succession, an ultrasound, a CT scan, and a needle biopsy, none of which produced a clear

result. So I turned to a Dr. Wang for an open biopsy, with local anesthetic. By this time, the lump had grown considerably beyond the swell-
ing I had noticed in Alaska.

The suspicion voiced by all the doctors who had seen me so far was
that I had lymphoma. The few friends I told about my worries were
quick to reassure me, citing other friends who had quickly bounced
back from such a malignancy. But now, as he completed his work, Dr.
Wang said, "I don't think it's lymphoma."

I felt a surge of relief. "What is it, then?"

The doctor hesitated. "I don't want to freak you out, but I think it
could be throat cancer."

That verdict was soon confirmed. The official name of my ailment
was squamous oropharyngeal carcinoma. In early July I was assigned a
trio of experts at Dana–Farber, one of the best cancer hospitals in the
world. My team was made up of a surgeon, a radiologist, and a general
oncologist. They seemed in a hurry to start treatment. I had been reading up on my diagnosis on the Internet, and now I asked my doctors,
"What stage?"

"Stage four," one of them admitted.

I sucked in my breath. The scale of stages, I knew, went no higher
than four. The general oncologist quickly added, "That's not the same
as, for example, stage four melanoma." Coincidentally, stage four melanoma was what my father had died of in 1990, at the age of seventy-four.
His last two years had amounted to a steady decline into pain and help-
lessness, punctuated by short bursts of hope for illusory cures.

"What are my chances, then?" I asked.

None of the doctors would answer. After an uncomfortable pause,
the radiologist said, "We believe that our treatment regimen can be
effective."

The experts did explain their choice of procedures. Surgery, normally the first resort, was ruled out in my case, because the carcinoma

was already widespread. Worse, it was bilateral—present on both sides of my neck and throat.

On July 20, I began treatment: six weeks of once-a-week high-dose chemotherapy, followed by a week or two of rest, followed by thirty-five doses of daily radiation (they would give me weekends off) stretching across seven weeks, with once-a-week chemo on top of the zapping. On October 29, the onslaught would end.

The treatment felt weird. Both the chemo and radiation were tedious though painless, but slowly my body grew weaker and weaker. In April, just two months before going to Alaska, I had joyously rock climbed with a gang of old friends near St. George, Utah. By November, I could barely walk a single city block, having to stop, sit down, and rest every fifty yards. Four times during the treatment, I had to go to the emergency room, for setbacks ranging from constipation to fainting. For weeks, I could eat almost nothing, yet I vomited my guts out almost every other day.

In October, I had to be admitted to Brigham and Women's Hospital (Dana–Farber's sister institution), after nausea, vomiting, and aspiration pneumonia left me unable to cope at home. For two weeks, I hardly left my hospital bed as, drugged with painkillers, fed intravenously, I drifted in and out of consciousness. In fourteen days, I managed to read only a third of a Lee Child thriller. Sharon, my wife, stayed with me as many hours of the day as she could, and slept most nights on a cot beside my bed. I clung to her desperately, as she dealt with nurses and doctors whose queries and ministrations only feebly pierced the miasma of my predicament.

The doctors had told me that recovery would last from one to three months. Perhaps the experts lay out that rosy prescription to allay the fears of the victims whose bodies they assault with poisonous rays and chemicals. Or perhaps my oncologists were reluctant to admit that the treatment they had had to marshal against my cancer had fallen on the severe end of the spectrum. But more than four months after my last submission to the smothering green plastic mask, bolted to the table, through which the techies aimed the lethal radiation, I still felt like a cripple.

By February I could walk a mile, slowly. My salivary glands were shot for good, so I knew I would have to carry a water bottle with me for constant sipping the rest of my life. I never felt hungry, and eating—mostly yogurt, soups, smoothies, soft pastas, and the like—was a daily chore, a pleasureless regimen through which I grimly tried to keep my weight at the emaciated plateau to which I had sunk after losing thirty pounds. To complement that intake, I used a feeding tube protruding from a hole in my stomach to force down cans of Ensure.

A dry, hacking cough that had begun in August was still with me. Radiation had ruined the hearing in my left ear and compromised what was left in the right. Movies were impossible, and my beloved classical music was reduced to screeching noise. Reading became my chief pleasure, as I tore through four or five books a week. During the seven months after I started treatment, except for stints in the hospital I spent not a single night away from home, and ate in a restaurant only once. On top of these deprivations, I felt a constant, overwhelming fatigue. After nine hours of sleep (plagued by dreams in which I was whole again), I would wake exhausted.

In February 2016, at Dana–Farber, I had CT and PET scans to ascertain how well the treatment had eradicated the cancer. The verdict was mixed. It looked as though the carcinoma in my throat and neck was gone, but several new nodules in my chest could be malignant. They were too small to biopsy, so I had to wait two months to see if they grew or diminished. At worst, they might herald the metastasis of cancer to a new part of my body. If so, I would start over, with tubes pumping newer poisons into my veins as chemotherapy made a last-ditch campaign to keep me alive.

In November 2015, my latest book had appeared. The publisher had set up a tour with my coauthor, the climbing wunderkind Alex Honnold, that would have taken me across the country, beginning with a launch at the Banff Mountain Film and Book Festival. I had been eagerly awaiting the tour, but now I had to cancel my part in it altogether. Likewise, I canceled an autumn trip to the Southwest, the latest installment in my biannual pilgrimage to the canyon country that has become my favorite place on earth.

Instead, cancer plunged me into a reassessment of life itself—of mortality, of the meaning of worldly aspiration, of the value of love and friendship. For more than fifty years, I had thought of myself as an adventurer. During the first two decades, adventure meant mountain climbing. And once getting up the west face of Mount Huntington had ceased to be the most important thing in life, I sought out other kinds of adventure all over the world.

For me, the passion was always allied to discovery and exploration. That was what made adventure so much more than a sport. Attempting a first ascent in Alaska, I was driven by the giddy awareness that no one before me had ever laid hand or foot on the perilous stretch of rock or snow I traversed. Later, I felt the same sense of discovery as I rode a raft down a river in Ethiopia that no one had ever run. And even now, in southeast Utah, when I climb to an alcove high on a sheer sandstone cliff where seven hundred years ago the Anasazi stored their precious corn, in rediscovering that *locus mirabilis* I taste a communion with vanished ancients whose worldview we only dimly comprehend.

From 1981 on, I made my living as a freelance writer. In magazine articles and books, I sought to explicate not only my own compulsions but those of kindred souls, whether they were today's elite practitioners of their esoteric trades or figures from history whose motivations I could fathom only through their deeds and their writings. The fun-house mirrors those men and women held up to me only deepened my grasp of the complex phenomenon of adventure.

Climbers and other explorers are notoriously inarticulate when it comes to explaining why they spend their lives pursuing phantom goals. Yet in the end, *why* is the ultimate question.

Cancer, with its foreshadowing of my own mortality, has injected a sharp new urgency into that eternal conundrum, on whose margins I have skated throughout my adult life.

Why have I spent my life trying to find the lost and unknown places of this world? What benefit has that pursuit brought to others? What has my passion cost me in missed opportunities to connect with those who do not share my desire?

And what have the passions of explorers across human history delivered to our understanding of life? What did it mean in 1911 to reach the South Pole, or the highest point on earth in 1953? What is the future of adventure, if any, in a world we have mapped and trodden all the way to the most remote corners of the wilderness?

Why do we do it? Why do we care? Why does it matter?

The purpose of this book is to grope toward an answer.

ONE

FARTHEST NORTH

"It is always hard to part," observed Fridtjof Nansen, "even at 84°, and maybe there was a tearful eye or two."

The date was March 14, 1895. The ship carrying the thirteen members of Nansen's expedition, the *Fram*, had been frozen fast in the sea ice for eighteen months. Theirs was far from the first vessel to be trapped in the crushing grip of polar ice. Seventy-six years earlier, in 1819–20, a pair of ships under Rear Admiral William Edward Parry, charged by the British government with discovering the Northwest Passage—the hypothesized shortcut north of Canada from Europe to the Orient—had spent the winter frozen in near Melville Island in the high Arctic. For that matter, any record of Viking warriors or Irish monks whose seacraft may have stuck fast in northern ice as early as the ninth or tenth centuries is lost to history. As far as well-documented exploratory missions go, Parry's was the first to face unrelenting entombment in a frozen ocean.

More often than not, such turns of nautical fate spelled catastrophe. The ultimate disaster of this kind befell the crew of the British ships *Erebus* and *Terror* under Sir John Franklin, who in 1845—charged like Parry with finding the Northwest Passage—steamed into a frozen trap in another forlorn corner of the Canadian Arctic. When two successive summers failed to deliver the ships from the ice, the surviving men set out on a desperate march, hoping to reach some outpost of settlement far to the south on the mainland. All 129 crew members died, not before some of them ate others.

The search for Franklin exhausted the finest efforts of the Admiralty for a decade and a half, turning a fiasco triggered by the commander's incompetence into an enduring myth of sacrifice and heroism. In the Victorian imagination, that quest blazed into a legend not unlike the panorama of the American Wild West half a century later.

On that late winter day in 1895, Nansen and his partner, Frederik Johansen, strapped on skis, harnessed dogs to sledges, and set out. All the hopes and prayers of the mission launched in the *Fram* nearly two years earlier rested on their shoulders. The world the thirteen Norwegians had left behind—their friends and loved ones, the joys of civilized life, the meaning that their deed might acquire—lay far to the south.

Nansen and Johansen headed north.

———

Thirty-one years old at the outset of the expedition, Fridtjof Nansen had been a champion skier and speed skater trained on the hills and lakes surrounding his birthplace, on the outskirts of Christiania (today's Oslo). In school he specialized in zoology, and his study of the nervous systems of such lowly marine creatures as sea squirts and hagfish eventually led to breakthroughs in the nascent science of neuroanatomy.

Nansen's real passion, however, was for adventure—skiing, hunting, and above all exploring. In the summer of 1888 he led a skiing expedition that accomplished the first traverse of Greenland, a challenge that had turned back more experienced veterans such as Robert E. Peary and Adolf Erik Nordenskiöld. Rejecting the conventional wisdom of a west-to-east journey—from the safety of inhabited villages on the west coast, and traveling for the most part downwind—Nansen had a ship drop his team off on the barren, iceberg-thronged east coast. The party's only half-ironic motto was "Death or the west coast of Greenland."

By the 1890s, Norwegians were nowhere near the forefront of Arctic exploration. Starting in the Renaissance, the boldest thrusts into the unknown North had been carried out by British, Dutch, Russian, American, and even Austrian expeditions. Between 1878 and 1880 the Finnish-born Swede Nordenskiöld seized the prize of the Northeast Passage (the Old World's equivalent of the Northwest Passage, which would not be navigated until 1903–06), by steering the *Vega* along a tortuous path north of Siberia and through the Bering Strait.

As early as 1550, the fantasy of a northern shortcut to the riches of Cathay had set European minds afire. When all attempts at the Northwest and Northeast Passages were defeated by impenetrable wastes of pack ice, the even more fanciful dream of a journey straight across the top of the world kindled the brains of monarchs and explorers. In the absence of any knowledge of the globe north of the coasts of Greenland, Ellesmere Island, and Russia, the theory of an Open Polar Sea gained a persistent vogue. Beyond the ice that thwarted mariners, pundits declared, must lie a temperate ocean and undiscovered lands, peopled perhaps by savages unknown to the rest of the world. Break through the frozen barrier into the open sea, and an easy voyage to the Orient would ensue.

Even before Columbus set sail from Spain in 1492, geographers recognized that a spherical earth (first demonstrated by the ancient Greeks) meant that there was a pole at 90 degrees north, a point on the surface of the globe where all lines of longitude converged and from which every direction pointed south. In the fifteenth century the notion of sailing toward that pole was a utilitarian dream among northern

European visionaries, a scheme by which traders might reach the riches of half-mythic Cathay without running afoul of Spanish and Portuguese warships.

According to Arctic historian Jeannette Mirsky, the first explorer explicitly to propose a quest to reach the North Pole was the merchant Robert Thorne, who petitioned King Henry VIII in 1527. The proposal sparked a feckless thrust toward the New World that reached the coast of Labrador after being thwarted by the eternal ice farther north. Thorne remains a footnote to history but for his bold vow, repeated again and again over the centuries: "There is no land unhabitable nor sea innavigable."

The voyages of such doughty explorers as Sir Hugh Willoughby, Willem Barents, and Henry Hudson likewise sought to reach Cathay via the North Pole, but ice wrote its stern *finis* to their hopes. On his three voyages in search of the Northwest Passage, Martin Frobisher claimed the European discovery of Baffin Island (though a Viking settlement long preceded him, and Inuit had thrived on the island for almost a millennium), but on his return to England Frobisher's journeys were greeted as utter failures. The chronicler on Frobisher's second voyage vividly evoked the hardships of Arctic navigation: "Whoso maketh navigations to those Countreys, hath not onely extreme winds, and furious seas to encounter withall, but also many monstrous and great Islands of yce: a thing both rare, wonderfull, and greatly to be regarded."

The toll of Arctic exploration during the Renaissance, not only in thwarted ambitions but in lost ships and lives, led to a hiatus of nearly two centuries in European probes toward the North Pole. Only at the end of the eighteenth century did mariners again take up the gauntlet. And by the early nineteenth century, the quest had taken on a life of its own. No matter that not a single ship had been able to defeat the ice or find the remotest hint of an Open Polar Sea. The rivalry acquired a new yardstick: the claiming of a "farthest north."

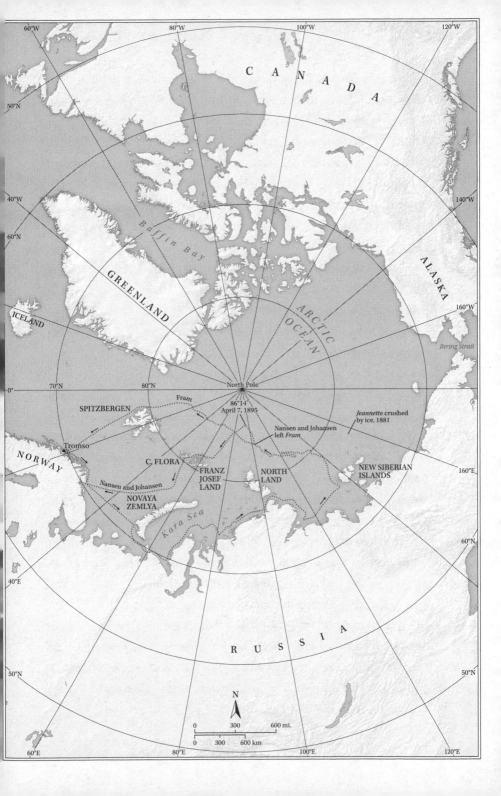

William Edward Parry, the same explorer whose ships had been the first to endure a frozen winter in 1819–20, won the support of the Admiralty for an expedition with the avowed goal of reaching the North Pole. Parry's plan seems in retrospect a bizarre one. He would sail to the northern edge of Svalbard (Spitsbergen), then set out across the ice with boats equipped with sledge runners, to be pulled by reindeer. When the reindeer failed to do their job, the men hauled the boat-sledges. Man-hauling became de rigueur on British expeditions to the Arctic and Antarctic during the next ninety years, to the disdain of Norwegians, who would perfect the use of dogs for the task. (Wrote Nansen, tongue in cheek, in 1897: "It would appear, indeed, as if dogs were not held in great estimation by the English.")

Nonetheless, on July 27, 1827, Parry's team reached 82° 45' N. It was a record that would stand for the next forty-nine years.

By the time Nansen got caught up in the quest, in the early 1890s, the record had advanced by only 38 minutes of latitude—a mere 49 miles. Ice had defeated the bravest thrusts of all the polar aspirants. A daunting 457 miles of *terra incognita*—more likely *glacies incognita*—stretched between the discovered pack and 90° N. The new mark had been set in 1882 by two members of an expedition led by the American army officer Adolphus Greely, whose 83° 23' N came at a terrible cost. Thanks to resupply ships that never arrived and to Greely's woeful leadership, nineteen of the twenty-five men died during their three-year ordeal, including a private who was executed for stealing food.

Rather than batter his boats and sledges against the unrelenting ice, Nansen came up with a plan that was breathtaking in its audacity. It was based on the fate of another American polar voyage that had spiraled into disaster—that of the *Jeannette* under Lieutenant George W. De Long of the U.S. Navy between 1879 and 1881.

De Long's plan was to strike north not from the conventional bases of Greenland or Svalbard but by sailing through the Bering Strait into the Chukchi Sea. The theory underpinning the expedition comprised another pair of *a priori* geographical assumptions: that Wrangel Island north of eastern Siberia ("discovered" in 1764, though humans inhabited it as early as 1700 BC) was actually a vast landmass whose coast the *Jeannette* could follow into the high latitudes, and that the warm Japanese Current flowing north through the Bering Strait would assure an ice-free path most of the way to the pole.

With thirty-three men aboard, the *Jeannette* set sail from San Francisco in July 1879. By September she was stuck fast in ice, still short of Wrangel Island. During the next twenty-one months, the ship drifted aimlessly in its frozen prison, as the thaws of two summers failed to release her. As one expedition after another learned throughout the nineteenth century and into the early twentieth, if a ship failed to break free of the ice, the crushing pressure would eventually destroy and sink her. The end for the *Jeannette*, which struck with dramatic suddenness, came on June 12, 1881.

The ship's final position was 77° 15' N, well short of Parry's farthest north from sixty-one years before. The failure of De Long's voyage would pound one of the final nails into the coffin of the hypothesis of the Open Polar Sea.

The crew set out on a grim trek toward the south, hauling heavy boats across slushy ice, hoping to reach the Lena delta on the Russian mainland. In the end, twenty of the thirty-three men died, including De Long.

So much for yet another ill-fated attempt to bash through the ice in quest of the elusive North Pole. But three years after the men bid farewell to the *Jeannette*, electrifying news emerged from Greenland. Near Julianehaab on the southwest coast, some Inuit discovered curious relics embedded in the drift ice on shore. Danish authorities soon identified them as fragments from the lost ship. Among the relics was a list of provisions signed by De Long and several pieces of clothing with the names of known expedition members sewn or written on them. The conclusion was unmistakable: these pieces of debris had been carried by the ice across the top of the world. The only possible force was a prevailing current that pushed the ice itself hundreds of miles from north of Siberia to Greenland.

The discovery was so outlandish that many observers, including several supposed experts, discounted it as a hoax or a case of mistaken identification. Yet further corroboration of the transpolar drift came in another discovery on the Greenland shore: that of an Inuit throwing-stick of a style unknown to Greenlanders but matching that of Alaskan natives, down to its decoration with Chinese glass beads of the kind regularly traded near the Bering Strait.

As the longitude of the *Jeannette* when it sank was nearly opposite that of the west coast of Greenland, it seemed unarguable that the drift must have carried the relics within several degrees of the pole.

Nansen's bold idea came to him in a eureka moment. Instead of fighting the Arctic ice, why not embrace it? What if a team deliberately let its ship get frozen in, so as to ride the newly discovered drift far closer to the pole than men with dogs and sledges and boats had yet been able to go? And if so, how could such a ship escape the usual fate of being crushed and sunk by the relentless pressure of the floes?

Most of the nautical attacks on the high Arctic had been launched in refurbished ships originally designed for other types of service. The truly radical notion Nansen brought to his quest for the pole was to build from scratch a ship that could withstand the worst the ice could do. The structure of the hull would call for a lattice of unusually stout timbers reinforced with iron. But its shape would be the critical factor. Design a hull that was far shallower and rounder than that of most ships, Nansen argued: instead of crushing it, the floes would force the ship upward, so that it would "be able to slip like an eel out of the embraces of the ice."

Nansen announced his plan in 1890 at a meeting of the Christiania Geographical Society. When his speech was published, experts from several countries weighed in. Most of them thought Nansen's idea was crazy. Among his harshest critics was Adolphus Greely, who, given the disastrous outcome of his own expedition in search of the pole, might have been wiser to bite his tongue. The whole conception, Greely judged, was an "illogical scheme of self-destruction." Not content to denigrate the plan, Greely sneered at the man himself. "As far as I know," he proclaimed, "[Nansen] has had no Arctic service." Apparently the crossing of Greenland didn't count.

Nansen blithely ignored the skeptics, and construction of the *Fram* (Norwegian for "forward") began at a shipyard in Larvik. Thanks to his fame from the Greenland expedition, Nansen's call for crew members elicited a deluge of applications. The hand-picked roster of twelve included Nansen's close friend and partner on the Greenland ice, Otto Sverdrup, who would be the captain of the ship.

———

On June 24, 1893, the *Fram* weighed anchor and began her long voyage. As the ship glided slowly northeast along the Norway coast, throngs gathered in ports and on hills to cheer her passage. The storage chests below decks were loaded with provisions for thirteen men for five years. Nansen was fully confident that after the *Fram* had completed an epic traverse of the polar regions, she would be delivered into ice-free waters somewhere in the North Atlantic, where the long-dormant engine could be fired up and the vessel could steam back to Norway. He had calculated the rate at which the *Jeannette* relics had floated in the ice as two miles per day. At a comparable rate, the *Fram* might complete her ice-bound drift in two years, so the ample provisioning built in a generous margin of safety.

The critical first leg of the journey would require a journey across the perilous seas north of Europe and Asia to reach the New Siberian Islands, near which the *Jeannette* had sunk twelve years earlier. In itself that was a formidable challenge, for many a mariner had been turned back by ice long before reaching that archipelago. In effect, Nansen's team would be retracing two-thirds of the Northeast Passage, still unrepeated after Nordenskiöld's landmark journey from 1878 to 1880. Should the *Fram* arrive at her goal without mishap, Sverdrup would then steer the ship straight north into the ice, whose grasp would transport her along the course of the hypothesized drift.

At age thirty-one, Nansen was in the prime of life, an athlete famed for his strength and stamina. Tall and solidly built—in the expedition photos, he looks almost portly—he exuded a brimming confidence that camouflaged deep doubts about his worth and achievements that would haunt him all his life. Handsome, with a penetrating gaze and an almost regal air, he dressed habitually in the "Sanitary Woolen Clothing" of the German health nut Dr. Gustav Jaeger, who trumpeted the virtues of garb that would allow "evaporation of the 'noxious' emanations" given off by the body.

Nansen was known as something of a ladies' man, who had formed a number of passionate if short-lived liaisons with Norwegian beauties. His biographer Roland Huntford rather harshly concludes, "He could only make friends with women, and never with a man." Yet in 1889, after an engagement lasting less than a month, he married Eva Sars, a professional singer and a first-rate skier. Only five months before setting out in the *Fram*, Eva gave birth to a daughter the couple named Liv. Being separated from his wife and daughter after June 1893 would prove a lingering grievance for the ambitious explorer.

With the radical design of her hull, as yet untried in any ocean, the *Fram* remained an enigma. Would she prove seaworthy in stormy conditions? A partial and discouraging answer came on only the fourth day of the expedition. Still skirting the coast of Norway, the ship was battered in the middle of the night by a sudden tempest. Seas flooded across the deck, all kinds of equipment was swept overboard, and several men came close to following the debris. The crew salvaged other cargo, but the scene was pandemonium. As Nansen drily recorded, "I am afraid the shares in the expedition stood rather low at this moment."

Nonetheless, as the ship plowed steadily eastward during the following weeks, the men adjusted to her quirks, and Sverdrup navigated skillfully through a chaos of free-ranging floes and foggy whiteouts. By mid-September, three months into the voyage, the *Fram* stood off the westernmost coast of the New Siberian Islands. Nansen ordered a course due north.

On September 25, the floes closed around the ship and froze her in their grip for good. The theodolite gave a latitude reading of 78° 50' N— about 770 miles as the crow flies from the North Pole. And now the great trial began.

Just how daring Nansen's scheme was can be gleaned via an anachronistic analogy. To submit to an icy prison in a ship whose design had never been tested, and to trust to an invisible current whose existence had been only indirectly deduced, might have been akin to setting out on the first manned mission to the moon if the type of spaceship the astronauts rode, unlike *Apollo 11*, had gone through no trial runs whatsoever, with the route across 230,000 miles of empty space only guessed at.

That the North Pole, like the moon seven decades later, should have loomed as a profoundly worthwhile goal for a mission of discovery seemed self-evident to the crowds that lined the seacoast to hail the *Fram*'s departure. And no doubts about the value of their quest troubled the sleep of the twelve men who had so eagerly sought places in the ship's crew. In the opening pages of *Farthest North*, the book Nansen would write about the expedition—one of the truly magisterial accounts of terrestrial exploration of his or any other age—Nansen nonetheless laid out the rationale for the voyage.

As did the moon, the Far North posed certain scientific questions. But a more fundamental motivation lay closer to the heart: "the limits of the unknown," Nansen wrote, "had to recede step by step before the ever-increasing yearning after light and knowledge of the human mind, till they made a stand in the north at the threshold of Nature's great Ice Temple of the polar regions with their endless silence."

That same yearning, Nansen was sure, gave voice to the cheers of the crowds who watched the *Fram* sail past: "the same thirst for achievement, the same craving to get beyond the limits of the known . . ."

Even as early as the 1890s, some skeptics voiced their doubts as to whether the arbitrary goal of 90° N—an abstract point on the surface of the globe, defined only by latitude—was worth the titanic struggle. In *Farthest North*, Nansen disavowed the North Pole itself as a paramount objective:

> it is not to seek for the exact mathematical point that forms the northern extremity of the earth's axis that we set out, for to reach this point is intrinsically of small moment. Our object is to investigate the great unknown region that surrounds the Pole . . .

Yet as the *Fram* drifted in her zigzag course, Nansen's veering moods betrayed that disavowal. Every second of latitude gained was a triumph, every second lost a setback. Breaking Greely's record farthest north became an all-consuming passion, and the only truly satisfying result of the expedition would be to stand at the "exact mathematical point" of the pole. For Nansen, the pull of 90° N outweighed even the pull of home, of the infant daughter and the wife who longed for his safe return.

___

When I first became aware, as a teenager, of the panorama of Arctic questing that unfolded between 1819 and 1909, I needed no persuading that the goal of reaching the abstract but precisely defined point at the top of the world was worth all the struggle, suffering, and even death that had been expended on it. And later, when I first read *Farthest North*, I drifted in my imagination along with the thirteen men aboard the *Fram* in a reverie of vicarious adventure.

Equally compelling to me was the quest for the South Pole, which spanned a much more concentrated era, from 1897 to 1912. In fact, Robert Falcon Scott, Ernest Shackleton, and Roald Amundsen became paragons for me before Nansen (or for that matter Robert E. Peary) did. For all the dire predicaments those pioneers plunged into on the Antarctic continent, the landscape across which their expeditions unfurled seemed somehow congenial: a steadily rising glacial plateau, fringed by dark mountains, seamed with dangerous crevasses.

The Arctic north of the shores of Greenland and Ellesmere Island, in contrast, figured in my imagination as an arena of unrelieved nightmare. There was nothing but ice, torn and twisted into chaotic pressure ridges by the winds and currents, hemmed by deadly open-water leads that could gape or close without warning. The flat surfaces of the floes, where unsuspecting men pitched their camps, could split into pieces with the booming reports of exploding shells. To travel across such a wilderness, one account after another revealed, was to wrestle monstrous sledge loads across boulder piles of ice, with constant terror as a ground bass.

By the age of five, I was already a veteran of snow. Three years before I was born, in 1940, my parents moved from the East to Climax,

Colorado—at 11,300 feet the highest town in the United States—where my father operated the first sun-eclipsing telescope deployed in the Western Hemisphere. On the ridges and basins surrounding Fremont Pass, the snows came in September and lingered past May. Dad turned dynamite boxes into sleds for me and my brother Alan, one year younger. To go out and play, we donned boots and mittens and woolen caps.

One day in May 1948, just before my fifth birthday, Alan and I set out to explore the gulf behind our house and adjoining observatory on Ceresco Ridge. That hollow was reputed to be a dump for old autos abandoned by the workers in the molybdenum mine that was Climax's raison d'être. In the warm sun, plowing our way across the saturated drifts, Alan and I discovered no rusty Model Ts, only a depthless sand-box of snow.

As we started to climb the slope back to our house, we blundered into the wettest drift of all. Thrashing to stay upright, we sank to our waists, then to our chests, in the slop. After half an hour of flailing, I realized with glum certainty that this was how I was going to die—the first time that the shadow of doom had darkened my otherwise charmed childhood.

Somehow Alan got loose, managed to struggle up the hill, and summoned the rescue squad of our mother. After yanking me out of my chilly trap, she warned both of us that the old car dump was not a safe place to play. We took heed, and thereafter confined our excursions to the toxic tailings piles surrounding the mine and the glory hole it had gouged out of the south face of Mount Bartlett.

I first felt the itch of exploration in my bones about three years later, after our family moved to Boulder. One bright spring day, provisioned with peanut butter and jelly sandwiches Mom had made for us, Alan and I set out to hike up Gregory Canyon, on the trail that rose between Flagstaff and Green Mountain. The mouth of the canyon opened where Baseline Road ended, after completing its traverse in a virtually uninterrupted straight line smack on top of the 40th parallel of latitude all the way from the Kansas border.

There, nestled in a small grove of apple trees, a sign informed us that the canyon was named after John H. Gregory, who in 1859 had pioneered the mountain route all the way to the future mining camp of Black Hawk. This scrap of history electrified me. Dad had mentioned Black Hawk, but the legendary settlement seemed to me impossibly remote. What a man Gregory must have been to find his way there alone, fighting off bears and Indians!

Alan and I made it about a mile up the canyon before fatigue and hunger (we'd polished off our sandwiches) brought us to a halt. My shoulders were already sore from the ten-pound pack I hefted. A forty-foot cliff of red sandstone stared over us on the south; in the shade at its base an old snowbank clung to the gravelly soil. How much more daunting must the snaking canyon ahead of us be!

Gregory Canyon did not turn me into an explorer. A few years later, I made it to the top of Green Mountain, which at an elevation of 8,150 feet towered half a mile above our house on Bluebell Avenue. But the trail to the summit was easy to follow and banked with runoff ditches, and on top there was a scrolled-up register housed in a cemented cairn whose brass plaque sported a sighting guide to all the much higher crests of the Indian Peaks to the west. This cozy nook among the pines was hardly *terra incognita*.

Rather than venture into the wilder outback above timberline— without a car and driver I was landlocked, and Dad was too busy with his scientific work to share any alpine rambles with his son—I turned Green Mountain into a fetish, hiking (usually solo) up it some fifty times over three or four years by every known trail from all the points of the compass. For the antisocial misfit I became in early adolescence, Green Mountain was a spiritual sanctum, not a world of discovery.

Because my father was an astronomer, at an age when other kids were learning the Ten Commandments in Sunday school I was absorbing the expanding universe. Even at eight or nine, I spent sleepless nights trying to fathom the concept of infinity. *There has to be a wall at the end*, I would tell myself, staring up at the darkness of my bedroom ceiling. A trim, mortared barrier of stones would pop into my brain. *But there has to be something beyond the wall*—and there I was, hopping over the border and gliding off into the limitless void.

By adolescence, outer space was more real to me than the Indian Peaks. But within a few years, I had turned to the sagas of polar discovery around the turn of the twentieth century—Scott and Shackleton at first, Nansen a little later. At the same time I had begun to read books about Himalayan expeditions—Maurice Herzog's *Annapurna*, Sir John Hunt's *The Ascent of Everest*, Paul Bauer's *The Siege of Nanga Parbat*. At last the exploratory itch that had lain dormant since Gregory Canyon stirred my blood again. At sixteen, liberated by a driver's permit, I reached Brainard Lake at dawn and hiked to the top of my first 13,000-foot peak. Mount Audubon, I would soon learn, was one of the easiest high "walk-ups" in Colorado, but on that June day the whole alpine panorama—conies whistling beside their lairs, elephantella and Parry's primrose peeping into bloom, winter snowbanks leaking crystalline trickles—enchanted me.

Scott and Shackleton were mythic heroes, but their portraits had a sepia tone. Hillary and Tenzing came in bright Kodachrome. From my vantage point in Boulder, the Arctic seas lay impossibly far away—more than 2,000 miles straight north, beyond the curve of the globe. The mountains began just beyond our front door on Bluebell Avenue.

By the late 1950s, moreover, Arctic and Antarctic discovery had stalled in a creative limbo. The South and North Poles had "been done"—by Amundsen in 1911, by Peary (or so we all thought) in 1909. But nearly all the hardest peaks in the Himalaya and the Karakoram were still unclimbed, and when I read Gaston Rébuffat's *Starlight and Storm*, I learned that even in the Alps, where the cavalcade of major first ascents had ended in 1865 with Edward Whymper's triumph on the Matterhorn, the best climbers alive, some of them less than a decade older than I was, were setting their sights on new routes the likes of which the previous generation had dismissed as impossible.

The played-out character of Arctic discovery would seem to me (and to my climbing buddies) confirmed in 1968, when a Minnesotan named Ralph Plaisted led a bunch of amateurs on a snowmobile expedition to the North Pole. The style of Plaisted's expedition struck us as deplorable, as his team was regularly resupplied by airplane, depended on navigational help from overflying pilots, and—worst of all—got picked up by plane at 90° N rather than return the way they had come. That denouement seemed to trivialize the pole itself. It was as if you could land a plane or a helicopter on the top of Everest. As *Annapurna* made gruesomely clear, the descent of a formidable mountain was often more perilous than the ascent.

I was ten years old when Everest was first climbed, in 1953. It was no wonder, then, that when I edged toward becoming an explorer myself in my early twenties, it was the great ranges that I chose as my undiscovered country—and in particular, Alaska, where all the most challenging mountains had yet to be climbed, or even attempted. The riches lay there for the taking.

———

Six weeks into the drift of the *Fram*, Nansen had grave doubts about the theory on which the whole expedition was premised. An observation on November 7 gave a latitude of 77° 43' N, which was actually south of the ship's position when she had first been frozen in. In despair, Nansen wrote in his diary, "My plan has come to nothing. That palace of theory which I reared, in pride and self-confidence, high above all silly objections has fallen like a house of cards at the first breath of wind."

The pressure of the ice, of which none of the thirteen men had any previous experience, could produce terror. On December 8, Nansen noted, "The ice creaked and roared so along the ship's side close by us that it was not possible to carry on any connected conversation; we had to scream." Yet the prevailing ambiance was one of darkness, silence, and monotony. To relieve the boredom, the men played the mechanical organ in the saloon, or read books from the well-stocked expedition library, or played cards, or composed verses about their plight, or drafted elaborate menus for each evening's dinner as if they were advertising a posh restaurant. In a tradition dating back to Parry's men on the *Hecla* and *Griper* in 1819–20, the team published an onboard newspaper.

Chores filled many of the men's waking hours: tending to the sails and rigging, retrieving foodstuffs from the hold, gathering salt-free ice to melt for drinking water, taking daily meteorological observations. Each man was charged with crafting his own pair of canvas boots. Feeding the dogs and keeping them from tearing one another apart in fights were especially onerous tasks. The keeping of a strict daily routine was deemed crucial to preserving the men's sanity. The round of activities gradually instilled a cozy sense of the ship as a safe haven in the limitless frozen sea, even though Nansen was so parsimonious of coal that the temperature in the saloon often hovered in the 40s Fahrenheit. Not all of the regimen was devoted to chores. The galley served as both kitchen and smoking room. "Out there [the men] had a good smoke and chat; many a story was told, and not seldom some warm dispute arose," wrote Nansen. "Afterwards came, for most of us, a short siesta."

The rare dramatic event punctured the tedium. On December 13, in penumbral darkness, a polar bear crawled on board, seized two dogs, and carried them back onto the ice. There the bear killed and partially ate the dogs before the men, carrying lanterns, were able to track it down and shoot it.

Slowly, the current asserted the fitful force that had carried the *Jeannette* relics across the top of the world. On February 1, the *Fram* at last passed 80° N. Yet for the perpetually impatient Nansen, the zigzag course was maddening. "We are going at the miserable pace of a snail," he wrote on February 25, "but not so surely as it goes. We carry our house with us; but what we do one day is undone the next." He calculated that at the current rate, it would take eight years for the *Fram* to complete its traverse and escape into North Atlantic waters.

Yet almost from the start, the ship had borne out the theory behind the experimental design of her hull. Less than two weeks after freezing fast, the *Fram* faced her first test by ice: "the ship trembles and shakes," Nansen recorded, "and rises by fits and starts, or is sometimes gently lifted. There is a pleasant comfortable feeling in sitting listening to all this uproar and knowing the strength of our ship. Many a one would have been crushed long ago."

At first the *Fram*, once an assault by the pressure ridges subsided, would settle back into her original berth in the pack. But as the winter wore on, the lifting persisted. With nothing for the ice to grasp, the round-bottomed hull was steadily squeezed upward. By February 1894 all the men were won over to the radical hypothesis by which Nansen had schemed the ship's survival. The only question was when and if the polar pack would finally deliver her into open waters.

On April 6 the men witnessed a solar eclipse. The event was vital for the team's navigation, as the onset of the moon's shadow, which had been predicted to the minute, allowed them to correct the ship's chronometers, without which they could not accurately reckon longitude.

The men greeted the spring, with rising temperatures and the return of the sun, with joy. But as the weeks wore on, their spirits wilted.

Midsummer's Day, for most Arctic expeditions a halcyon occasion, gave them little cheer. "A dismal, dispiriting landscape—nothing but white and gray," noted Nansen. "No shadows—merely half-obliterated forms melting into the fog and slush." June 24 marked the passage of a year aboard the *Fram*. There was no ignoring the fact that the drift had accomplished far less northward progress than Nansen had predicted.

Between May 1 and June 18 the ice-bound ship hovered around 81° N, gaining a paltry 6' of latitude during seven weeks of aimless to-and-fro. Then, between June 18 and September 5, the *Fram* actually retreated southward by 38', or some 44 miles.

Throughout the spring and summer, the men practiced all the means of travel across the pack at their disposal, slowly attaining at least beginners' proficiency on snowshoes and skis. The ship was equipped with boats and sledges, and the men practiced hauling these as well. In addition, starting in July, Nansen supervised the construction of light two-man kayaks, made of wooden frames covered with sealskin and sailcloth.

No matter how confident the men grew in the *Fram*'s capacity to survive the gripping ice, they had to rehearse the grim course to which they would resort if the ship sank. Nansen pondered again and again the paradox at the heart of the voyage. All other crews frozen into the Arctic ice had prayed each summer for release, while the men on the *Fram* hoped instead for more solid entombment and a current to ride north.

Should the ship sink, the team would have to set off across the ice with sledges and boats in a desperate bid for escape. By June the nearest land was 70 air miles from the *Fram*; the nearest inhabited land was much farther. All the previous expeditions whose ships the ice had doomed had attempted such retreats, with catastrophic results. The precedent lodged in all the men's minds was the denouement of the Franklin expedition after 1845, when all 129 men had died either on or near the *Erebus* and *Terror* or on the hopeless march south after the ships had gone to the bottom.

Although the team kept up its rehearsals of their last-ditch scenario, Nansen confided to his diary the conviction that in the event of a retreat, there would be "little doubt as to our fate." Only thirteen of the thirty-three men from the *Jeannette* expedition had survived, and the American ship had sunk at 77° N, not 81°. Such musings only reinforced Nansen's faith in the perfect plan and the indomitable ship: "But the *Fram* will not be crushed . . ."

From the start of the journey Nansen had plotted a logistical gambit that he kept up his sleeve as the crowning tour de force of the expedition. Why he felt it had to be kept secret is unclear. He hinted at the scheme to Sverdrup, but kept his silence with the rest of the team. (They guessed the outlines of the plan anyway.) There was, of course, little chance that the drift of the pack would carry the *Fram* straight to the North Pole. At some point, no matter how well the hypothesized course of the frozen ship conformed to Nansen's predictions, the *Fram* would reach a highest latitude before gliding south and west. That apogee would have to be seized. From that point, Nansen and one or more partners would leave the ship, setting off with skis and kayaks and dogs and sledges on a determined jaunt to the pole.

As always, Nansen's ambivalence about his goals left him of two minds. As he wrote in his diary on September 25, as if the expedition sponsors were looking over his shoulder, "Our aim, as I have so often tried to make clear, is not so much to reach the point in which the earth's axis terminates, as to traverse and explore the unknown Polar Sea; and yet I should like to get to the Pole, too . . ."

In Nansen's mind, the ideal time for the departure would be February or March, to take advantage of the waxing daylight yet complete the trek before summer turned the ice to slush and melted fiendish open-water leads between the floes. He considered setting off in March

1894, after a drift of only five months, but the poor progress of the *Fram* to that date dictated delay. Another year's zigzag in the ice ought to gain several degrees of latitude. Privately Nansen dreamed of 87.5° N, but he hoped realistically for 85°, and would settle for even less.

Throughout 1894, the tedium of passive life aboard the ship drove Nansen into frenzies of impatience. The lure of the grueling dash toward the pole tugged constantly at his feelings. As he wrote on March 26, "this inactive, lifeless monotony, without any change, wrings one's very soul. No struggle, no possibility of struggle! All is so still and dead, so stiff and shrunken, under the mantle of ice.... What would I not give for a single day of struggle—for even a moment of danger!"

For the men under Nansen's command, the prospect of their leader abandoning them was fraught with dismay. But they also fully appreciated what a bold gamble the men skiing off to the north would be undertaking. Once more than a few days away from the ship, the party aimed at the pole would have no chance at returning to that tiny island of safety and comfort in the vast sea of ice, because the course of its drift was utterly unpredictable. The *Fram* would be harder to find than the proverbial needle in a haystack.

Instead, the returning polar party would have to head south until it reached terra firma. Nansen hoped for Franz Josef Land, lying between the longitudes of 50° and 60° E, and for the seemingly remote chance that some passing whaler or explorer might come upon the men and pick them up, or if not, that they might hunt and scavenge and live off the land indefinitely. The difference between those skiers and the refugees from the *Jeannette* and other stricken ships would be, Nansen judged, the fact that they would be fit and healthy, as opposed to starving and demoralized. Still, even Nansen recognized what an audacious program, the likes of which the Arctic had never seen, he was proposing.

On September 25, 1894, the *Fram* marked a full year of frozen drift. Nansen made the gloomy calculation that during that year, she had gained only 189 miles in her northward quest. The daunting span of some 550 miles of pack still stretched between the expedition and the pole. On October 21, the *Fram* finally passed the 82nd parallel of latitude. The team celebrated with a "grand banquet," whose printed menu extolled the courses ranging from "fish pudding, with melted butter and potatoes" to honey-cakes specially baked for the occasion. "[T]here is not a soul aboard who doubts that we shall accomplish what we came out to do," Nansen boasted to his diary, as he suppressed his dark misgivings about the ship's wayward wandering in the ice.

Greely's record of 83° 23′ N still posed the challenge of 95 miles of further progress. Indeed, it would take another two and a half months for the *Fram* to break the record, and when that landmark event arrived, the men were in no mood to enjoy it. On January 3, 1895, a huge pressure-ridge of ice bore down on the ship, threatening a catastrophic collision. The *Fram* began to list dangerously to the port side. The advance of the pressure-ridge was signaled by louder roaring than the men had heard before. Slowly, over three days, the crisis intensified. On January 5, Nansen was awakened by Sverdrup at 5:30 AM. In the darkness the commander "heard a thundering and crashing outside in the ice, as if doomsday had come."

The nightmare scenario had arrived. Nansen ordered all the equipment and provisions for a retreat placed on the ice or on the deck ready to be offloaded at a moment's notice. By now the pressure-ridge had closed with the ship, not in a collision but with the grip of a gigantic vise. Massive blocks of ice rose so high they spilled over the railing onto the upper deck. The men futilely attacked the encroaching tons of ice with shovels and spades. "We are now living in marching order on an empty ship," Nansen wrote in his diary.

Yet when January 6 passed with no worsening of the *Fram*'s predicament, the men began to believe that the ship would survive. That day, a meridian observation revealed that the expedition had broken

Greely's record by eleven minutes of latitude. The men attempted a nervous celebration with punch and cigars, but never let down their guard. "Perhaps the growth of this ridge has come to an end now, perhaps not;" wrote Nansen, "the one thing is as likely as the other."

It was not until January 15 that the team could rest in the conviction that the crisis had passed. At once Nansen pushed forward his preparations for the jaunt toward the pole. He had decided that he would take only one companion. Sverdrup might have been the obvious choice, but the team could not part with both its leader and the captain of the ship. Privately, Nansen had settled on Frederik Johansen, officially the expedition stoker, a twenty-seven-year-old with a military background. "[H]e is in all respects well qualified for that work," Nansen wrote. "He is an accomplished snow-shoer, and few can equal his powers of endurance—a fine fellow, physically and mentally."

Before announcing his choice to the team, Nansen sought out Johansen in private to invite him. He warned his comrade that if he agreed to go, "neither of us may ever see the face of man again." Johansen accepted on the spot. Nansen asked him if he would like to think over his decision. "He did not need any time for reflection, he said; he was quite willing to go."

In his thoroughly methodical way, Nansen had plotted the logistics of the polar dash. The two men would take twenty-eight dogs to haul the sledges, food for 110 days—2,100 pounds of gear and food altogether. At an average rate of 9½ miles per day, the men should be able to close the nearly 500 miles to the pole in sixty days. (In Greenland, Nansen's team had covered 345 miles of glacier in sixty-five days, but that was "at an elevation of 8000 feet, without dogs and with defective provisions, and [we] could certainly have gone considerably farther." As the loads dwindled and the dogs were played out, Nansen and Johansen would not hesitate to supplement their rations by killing and eating them.

Nansen fixed a tentative launching date of March 1. As spring crept over the Arctic, his congenital impatience surged. But it was tempered by an existential sense of fate, sharpened by the strange conundrum that his team's lonely mission in an inhuman wasteland posed. "What is life thus isolated?" he asked his diary. "A strange, aimless process; and man a machine which eats, sleeps, awakes; eats and sleeps again, dreams dreams, but never lives. Or is life really nothing else? And is it just one more phase of the eternal martyrdom, a new mistake of the erring human soul, this banishing of oneself to the hopeless wilderness, only to long there for what one has left behind? Am I a coward? Am I afraid of death?"

———

The polar duo suffered false starts on February 26 and 28, when their first trials with dogs and sledges revealed glaring flaws in Nansen's program. Back on board the *Fram*, he reduced the cargo loads and strengthened the fragile sledges. As disheartening as those setbacks were, Nansen tasted his ambivalence about the daring thrust he and Johansen were determined to pursue. "It was undoubtedly very pleasant once more to stretch my limbs on the sofa in the *Fram*'s saloon," he wrote on March 6, "to quench my thirst in delicious lime-juice with sugar, and again to dine in a civilized manner."

At last, on March 14, the two men set out for good. Some of the crew went with them on the first day's leg of their journey. Again Nansen was awash in ambivalence. Watching Sverdrup stride back toward the ship from an ice hummock where they bid each other farewell, Nansen reported, "I half wished I could turn back with him and find myself again in the warm saloon . . ."

The last reading aboard ship had given a latitude of 84° 4' N. For the utterly uncertain future Nansen and Johansen faced—a trek that might last months or even years—their choices of clothing, gear, and food were absolutely crucial. Some of their decisions would prove inspired, others sadly misjudged.

Because they had sweated profusely during their trial runs on the ice, Nansen decided at the last minute not to take the wolfskin outer garments that so effectively warded off the cold and wind, relying mainly on wool instead. Within a week, the men would bitterly regret that omission, as their clothes got soaked, then froze into mantles of ice. On the other hand, Nansen decided to take not only skis but snow-shoes, which ended up being vital for much of the march over broken pressure ridges.

Twenty-eight dogs, as planned, took to the ice along with the men. But in the end, only three sledges, as opposed to the original six, were deployed to carry the considerable weight of food and gear. Nansen requisitioned two of his beloved kayaks, built from scratch on board the *Fram*, for the journey. Hauled on top of the sledges, they suffered punctures in the rugged jostling inflicted by the pressure ridges that rendered them almost useless for crossing leads of open water.

Nansen opted for a silk tent without a floor (since the built-in can-vas floors he had tried out earlier on the expedition tended to absorb moisture and add unwanted weight), but this meant that the men's sleeping bags lay directly on the ice. (Air mattresses, though invented in Massachusetts in 1889, were still far from becoming standard items on polar voyages.) Having also tried out lightweight calfskin sleeping bags, Nansen wisely chose a bulkier double bag made out of reindeer skin with the hair intact. Even so, each night the two men lay shivering in their cocoon as they went to bed, until body heat raised the tempera-ture enough so they could sleep.

For boots the men relied on *finnesko,* a Norwegian specialty, made of reindeer skin with the hair turned inward. They were lined with sen-negrass, a sedge that had the additional virtue of drying up perspiration from the feet. Though too soft and flexible to be of much use for mountaineers, *finnesko* were ideal for Arctic travelers. Despite the extreme cold Nansen and Johansen would soon face, neither man developed frostbite of the toes or feet.

Nansen swore by Dr. Jaeger's woolen shirts and drawers, topped with camel's hair coats and canvas leggings. Felt hats protected the men's heads. The only concession to wolfskin garb came in outer mittens worn over woolen inner mitts.

Nansen designed the all-important cuisine to be as rich as possible in calories. The store of butter alone weighed twice as much (86 pounds) as the sledge that carried it. Among the staples were foods that few explorers in our own day have ever tasted, including Våge's fish flour. (Nansen wrote, "if boiled in water and mixed with [corn or wheat] flour and butter or dried potatoes, it furnishes a very appetizing dish.") That Arctic standby, pemmican (a concentrated mixture of dried meat, animal fat, and berries), scored high with Nansen. On the pack ice, the men soon craved their favorite dinners—"lobscouse" (pemmican and dried potatoes) and *fiskegratin* (a melange of Våge's fish flour, regular flour, and butter). "Johansen preferred the 'lobscouse,' while I had a weakness for the 'fiskegratin.'"

Rounding out the gear were ample repair and medical kits ("chloroform in case of an amputation"), surveying instruments, and a rifle with a generous but not unlimited supply of cartridges.

The first few days on the ice filled the two men with joy. On March 22, Nansen calculated their day's jaunt to have covered 21 miles. "If this goes on," he wrote in his diary, "the whole thing will be done in no time." Temperatures hovered around minus 40 Fahrenheit, with clear skies. "Beautiful weather for travelling in, with fine sunsets; but somewhat cold, particulary in the bag, at nights . . ."

That same day the men killed their first dog after she failed to recover from some mysterious illness. They tried to feed Livjaegeren's carcass to the other dogs, but "many of them went supperless the whole night in preference to touching the meat." Later the dogs would grow less squeamish, wolfing down their dead companions "hair and all."

Johansen had a close call on March 31, when the pack split under his feet and he went up to his waist in seawater. The men set up camp as soon as possible. "Johansen's nether extremities were a mass of ice and his overalls so torn that extensive repairs were necessary."

Thanks to their own sweat, the men's wool clothing gradually froze and restricted movement. The aggravation was extreme. Their outer layers were "transformed into complete suits of ice-armor," wrote Nansen. "These clothes were so stiff that the arm of my coat actually rubbed deep sores in my wrists during our marches."

Bedding down inside the tent each evening became a dreaded ordeal. "We packed ourselves tight into the bag, and lay with our teeth chattering for an hour.... At last our clothes became wet and pliant, only to freeze again a few minutes after we had turned out of the bag in the morning."

The smooth going across flat ice over the first few days degenerated into a gauntlet of pressure ridges. Across the worst of these, the men had to seize the sledges by hand to keep them from capsizing and to force them over talus piles of ice blocks. "[T]he dogs are growing rather slow and slack, and it is almost impossible to get them on," wrote Nansen. "And then this endless disentangling of the hauling-ropes, with their infernal twists and knots, which get worse and worse to undo!"

The men beat the dogs with lashes and wooden sticks to make them obey, a treatment that went against their better natures. "It made one's heart bleed to see them," wrote Nansen, "but we turned our eyes away and hardened ourselves.... [O]ne systematically kills all better feelings, until only hard-hearted egoism remains."

Still, Nansen and Johansen were full of optimism as they gamely drove north in the face of all their obstacles. The first hint that something was drastically wrong came on March 28, after Nansen took a noon sighting that gave a latitude of 85° 30' N. "I could not understand this," he wrote in his diary; "thought that we must be in latitude 86°, and, therefore, supposed there must be something wrong with the observation."

That discouraging discovery was reinforced six days later, just after the men killed their second dog, when the theodolite gave a reading of 85° 59' N. "It is astonishing that we have not got farther; we seem to toil all we can, but without much progress." Slowly the explanation, which had been nagging at the back of Nansen's mind, came to the fore. There was nothing wrong with the theodolite. "It was becoming only too clear to me . . . that the ice was moving southward, and that in its capricious drift, at the mercy of wind and current, we had our worst enemy to combat."

The heroic daily marches the men were making, fighting the cold in frozen "armor," manhandling the sledges over chaotic ridges, beating the dogs to summon their best efforts, were being stymied by the inexorable southward drift of the pack. The team was fighting a treadmill that reduced each day's dogged thrust to a pitiful increment of progress. Even as they slept inside the tent in the icy "cocoon" of their double sleeping bag, the drift robbed them of minutes of latitude.

On April 8, Nansen succumbed to the inevitable. "There is not much sense in keeping on longer," he wrote in his diary; "we are sacrificing valuable time and doing little." The men pitched a last camp and tried to cheer themselves with a final "banquet" of lobscouse, chocolate, and red whortleberries. A careful sighting gave their final latitude of 86° 13.6' N. They had broken Greely's record by two degrees and fifty minutes, or some 144 miles.

The new farthest north offered Johansen and Nansen scant satisfaction. As they turned southward, the only challenge they now faced was survival.

———

In the twenty-first century, the North and South Poles have been in some fundamental sense trivialized. The main agent behind this transformation is modern aircraft, whose capacity to reach previously inaccessible places on the surface of the earth could scarcely have been imagined in 1895. The unknown loci that Nansen and his twelve companions—and Greely and De Long and Peary and countless others—were willing to risk their lives to attain have become landing strips for latter-day "explorers" dabbling in watered-down versions of adventure.

In 2017 the bustling Amundsen–Scott South Pole Station, a research facility regularly resupplied by giant Hercules cargo planes, occupies the barren plateau at 90° S. And a number of so-called adventure travel companies offer "last degree" expeditions, on which clients are plunked down by plane at 89° N, shepherded by guides on a sixty-nine-mile ski jaunt to the pole, and picked up there by helicopter, not before celebrating with champagne, photographs, and diplomas.

From the vantage point of more than a century of motorized progress in the exploration of the globe, the quests of Scott and Amundsen and Nansen seem somehow quaint, the earnest heroics of their struggles with ice and storm reduced to historical oddities. If those men could have anticipated how aircraft would reconfigure polar discovery, would they have committed their lives to their bold voyages?

Nansen at least anticipated the brave new world of aerial discovery. In 1897 the Swede Salomon Andrée, with two companions, set off by balloon from the shores of Svalbard, intent on flying to the North Pole. His scheme was dismissed by experts as foolhardy and suicidal, but then kindred pundits had said as much about the voyage of the *Fram* four years earlier. Nansen awaited the outcome with a gloomy premonition of the eclipse of his farthest north. But no news came from the balloonists.

It was not until 1930 that the fate of Andrée's team was learned. The men had stayed airborne for only three days before their balloon crashed at 83° N. Making their way to remote White Island, the trio had prepared to live off the land. Diaries and photographs (developed, remarkably, after thirty-three years in the cold) suggested that they may have perished from trichinosis after eating undercooked meat from a polar bear they shot.

Even the most hardened polar adventurers today, seeking new firsts in the Arctic and Antarctic, must recognize a fundamental difference between their own exploits and those of their paragons from a century before. As much as aircraft have transformed terrestrial exploration, electronic communication by means of satellite phones, radios, and the Internet has changed the exploratory game even more profoundly.

Mountaineers attempting Everest today, as well as skiers man-hauling sledges on "unsupported" journeys in the polar regions, count on daily contact not only with their backup teams but with audiences in the outside world that hang on every up-to-the-minute dispatch. Yet surprisingly few of these latter-day adventurers really own up to the gulf between what they hope to achieve and what Nansen and Amundsen undertook.

No watershed in exploratory history has been more dramatic than the revolution in what might be called connectedness. Thanks to the radio and the sat phone and EPIRB gadgets that send out automated distress calls with precise coordinates, today's polar trekkers not only get rescued by plane and chopper, they count on such exit strategies when they get in trouble.

The only kind of connectedness the men on the *Fram* could hope for was inscribed in the letters they sent back with the last supporters on the Arctic coast who saw them off into the unknown—one-way messages to the loved ones they left behind.

———

Between 1963 and 1975, I led or co-led thirteen expeditions to the mountain ranges of Alaska and the Yukon. On none of those journeys were my companions and I connected with the outside world except by a handshake agreement with the bush pilot to pick us up on a certain date. On three of the expeditions, eschewing the pilot, we hiked into and out of the ranges. On four others we hiked or boated out of the mountains.

In recent years, when I've chatted with much younger climbers about their cutting-edge forays in Alaska or the Andes or the Himalaya, I sometimes twit them with the change in expeditionary connectedness since my day. How come, I needle, they didn't choose to do without the radio and the sat phone? How come they had to stay in daily contact with the spouses or lovers they left at home?

Beneath the raillery, I nurse the memory of the blissful state that disconnectedness imbued. How could I convey to my younger friends what they missed? For the first few days in the mountains I would be jittery with the change, as half-formed fears and guilt about duties left undone jangled my nerves. Then contentment seeped in. The absolute distinction between "out" (the world I left behind) and "in" conferred its benediction. The petty aggravations of normal life fell away. The knowledge that if we got into trouble, we could count only on ourselves for rescue delivered a paradoxical boon in self-reliance. At the end of the trip, it was always wrenching to return to "out."

In the midst of such exchanges with today's alpinists, the phrase from Marvell seizes my brain: "But at my back I always hear..." Not

time's wingèd chariot, but rather the stern put-down of my vanity that
Nansen and Amundsen and their kin embody. The longest I ever spent
disconnected in the mountains was fifty-two days. That seemed plenty.
Yet Nansen and his teammates submitted without an apparent qualm
to the prospect of *five years* with no word to or from the "real" world
left behind.

Between 1819 and 1917, scores of expeditions wintered over in the
Arctic and Antarctic. More than a few spent two or even three years
disconnected from the world back home. The record may have been
held by the men aboard the *Victory* under Sir John Ross, who endured
four winters between 1829 and 1833 in the Canadian Arctic before
returning to England with the loss of only three crew members.

In all the rich literature of these polar campaigns, there is scant
discussion of the sacrifice those sailors and sledgers made in going so
long without outside contact, though the principals in several of the
more ill-starred expeditions (the *Belgica* off the Antarctic coast in
1897–99, among others) went insane from the stress, and "polar madness" was a semi-official diagnosis of mental derangement inflicted by
such ordeals.

In the twenty-first century, the number of explorers willing to sign
on for a three- or four-year exile from the civilized world has dwindled
to absolute zero. It is hard to think of any adventurer in recent years
who has gone thus disconnected for even twelve consecutive calendar
months. Yet when Nansen had announced the journey, hundreds of
applicants clamored to join.

The polar explorers of the nineteenth and early twentieth centuries
put us all to shame. We have grown addicted to contact. (American
teenagers in recent experiments have gone bonkers trying to survive
without social media for twenty-four hours at a stretch.) Not many of
my younger climbing friends today would be psychologically equipped
to handle fifty-two days in the wilderness without a radio or sat phone.

But, in turn, in the 1960s I could not have countenanced the threat of two years of isolation aboard an ice-locked ship in the Arctic.

Nansen's account of his landmark voyage verges at regular intervals into personal confession. Leaving behind his wife and infant daughter amounted for him to an almost unbearable tribulation. In *Farthest North*, he calls June 24, 1893, when he waved goodbye to them from the ship, "the darkest hour of the whole journey." Yet throughout the epic voyage, he never wavered from his goals, never succumbed to the lure of the south by cutting short the audacious program he had devised to seek the North Pole.

Perhaps we modern adventurers have lost for good the character traits that would tolerate all-out commitment to the prolonged separation from the cherished world a polar voyage once demanded. Perhaps we have lost the art of disconnectedness. In terms of psychological endurance, perhaps we have all gone soft. Neither in 1963 nor in 2016 would I have signed on for an expedition like the *Fram*'s. But the loss, I know, is mine.

With my diagnosis of throat cancer in July 2015, the awareness of ever-fleeting time took on a new acuity. I no longer worried about what I might be doing a year from now: what I might be capable of in three months seemed a more urgent concern. At the age of seventy-two, I had long since renounced any ambitions to set off into the Alaska ranges and forge first ascents. But now the question of whether I should ever again hike a favorite canyon in Utah loomed uncertain.

In my twenties and thirties, each time I headed into the mountains, I pondered the possibility that I might not come back alive. Climbing is dangerous, expeditionary mountaineering especially so. By the age of twenty-two I had lost friends in fatal accidents. After 1965, parting with Sharon, my wife, each time I stepped on board the bush plane seared my soul with ambivalence. And during storm days in the tent, I whispered a plea to her not to worry, or wrote to her in my diary.

Nansen's men were in their twenties and thirties when they sailed north from Norway in 1893. And though their anguish goes unarticulated in *Farthest North*, we can be sure they spent many a sleepless night aboard the *Fram*, wondering anew whether the bargain with fate they had sealed was worth all the privation and sacrifice, and wondering whether they would return alive. Seven of the twelve men were married with children.

Nansen speaks for all of them in his dark nights of the soul. Setting off on that serene June morning, he tells himself, "Behind me lay all I held dear in life. And what before me? How many years would pass ere I should see it all again?"

Four months later, drifting in zigzags aboard the frozen ship, on the eve of his thirty-third birthday, Nansen pondered primal matters: "in these nights such longing can come over one for all beauty, for all which is contained in a single word, and the soul flees from this interminable and rigid world of ice. When one thinks how short life is, and that one came away from it all of one's own free will. . . . We are but as flakes of foam, helplessly driven over the tossing sea."

———

Nansen and Johansen's southward retreat, an expedition unto itself, is the stuff of legend. Seizing the reprieve of turning back from their hopeless quest, at first they flew across the ice, sledging for thirty-six hours without stopping to camp. In the process, they made a tiny mistake, one that might well have proved fatal. They forgot to wind their watches.

Without an accurate timepiece, the men had no way of determining their longitude. And without longitude, they might veer so far to the east or west that they could miss Franz Josef Land altogether. Without longitude, they were effectively lost.

Minimizing the setback in his diary, Nansen tried to guess the time by watching the sun as it neared its noon zenith and by recording sunrise and sunset—at least during the days when clouds and snowfall held off. He noted down his educated guesses as to the men's longitude. (So canny was Nansen's dead reckoning that he was later able to ascertain that his estimates were off by only 26 minutes, or less than half a degree!)

One by one the dogs, famished and played out, had to be killed. To save ammunition, the men resorted to means of execution other than shooting. "The killing of the animals, especially the actual slaughtering, is a horrible affair," Nansen wrote on April 19. When several of the huskies failed to succumb to strangulation by rope, Johansen had to finish them off with a knife. Still confident that their rations would hold out for many weeks, the men fed the slain dogs only to the others. By June 5, only six of the original twenty-eight were alive.

That day Nansen got a latitude reading of 82° 18' N. From their farthest north on April 8, in two months the men had gained almost four degrees in their southward dash, or some 270 miles. Yet Nansen complained to his diary, "I cannot understand why we do not see land. The only possible explanation is that we must be farther east than we think . . ."

It was not Franz Josef Land that the men expected to sight, but Petermann Land. The Franz Josef archipelago had been discovered by an Austro-Hungarian expedition only in 1873, and then quite by accident. The expedition ship, the *Tegetthoff,* frozen into the pack the previous November, had drifted aimlessly north of the Russian archipelago of Novaya Zemlya for a year until its men touched the shores of the southernmost island of a previously unknown landmass. The team named this new discovery (191 islands all told, stretching across some 6,200 square miles) after their emperor, Franz Joseph. Despite their dire predicament, the men explored the archipelago, reaching its northern tip at Cape Fligely, from which its co-leader, Julius von Payer, stared across the frozen sea and spotted another sizeable land mass dead north, which he named after Augustus Petermann, a German geographer who had divined a temperate branch of the Gulf Stream that ought to promise easy passage north of Novaya Zemlya (one more last gasp of the Open Polar Sea). The official expedition map sketches in the southwestern shore of that presumably massive tract, centered at 83° N, even naming a western promontory Cape Vienna.

From wondering whether the two men had missed Petermann Land by veering eastward, Nansen became convinced during the following days that a prevailing wind was driving them west. If so, they might stand a better chance of reaching Svalbard than Franz Josef Land, though the prospect seemed almost hopeless. "We do not know where we are, and we do not know when this will end," Nansen lamented on June 11.

It would take Nansen and Johansen's retreat, as well as the probings of subsequent expeditions, to prove that Payer's Petermann Land did not exist. It was one more illusion, born of the hunger for discovery, by which explorers in the Arctic and Antarctic again and again turned mirages into previously unknown lands.

With the southern push and the approach of summer, the two men saw the icescape in which they lived transformed. The temperatures rose steadily, until the norm hovered just below freezing rather than forty below. With the thaw, the once solid ice disintegrated, until vast stretches were reduced to "brash," a slushy melange of chunks and water. Even as they crossed seemingly solid snowdrifts, the men regularly sank to their knees, soaking their legs.

They realized that in order to complete their quest for terra firma, they would have to repair the kayaks, carried so far as dead weight aboard the sledges. Sewing and patching the torn kayak skins inside the tent each night, they tackled this renovation.

By now the men were almost out of food, nearly 800 pounds of which they had hauled away from the *Fram* in March. Fortunately seals began to appear in the open leads, some of which they were able to kill and haul onto the ice before they sank. Butchering these beasts was a nasty and onerous business, but the taste of fresh meat sent the men into transports of delight. Eventually they were able to supplement their larder with walrus and polar bear.

On July 24, as they began to give up hope, they sighted land—the first they had seen in two years. "It has long haunted our dreams, this land, and now it comes like a vision," Nansen wrote. But so treacherous were the channels full of brash ice, and so fickle the winds, that it took them thirteen days to close the short distance to the shore.

It was in the midst of this arduous toil, on August 5, that Nansen and Johansen suffered their closest call of the expedition thus far. Without their noticing it, a polar bear had stalked the men as they struggled to ferry their loads by kayak across a slushy lead. Johansen turned to pull up his sledge just as the bear, towering over him, made a lunge, cuffing him on the head and knocking him onto his back. In the best tradition of explorers' understatement, he quietly urged his partner, "You must look sharp if you want to be in time."

Fumbling to retrieve the rifle from the kayak, Nansen almost let it slip into the sea. The bear was momentarily distracted by one of the two remaining dogs, which was barking fiercely. One shot behind the ear from the marksman who had trained among the Norway hills felled the great mammal.

At last, on August 6, the men set foot on land. Undercutting their joy was the necessity of finishing off the last two dogs, Suggen and Kaifas, for there was no way they could be carried on sledge or kayak, and they were too weak to walk. "Faithful and enduring, they had followed us the whole journey through," wrote Nansen, "and now that better times had come, they must say farewell to life." Out of pity the men squandered cartridges on the executions. "I shot Johansen's, and he shot mine."

They could only guess what land they had discovered. "I am more than ever at a loss to know where we are," confessed Nansen. So true had been his dead reckoning, however, that the small island on which the men first set foot, which Nansen named after Eva, his wife, was in actuality part of Franz Josef Land, an outlying isle only 40 miles southeast of Cape Fligely.

During the next month, the men made their way south and west, traveling more by kayak than by sledge. Coasting the shores of much larger land masses than Eva Island, they began to believe they must after all have stumbled upon Franz Josef Land. But Payer's sketchy map was impossible to fit to the terrain they came across. With the waning of summer, they reconciled themselves to wintering over, as they searched for the ideal location to build a rude hut.

Construction took a week. They quarried stone for the walls, and dug into the turf to hollow out a space in which eventually they could just barely stand erect. A walrus shoulder blade tied to a broken snowshoe piece served as their shovel. They chinked the stones with moss and dirt. For a roof, they rigged a ridgepole out of a driftwood log, over which they stretched walrus skins.

Almost out of food, the men dug a hole in the turf and buried a cache containing the last of the provisions they had hauled all the way from the *Fram*—a treat to be saved for the spring of 1896. They counted on surviving off the land, principally the walruses they were able to kill just offshore from their hut. For light, the men fashioned stone lamps in which they burned smoky oil from the walruses, scavenging bits of cloth from their medical kit for wicks. They had hoped the lamps would give off heat as well, but after the sun disappeared for good on October 15, the men shivered in perpetual cold.

Nansen and Johansen spent the next *eight months* confined to their domicile. For the first time during the expedition, Nansen stopped writing in his diary. If depression seized the men's spirits, *Farthest North* gives no hint of it. Instead, Nansen claimed, "our life was so monotonous that there was nothing to write about."

The men tried to sleep as much as they could, sometimes managing twenty hours out of twenty-four. They tried to take interest in the winter sky, attending to Northern Lights, meteors, and the wandering of the planets. On Christmas Eve, Nansen "washed myself . . . in a quarter cup of warm water." Their dreams dwelt on banquets back in Norway, packed with friends and family. By day they endlessly discussed a myriad of topics, skirting the gut-level questions of survival and rescue. They speculated for hours about what had happened to the *Fram* and the eleven comrades they had left behind.

And Nansen, once he had resumed writing in his diary, went off on his metaphysical flights, pondering the place of human beings in the cosmos: "Is, then, the whole thing but the meteor of a moment? Will the whole history of the world evaporate like a dark, gold-edged cloud in the glow of the evening—achieving nothing, leaving no trace, passing like a caprice?"

In May, as they prepared to continue their southward journey, the men dug up their cache. All the precious food was spoiled: "the pemmican—well, it had a strange appearance, and when we tasted it— ugh! It, too, had to be thrown away."

On May 19, after their third winter in the Arctic, the men bade farewell to their hut and started onward. For a month they made their way farther south, eventually crossing the 80th parallel. During this peregrination, on June 12 they blundered into a disaster as perilous as men in the Arctic have ever survived. All it took was a moment of careless inattention.

After a long day of paddling, Nansen and Johansen pulled up to an ice shelf "to stretch our legs a little" and to climb a hummock to scout the route ahead. Having grown casual about tying off the kayaks, they anchored them to a flimsy stake. When they returned, they found the boats floating out to sea. Without the kayaks, the men were as good as dead.

Without hesitation, Nansen stripped off half his clothes, dived into the water, and swam toward the drifting kayaks. The cold shocked his whole body. Before he could reach the boats, "I felt ... that my limbs were gradually stiffening and losing all feeling, and I knew that in a short time I should not be able to move them." There was no alternative but to swim on. With a desperate last surge, he caught the nearest kayak and managed to clamber aboard, but he was shaking so uncontrollably that he could paddle only in short bursts. Once on shore again, Nansen let his partner strip off his clothes, pack him into the sleeping bag spread on the ice, and stand vigil as he shivered for hours before his body regained its warmth.

On June 7 the men's provisions were reduced to a single day's supply of meat. Yet once again, they were able to shoot a walrus and replenish their store.

They still wondered where exactly they were, though Nansen became convinced not only that they were on Franz Josef Land, but that they might be nearing the spot where an English yachtsman named Leigh Smith had wintered over in 1881–82, after his boat had been crushed in the ice. On June 17, as he crawled out of the tent to fix a breakfast of walrus meat, Nansen froze in incredulity: "[A] sound suddenly reached my ear so like the barking of a dog that I started." He returned to the tent to report the event to a disbelieving Johansen. The two men set out to investigate.

They followed dog tracks in the sod, heard more barking, turned a corner, and saw "a dark form moving among the hummocks farther in." It was indeed a dog. And moments later, Nansen and Johansen waved their hats at the first other human they had seen in fifteen months. They closed the gap.

With Victorian formality, the stranger shook Nansen's hand, murmuring in English, "I'm immensely glad to see you."

Nansen rejoined, "Thank you; I also."

The man kept staring. Suddenly he blurted out, "Aren't you Nansen?"

"Yes, I am."

"By Jove! I am glad to see you!"

———

The stranger was Frederick Jackson, in charge of an expedition tasked by the Royal Geographic Society with exploring Franz Josef Land. The meeting point was Cape Flora on Northbrook Island, the very same place where Leigh Smith had wintered over.

Nansen and Johansen were back in Norway by mid-August. There was still no word of the *Fram*. But meanwhile, Sverdrup had piloted the frozen ship through another year's vicissitudes, and had been at last able to fire up its engine and cut through disintegrating ice into the North Atlantic. The ship completed its voyage just as planned. Nansen and Johansen got the welcome news by telegram on August 20. The next day they boarded the *Fram* and embraced their teammates.

In the strict terms of completing the mission on which Nansen had set his heart—being the first to reach the North Pole—the expedition had failed. Yet the whole world saluted the triumph of the extraordinary voyage, and of the team's establishing a new landmark farthest north.

Nansen lived for the rest of his life on the fame his expedition had won him. The *Fram* went on to a lasting renown of her own, serving the 1910–12 expedition under Amundsen that attained the South Pole.

For Johansen, however, the glory was fleeting. According to Nansen's biographer Roland Huntford, he bitterly resented Nansen's treatment of him in *Farthest North*, though the modern reader can find little in the book to warrant such disenchantment. Chosen for Amundsen's Antarctic voyage more than a decade later, Johansen had a falling out with his leader and was left behind at the base camp hut by the party that reached the pole.

Johansen declined into heavy drinking and depression. Back in Norway in early 1913, he committed suicide by shooting himself, leaving behind a wife and four children.

Nansen went on to as storied a career as any explorer ever enjoyed. After World War I, he became Norway's delegate to the League of Nations, and for his work in resettling refugees from the war, he won the Nobel Peace Prize in 1922.

For the rest of his life (he died in 1930), Nansen was the leading *éminence grise* among polar explorers. Yet his record farthest north lasted only five years. On April 25, 1900, members of an expedition led by another great explorer, Luigi Amedeo, the Duke of the Abruzzi, pursuing a more conventional campaign launched from none other than Franz Josef Land, reached 86° 34' N, besting Nansen and Johansen's mark by a mere 25 miles.

According to Huntford, Nansen was inconsolable. He later agonized over whether Amundsen, once his protégé, had stolen his place as Norway's greatest explorer.

For more than half a century, the world accepted Robert E. Peary's claim to have been the first to reach the North Pole in 1909. Yet beginning in the 1970s, long-simmering doubts about the extraordinarily rapid times on Peary's final dash prompted a rigorous reexamination of his data. The consensus today is that Peary probably got within 100 miles of the pole, but faked the rest. Worn out by seven previous attempts to reach 90° N, his toes sacrificed to frostbite, he took refuge in a hoax rather than confess another failure to the world.

The first human beings to stand at the North Pole, then, were the crew of a Soviet military plane that landed there in 1937. The first "explorers" to reach the pole by travel across the ice were Ralph Plaisted's self-taught amateurs, who arrived by snowmobile on April 20, 1968. A few days later, they were downing beers back home in Minnesota.

TWO

BLANK *on*
the MAP

Between 1933 and 1951, Eric Shipton was a member of five Mount Everest expeditions. In 1933, he reached 27,400 feet on the northeast ridge. By 1953 there was no other Everest veteran half so experienced on the world's highest mountain, yet at the last minute he was fired from leadership of the team that placed Hillary and Tenzing on the summit. He was replaced by Colonel John Hunt, who organized the massive overkill of the successful first ascent along strict military lines.

Shipton always disdained big teams and regimented ranks. He once said, "If an expedition cannot be organized in a pub on the back of an envelope in a couple of hours, it isn't worth going on." By 1953, his notions were considered quaint and out-of-date. Ironically, he is now seen—along with his best friend, H. W. (Bill) Tilman—as a retroactive hero of the avant-garde. The two men pioneered the light-and-fast alpine style that would eventually supersede the heavy logistical assaults that claimed the first ascents of all but one of the fourteen highest mountains in the world between 1950 and 1964.

Despite his identification with Everest, Shipton preferred exploring unknown regions to making first ascents. In 1937, with his pal Tilman, on one of several expeditions the two masters of light-and-fast travel would share, Shipton realized his dream to near perfection. In the rugged Karakoram Range of Pakistan, a vast region north of the Baltoro Glacier and K2, the world's second highest mountain, had never been mapped. On the charts of the day, as Shipton later wrote, "Across this blank space was written one challenging word, 'Unexplored.'" Expeditions trying to climb K2 had followed the Baltoro to the mountain's southern approaches in 1902 and 1909. The first two thoroughgoing attempts on the peak would follow the same route in 1938 and 1939. But no explorer had penetrated the maze of peaks and glaciers to the north, a region that constituted the bulk of the great Karakoram, a realm that still challenges the best alpinists today. A few intrepid travelers—Sir Francis Younghusband in 1887, Kenneth Mason in 1926, Ardito Desio in 1929—had touched on the borders of that *terra incognita*, leaving behind a handful of wildly inaccurate sketch maps and scraps of geographical certitude.

Shipton's plan to explore and map the region was an immensely ambitious one, but in his typical jaunty fashion he at first proposed tackling it with a single companion, the redoubtable Tilman. In the end, he put together a four-man party. The two other principals happened to be the brothers of two of England's most famous poets. John Auden was a geologist who had traveled extensively in the Himalaya and had done a fair amount of climbing in Europe. Michael Spender was a surveyor with experience in Greenland; he had also been a member of Shipton's 1935 expedition to Everest. One would give much to be able to listen in on the conversations the four men must have had in many a camp that summer about art and literature and politics, but Shipton's expedition narrative is silent on the subject.

From his previous expeditions Shipton knew how valuable Sherpas were in high-altitude exploration, and he managed to recruit seven of the best, even though it meant arranging their passage by railroad from Darjeeling across India to Srinagar. As Shipton later vowed, "During the expedition I frequently regretted that I had not brought double the number of Sherpas." As sirdar, or head Sherpa, Shipton enlisted Ang Tharkay, already a veteran of five expeditions with Shipton. Ang Tharkay would become a legend in Himalayan annals on a par perhaps only with Tenzing Norgay. He would leave his own account of the 1937 expedition in a fugitive memoir dictated in English, published in French, and translated back to English only in a 2016 edition. Rounding out the party were four Balti porters whose knowledge of their home country on the fringes of the Karakoram would prove invaluable.

Blank on the Map is not the best of Shipton's six mountaineering narratives, but it remains a blithe evocation of an exploratory experience the likes of which no one can have today. Yet Shipton was convinced that he lived in a decadent age, and he rued the fact that explorers before him had lived more boldly and more truly. In a curious chapter early in the book, titled "Of the Real Value of Climbing," he laid out a manifesto for his vagabondage. "Every time I start an expedition," he wrote, "I feel that I am getting back to a way of living which is now lost." He wished he had climbed in the Alps in the days of de Saussure, at the end of the eighteenth century, "before they had been civilized out of their wild unspoiled beauty and tamed into a social asset." Unabashedly, Shipton hankered for the "good old days." In the 1930s, he complained, so many human activities were undertaken for all the wrong reasons: "for publicity, for sensationalism, for money, or because it is the fashion to do them." Only in the great ranges such as the Himalaya and the Karakoram could an explorer discover a world as unspoiled as the Alps of de Saussure. In the summer of 1937, Shipton claimed, the wilderness taught him and his companions "a way of living in the beauty and solitude of high remote places."

Reading those words today, I long to set Shipton straight. He lived in a golden age that we moderns would give much to recapture. There are no more blanks on the map of the world in 2017. And there are few adventures as stirring and all-encompassing as the lyrical summer he and his teammates spent wandering among the unknown peaks and glaciers of the Karakoram. It is we who were born too late.

———

There seems to be an organic linkage between the style in which Shipton and Tilman traveled and the style in which they wrote. The expedition books of the 1930s, chronicling German attempts on Kangchenjunga and Nanga Parbat and the British on Everest (unless Shipton was the author), tended to portray the efforts in grimly serious, military language. The prose is full of siege and assault, advance and retreat, conquest and defeat. But Shipton and Tilman chose an ironic tone, glossing lightly over hardships and celebrating successes in the most modest language. It is a style that has been much imitated in adventure narratives ever since, but seldom with the dexterity and panache of the original masters. In Srinagar, for instance, the team shops for eating utensils, determined to keep the weight at an absolute minimum. The men debate whether each of them needs his own knife, rather than sharing a knife between two members. Writes Shipton, "Tilman was strongly opposed to our taking plates, insisting that one could eat everything out of a mug. I maintained that if we happened to be eating curry and rice and drinking tea at the same time it would be nicer to have them served in separate receptacles."

Climbers attempting K2 today usually fly to Skardu, then take trucks to Askole, near the foot of the Baltoro Glacier. The 1937 party had to walk all the way from Srinagar, 416 miles to Skardu and another 70 to Askole. To carry the gear and food the team would need for four months in the Karakoram, the men hired porters and ponies in Srinagar. Such a trek today might well be worth a book in its own right, but one has to read between the lines of Shipton's account to conceive of the monumental effort it took simply to get to the launching point of the expedition itself. "Mountaineers are notoriously bad walkers," Shipton claims, and "Tilman declared dejectedly that we would certainly be turned out of any self-respecting hiking club in England." The entourage, however—"sahibs," Sherpas, Baltis, porters, ponies, and all—covered the march from Srinagar to Skardu in fourteen days. Shipton does not bother to calculate the rate, but the reader can easily do the math and discover that the average march was 30 miles per day. So much for bad walkers.

The dusty ride by jeep or truck from Skardu to Askole takes about seven hours today. Shipton's team needed five harrowing days. The biggest obstacles were two huge rivers, the first of which was the mighty Indus. The only ferry was a big wooden barge propelled with oars and paddles.

> *The Sherpas were in a great state of excitement as we cast off, shouting wildly and bombarding those on shore with dried dung. They then seized the paddles and wielded them in the wrong direction. However, as the craft relied for its progress mostly on the oars and the poles, their efforts did not hinder us much, and soon they abandoned paddling for the better sport of splashing each other with water. We were carried downstream by the current at an alarming rate and seemed to make very little progress across the river. However, we eventually stuck in the mud on the opposite side and landed our belongings.*

It took two relays and three hours to get the entire party across the river.

The Shigar River was even more dicey. Instead of a wooden barge, the natives relied on rafts made of twenty sheepskin bladders each, tied together and reinforced with strips of wood. Writes Shipton, "It was a terrifying experience to entrust our lives and our belongings to such ridiculously frail craft, on a racing river with ugly rapids in sight ahead.

The most alarming moment occurred when the crew downed [paddles] to blow up the leaking bladders!" The ponies had to swim the torrent. After four haphazard ferries and many heart-stopping moments, the team gathered itself on the far bank.

Askole stood as the last outpost of civilization. The first major challenge for the team was to get its one and a half tons of gear and food up the Baltoro and across a virtually unknown pass into the huge, unexplored labyrinth of glaciers that drained into the Shaksgam River. Shipton had counted on hiring porters in Askole. At first, this seemed like a routine matter, as the locals assumed the team simply wanted to ascend the Baltoro the way the parties attempting K2 had previously done. "When at last it dawned on them," Shipton noted, "that we intended to cross the range, their faces fell, and they told us no one would consent to come with us." That pass, the natives swore, had only once been traversed, and that by a much better-equipped party, and in the proper summer season. Yet "after some hours of diplomatic argument we managed to convince them that we were not so incompetent as we looked, and that we were willing to pay well for any help we received."

Readers of the classic expedition narratives of attempts from the 1930s through the 1960s on the world's highest mountains tend to hurry through the first hundred pages or so. The details of load carries, porters, negotiations to forestall strikes, and the endless problems of getting enough food, stoves, and tents to the right camps make for tedious going. Yet only after scaling this mountain of logistics can the actual mountain be attempted. Shipton's challenge in 1937 was several times more difficult than those that had faced the previous attempts on K2 or Everest. He needed to get all the impedimenta that his reconnaissance required not to some base camp on a straightforward glacier, but across the main spine of the Karakoram, simply to begin the team's explorations. In Askole, the men hired one hundred porters—ethnic Baltis, whom in the language of the day Shipton often refers to as "coo-

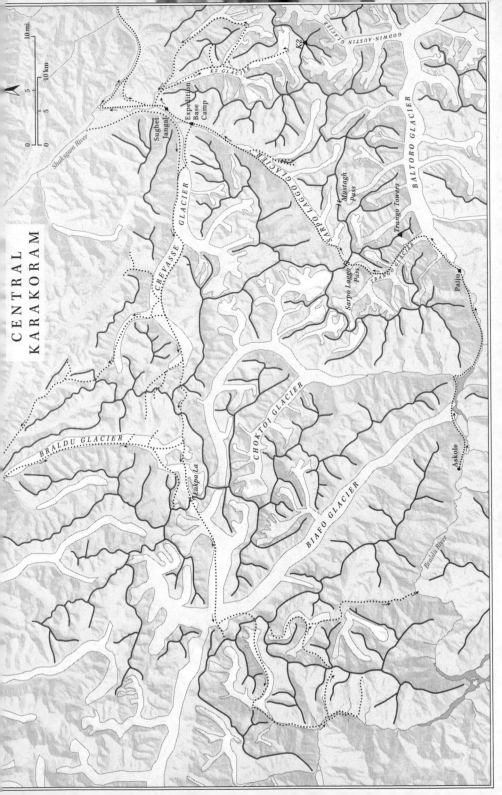

lies." Even with so much manpower, the task was herculean. Once again, loads had to be stripped to the bare minimum.

Reading between the lines once more, one realizes that sorting out the massive piles of gear and food and porter assignments must have been a nightmarish task. But Shipton recounts it with his usual droll humor. The leaders imposed on themselves a strict limit of thirty-five pounds apiece for personal gear, including sleeping bags and ground sheets. (Thirty-five pounds for more than three months in the field, as any expeditioneer today can testify, is spartan in the extreme.) "Spender cut his tobacco allowance down to one pipeful a day," Shipton observed, "in order to take with him Tolstoy's *War and Peace* and Forster's *A Passage to India*. These were a great boon to us in our few bouts of bad weather, though Tilman and I felt ourselves morally obliged to pay with tobacco for the luxury of reading." There was no use imposing the same regimen on the Sherpas, who had been gathering knickknacks to add to their personal stashes all the way from Srinagar. In Askole their packs weighed twice as much as they had at the start. "They were bursting with an amazing assortment of junk: wooden spoons, packets of snuff and spices, electric torches, nails, filthy rags, and other treasures which they were reluctant to leave behind."

The team left Askole on May 26. The next eight days would throw so many obstacles across the team's path that they seriously considered abandoning the whole expedition, or at least whittling its ambitions vastly down to an easy reconnaissance of the country south of the Baltoro Glacier. It did not help that on the second day of the march, Tilman (normally the toughest man on any expedition) fell ill with a high fever. The men deliberated solemnly and at last decided that Auden would stay with Tilman at the Paiju camp just below the snout of the Baltoro, while Shipton and Spender pushed the army of porters and loads onward to the north. It is a measure of just how canny and independent all four Britishers were that at times during the following months, they happily split up and pursued separate explorations hither and yon, with only a promised rendezvous at a certain spot in the unmapped wilderness to ensure a reunion.

During most of the next week it snowed heavily. The Balti porters shivered around their campfires fed by juniper boughs, and on the marches, the leaders usually broke trail through knee-deep snow. The pass that the Baltis swore had been crossed only once before, Shipton decided, was out of reach. Instead, the team proceeded only a little way up the Baltoro before taking a sharp left turn at its tributary, the Trango Glacier. This icy corridor climbs northwest between dazzling granite walls that rise sheer as much as 7,000 feet to distant, spiky summits. Not until the 1970s and 1980s did climbers dare tackle such peaks as Nameless Tower, Great Trango Tower, and Uli Biaho. Indeed, the Trango massif is regarded today as harboring perhaps the greatest collection of severely technical, high-altitude alpine routes of any range in the world. Somewhere near the head of the Trango Glacier, Ardito Desio had in 1929 seen from a distance a pass that ought to lead to the Shaksgam drainage. On that elusive goal all the expedition's hopes depended.

Day after day, the terrified porters threatened mutiny, insisting that they be paid and discharged on the spot. Shipton described the "incredible confusion" that ensued. "Everyone shouted at once. No one listened to what was said. Occasionally blows were exchanged between the coolies themselves." Despite meticulous outfitting by the Englishmen, the Baltis wailed about their shortages: "Some had no glasses; some no warm clothes; some no gloves; some no boots; some no blankets; some had sore eyes; some had boils; and everyone had too much to say." It was here that the Sherpas played a vital role, as Ang Tharkay and Lobsang berated the Baltis with "torrents of abuse."

The fugitive pass, if it existed at all, was invisible from below. On June 2, Shipton, Spender, and several Sherpas ploughed a track through the deep snow of the upper Trango Glacier. Ang Tharkay turned back

to exhort the straggling caravan of porters onward. Finally, at an altitude of 18,650 feet, Shipton and Spender stood on the col that led to the
unmapped greater Karakoram. Wrote Shipton, "It was a thrilling
moment; and all the exasperation and worry of the last few days slid
away from our minds. To the north, the Sarpo Laggo glacier curved
down towards the desolate rust-coloured ranges of Chinese Turkistan.
This was our first view into the country which we had come so
far to see."

But there was no room for a campsite on the pass, and the porters
were closer to mutiny than ever. The fate of the whole expedition was
still very much in doubt.

———

The Shipton–Tilman style of writing, like the fast-and-light ethos of
expeditioneering the two men espoused, took decades to catch on.
During the so-called Golden Age of Himalayan Mountaineering (1950–
64), the chronicles that recorded the triumphs on the highest peaks in
the world, such as Maurice Herzog's *Annapurna*, Sir John Hunt's *The
Ascent of Everest*, and Ardito Desio's *Victory over K2*, treated the ascents
as masterworks of logistical buildup capped by gutsy summit pushes
by a stalwart pair of climbers. These books postulated that the success
of only two men in reaching the highest point on the mountain spread
its benediction to the whole team, and indeed served their country as a
clarion declaration of national pride and supremacy. There was precious little humor in the prose; instead, martial metaphors on every
page supported a narrative that veered closer to melodrama than to
understatement.

The Shipton–Tilman vein of dry, whimsical wit came into vogue
only in the 1970s and '80s, partly as a reaction against the jingoism of
international mountaineering as it had been waged throughout the
Golden Age. Four decades later, climbing writers still strive to hit the
Shipton–Tilman note of happy vagabondage laced with gentle self-

deprecation. Yet today's climbing panegyrists all too often go overboard, indulging in the affectation of treating real danger and narrow
escapes as slapstick buffoonery. The genuine lyricism that anchors
Shipton's and Tilman's books gets lost in a self-conscious straining for
effect. The difference is a matter of subtlety—Buster Keaton versus the
Three Stooges.

Irony is a delicate technique, and no mountain writers ever han-
dled it better than Shipton and Tilman. The *locus classicus* of their style
is the famous line in Tilman's *The Ascent of Nanda Devi*, recording the
moment in 1936 that he and Noel Odell stood on the summit of the
highest peak yet climbed anywhere in the world: "I believe we so far
forgot ourselves as to shake hands on it."

Having crested the all-important pass to the Shaksgam drainage,
Shipton and Spender and the Sherpas stumbled down the far side to a
cheerless camp at the head of the Sarpo Laggo Glacier. The "thrilling
moment" of crossing the pass was tempered now by the daunting challenge of getting all the Balti porters with their loads across the
same divide.

On June 4, an exhausted John Auden arrived in camp with the
happy news that Tilman had recovered from his high fever and was
following a day or two behind. (About the self-sufficiency of the four
principals on the expedition, with their blithe ability to find one
another after days apart and across unmapped terrain, Shipton makes
no bones. It is left for the reader once more to discern and admire
their skill.)

That day Shipton led his advance party farther down the glacier to
find a hospitable site for what would in effect become the team's
advance base camp. Within an hour, he had arrived at a grassy glade
beside the massive glacier where there was running water, flowers in
early bloom, and birds in full song.

The glade was known Changtok. Both Younghusband in 1889 and
Desio in 1929 had camped here on their glancing reconnaissances of

the greater Karakoram. The Sarpo Laggo Glacier, though essentially unexplored, was thus known to Westerners before Shipton, and he was not surprised to find vestiges of both camps. The name presents a puzzle: it is Uzbek for "young husband," though whether Sir Francis himself or someone else so labeled it remains uncertain.

What stunned Shipton on arriving at Changtok was not the old campsite of his predecessors but the much older remains of stone circles and even the foundations of stone buildings. This was the first of a number of discoveries the 1937 expedition would make of prehistoric, non-Western presence in the middle of this severe wilderness. Musing on the ruins, Shipton concluded that Changtok must have been a regular stopping place on the passage between Baltistan and Yarkand, an ancient trading route so lost in time that its memory persisted (even among the Balti natives) only as rumor and myth. Yet the remoteness of the place, and the difficulty of reaching it, filled Shipton with astonishment at the unknown traders who had pioneered such a thrust into one of the most dangerous regions in all of Asia.

Ang Tharkay's account of the 1937 expedition takes up a mere nine pages of *Mémoires d'un Sherpa*. It is short on the geographic minutiae that Shipton so lovingly details in *Blank on the Map*, but it reveals a side of the expedition that Shipton largely glosses over. That is the conflict between the Sherpas and the Balti porters, which at times broke out in physical violence. Thus, even before the team reached Askole, an incident occurred that could well have wrecked the whole expedition. Seventeen years later Ang Tharkay recalled it vividly:

> One of the coolies stumbled and fell with his load of ghee and cigarettes. The cigarettes and melted butter fell in a heap together, both of them rendered unusable. This made me angry, and I reprimanded

the man for his carelessness. He responded by threatening me with
a large stick that he held in his hand. I flew into a rage, ripped the
stick out of his hand, and hit him several times with it. His thirty
comrades, plus a crowd of villagers, threw themselves upon me. The
situation was about to turn ugly when my six Sherpas pulled out
their kukris [knives]. They also brandished their pistols. This brought
our assailants back to reason.

Once the "sahibs" learned about the conflict, they lined up the
Sherpas like truant schoolboys, scolded them in front of the villagers,
and "made us promise to avoid any quarrels in these barbarous environs, where the law of the jungle reigns."

Shipton devotes a paragraph to this debacle, but makes it sound as
though the incident had been a simple case of cultural misunderstand-
ing. But Ang Tharkay unwittingly reveals just how entrenched even a
Shipton–Tilman expedition was in the hierarchical assumptions of
Empire. The fact that Ang Tharkay unblushingly refers to his inferiors
as "coolies," his betters as "sahibs," indicates how imbued even the
Sherpas were with that colonial sensibility.

Weeks later, on the Sarpo Laggo Glacier, another serious conflict
arose. Shipton's narrative laments the difficulty the men have throughout this crucial part of the journey in keeping the porters from mutiny-
ing, and he glumly notes the times at which five or six or eight of the
Baltis refused to continue and demanded to be paid on the spot. But
Ang Tharkay heightens the conflict:

The coolies became intractable, so Mr. Shipton decided to send them
home. For safety reasons he asked Lhakpa Tenzing and me to walk
with them to Askole [unlikely, since the team needed the Sherpas at the
front]. Lobsang, another Sherpa porter, followed us for some distance,
and we had gone barely a mile with the coolies when he shouted at us

to stop, because he realized that the coolies had smuggled a load of
food and cigarettes as well as a roll of blankets. We tried to stop them,
but they rushed ahead until Lobsang and I caught up with them. We
had to come to blows in order to recover what they had stolen. One of
them pretended to faint, in order to incite his comrades against us and
escape with his stolen goods.... You could see the extent to which the
coolies' moods and whims complicated our expedition.

For Shipton, despite the nuisances of load-hauling, the days spent on the Sarpo Laggo Glacier were rapturous. The full team of four was united again. Every day the men could see the summit of K2 soaring in the east. Since that was a fixed point whose latitude and longitude were known, Spender could use it as a base as he plotted all the unmapped peaks and glaciers the team discovered into a comprehensive survey.

Beyond the snout of the Sarpo Laggo Glacier to the northeast lay the surging Shaksgam River, which flows from southeast to northwest across the high plateau. If the team could get to its banks early enough in the season, they might ford the river to explore a whole separate constellation of peaks, the Aghil Range. In any event, Shipton intended to make an oasis of snow-free land near the Shaksgam, at a place Younghusband had called Suget Jangal, the base camp for the whole four-month reconnaissance.

Shipton's account of these days mingles frustration with the porters and the obstacles of glacier travel with a dawning anticipation of success. On June 13 the team camped within a short march of Suget Jangal. For once, the dry restraint of *Blank on the Map* gives way to a passage of unalloyed joy:

That evening was for me one of the greatest moments of the expedi-
tion. Warmed by the unaccustomed luxury of a blazing fire, its leap-
ing flames fed with unstinted wood, I felt that after long days of toil

and disappointment we had at last arrived. East and west of us stretched an unexplored section, eighty miles long, of the greatest watershed in the world. To the north, close at hand, across the Shaks- gam river, was the Aghil range, with its romantic associations and unknown peaks and valleys. To share all this, I had with me three companions as keen as myself, supported by seven of the most stout- hearted retainers in the world. We had food enough to keep us alive for three months in this place of my dreams, and the health and experience to meet the opportunity. I wanted nothing more.

When I first read *Blank on the Map*, I felt the same kind of wistful sorrow that Shipton had when he imagined climbing in the Alps in the time of de Saussure. By 1963, the first year I climbed in Alaska, every square mile of the forty-ninth state had been mapped. This remarkable achievement had come about not thanks to the gutsy work of teams such as Shipton's, plunging into unknown places and surveying their way from camp to camp, but rather through the high-tech wizardry of aerial photography. In 1963 in Alaska, there were still wilderness tracts that no human being had ever set foot in, but you could buy a very accurate map of every one of them from the United States Geological Survey in Washington, DC. Much of the state was covered by the 1:62,500 series, on which an inch equaled a mile of real terrain. But even the farther-flung regions, such as the Brooks Range north of the Arctic Circle, had been mapped on vast 1:250,000 quadrangles (1 inch = 4 miles).

By 1963, I suspect, there were still parts of the globe—in Africa, perhaps, or Antarctica—that had not been adequately mapped. But by 2017 every inch of the surface of our planet has succumbed to the dream of the cartographers. Today, there are no more blanks on the map.

In 1967, however, I was granted an exploratory adventure as close to Shipton's idyll as a young climber could have hoped for. The year before, our team of five had made the first ascent of Kichatna Spire, the highest peak in a compact cluster of granite monoliths rivaling those of the Karakoram. The tiny range, 70 miles southwest of Denali, was officially known as the Cathedral Spires. Today, climbers simply call it the Kichatnas.

From high on Kichatna Spire's north ridge in late September, on a rare clear day, I spotted a kindred agglomeration of fierce summits thrusting into the sky some 80 miles farther southwest in the Alaska Range. In four trips to Alaska, I had never before seen those peaks, nor, I would later deduce, could they be viewed from any inhabited place in the Great Land.

Thrilled by my discovery, I ordered four 1:62,500 quads from the USGS, titled Lime Hills C-3, C-4, D-3, and D-4. To my astonishment, there were only three named peaks in a vast sprawl of glaciers and mountains rising as high as 7,000 feet above their bases. The highest summit in the range stood a mere 9,828 feet above sea level. But I could tell from the dense contour lines that here lay hidden a fairyland of unclimbed peaks, enough to challenge my own and several future generations.

Two of those peaks had been given the meaningless names North Buttress and South Buttress, but the third—evidently a formidable pyramid of steep rock walls and icy couloirs—was labeled Mount Mausolus. Only one of the dozens of glaciers in this mysterious range bore an official name—the Stony Glacier, lapping against Mausolus on the east.

To plumb the provenances of this odd assortment of names, I turned to Donald J. Orth's magisterial *Dictionary of Alaska Place Names*. North Buttress and South Buttress bore the unhelpful tag, "Local name reported in 1958 by USGS." That was the year in which the quad maps had been compiled, but what "local name" could possibly mean, with no residents within 70 miles of the mountains, was puzzling. My best guess was that some soulless surveyor out in the lowlands to the west, where the Big River churned through tundra barrens toward its junction with the mighty Kuskokwim, had slapped the names on a pair of distant summits in a moment of bureaucratic taxonomy. Stony Glacier was also attributed to the faceless USGS in 1958.

Mount Mausolus, however, suggested deep personal history. According to Orth, Mausolus was a "name shown on a manuscript map, probably done by a prospector, dated 1917. He must have been a classicist, because several of his names come from classical history." Mausolus, ruler of Caria in the fourth century BC, was the builder of the storied Mausoleum.

Who was the prospector? Where was his map? I should have written to Orth for clarification, but I was too eager to go climbing.

The wilderness I had become infatuated with stretched some 15 miles east to west and 20 north to south just on the four quads I had purchased. Evidently it spread even farther to the east, north, and south off the edges of those maps. Perhaps a handful of prospectors or surveyors had ventured into the fringes of this range, and maybe in even earlier times bold Native American hunters (Athapaskans from the Kuskokwim?) had nosed against its western ramparts, but I grew increasingly convinced that this sizeable range, promising top-notch climbing, was essentially unexplored.

According to Orth, the Cathedral (Kichatna) Spires had been named in 1898 by Josiah Edward Spurr, a tough USGS explorer who had passed just south of the stunning cluster of peaks on his ambitious reconnaissance of southwestern Alaska. But the much larger range on which I fixed my obsessive attention through the winter of 1966–67 was unnamed. I couldn't wait to go there.

I rounded up five friends for the expedition, four of them old cronies from the Harvard Mountaineering Club, the fifth, Art Davidson, fresh off the first winter ascent of Denali. From the USGS I also ordered the aerial oblique photos from which the maps had been made. I had taught myself the stereo trick of crossing my eyes and focusing at a distance, so in each pair of photos I could suddenly see the mountains in three-dimensional relief, as they would have looked from about 25,000 feet. In a letter to Art, I raved, "The finest-looking peak spreads these perfect ridges over the head of the glacier, just like the wings of an angel." Art wrote back, "Does the Angel have a reasonable route?" Thus even before we got there, we had named the peak that would become our principal objective the next summer.

In 1967, we were only thirty years removed from Shipton's exploration of the greater Karakoram, yet much had changed since his day. Not only did we have the huge advantage of the maps and aerial photos; I was pretty sure we could fly in and land on the glacier that flowed north from the Angel, as we had flown in to a similar glacier in the Spires the year before. In 1937, to explore our range, we would have had to fly to the dirt landing strip of Farewell, 70 miles to the north, then ferry loads across boggy, trackless wastes of taiga and tundra, fording two big rivers just to get to the snout of the glacier I had planned for our base camp. That, to be sure, would have been a much shorter trek than Shipton's team had braved all the way from Srinagar in 1937; but on the other hand, we could have found no native porters to carry our loads.

The plan was for Matt Hale, Ned Fetcher, and me to get a three-week head start on the rest of the team. On July 11, I flew into the unknown range with a very jittery pilot. The fellow, I realized, was effectively lost once we passed over the dormant volcanoes of Spurr and Gerdine, which you could see from Anchorage. I monitored the maps carefully, and at last we came in sight of North Buttress, the highest peak in the range. I'm not sure the pilot would have attempted a landing at the head of the glacier had I not coaxed him into trying it with my cries of excitement. As he stepped out of the plane he exclaimed, "Wow! What a place!"

During the several hours it took for the plane to return with Matt and Ned, I fell into a weird depression. I was unable to walk more than a few yards from our small pile of gear for fear of crevasses, and a single thought surged through my brain: *This is the most remote place I've ever been.*

Yet by late that evening I had warmed to my surroundings as to a second home. The three of us would spend fifty-two days in this unknown range, with no radio or other means of contact with the outside world. Just as the Karakoram had for Shipton, during those seven weeks this corner of Alaska came to be to me the only world that mattered.

For two days we poked around the nearby branches of our glacier, plotting routes on the half-dozen imposing peaks that hung over base camp. We started up the Angel, but bad avalanche conditions scared us off. Above all, even more than to get to the summits of the peaks, I wanted to explore.

So on July 14 we set off on a long backcountry loop, intending to circle the main spine of the range's proudest peaks, just to see what was there. On the maps, it looked like a 45-mile circuit, traversing the lengths of four separate glaciers. We reckoned that it would take us six to ten days. The only possible glitch in our plan, we thought, was a thousand-foot climb up the steep rock-and-snow slope at the very end of the loop that we would need to perform to regain our base camp glacier, so on July 12, Matt and I roped up and climbed seven pitches down that slope to check it out. It proved easier than we had anticipated.

The Butterfly Traverse, as we jauntily named our reconnaissance, would nearly cost us our lives.

The first four days mingled delight with challenge, as we spent three and a half hours crawling through a hideous alder thicket to gain a single mile and worried about fresh grizzly tracks we followed along the sandbars of the Big River. By the evening of the fourth day, we were camped just below the pass at the head of the second glacier, halfway through our loop.

Without the maps, we might have headed blind from one valley to another, as Shipton's team had in 1937. That would have meant finding out whether a loop back to base camp even existed, with no guarantee the route would "go." Thanks to the maps, I was sure the Butterfly Traverse was feasible. The great joy so far had lain not in discovering terrain no one knew existed, but in being the first human beings to travel across a landscape the maps announced in exquisite detail.

In the night at our fourth camp, however, the weather drastically turned. A fierce wind drove sleeting rain in an alpine hurricane, as the visibility radically shrank. We could no longer see the dark granite walls that loomed over us on the west, only the gray ramp of our third glacier sloping off into whiteout. The storm would not let up.

We had a compass, but GPS had yet to be invented. It was crucial to keep the one set of maps I carried from getting soaked into illegibility. But the great problem was our clothing and camping gear. Once our down jackets and sleeping bags became sodden—impossible to prevent in the gale—they did very little to ward off the cold. Our tents lacked fitted rain flies—instead we had scrounged plastic tarps to keep them dry, but the wind ripped them loose like unfurled sails.

That night, unable to sleep, with the edge of hypothermia creeping into my bones, I talked Matt and Ned into packing up and pushing on in the wee hours. We hoped that movement would stir our blood and cure the shivers, and if we could get down to the lowlands, we might be able to build a fire. All day we stumbled south, losing altitude in the obscure valley. At last we found willow thickets among the boulders, but the wood was too soaked to start a fire. That fifth night's camp was a trial by hypothermia.

To find our way back to base camp, we had to identify the correct side-valley coming in from the west among four identical-looking gorges. Here precise map-reading might be the key to survival, for all three of the wrong valleys would lead us into steep ice fields dead-ending against granite walls. Shivering and sleepless, we chose the right valley, and at 1 PM on July 19, we started up the thousand-foot cliff Matt and I had judged a piece of cake the week before.

We gave Matt the lightest pack, and he led all ten pitches up the rock-and-snow precipice. Coming second, I belayed Matt with one rope and one hand, Ned with another. I guessed that Ned's and my packs, with all our soaked gear, weighed 65 to 70 pounds each. Everything felt desperate. If one of us did nothing worse than sprain an ankle, I remember thinking, the other two would have to leave him for dead.

Matt did a brilliant job. At last we crested the col, coiled up the ropes with numb fingers, and sprinted (at a crawl) back to base camp. It took three more days to get warm, as we often kept our camp stoves running through the night just for heat. Later we would learn that the same storm had trapped the Wilcox party high on Denali, snuffing out the lives of seven climbers—still the worst disaster in the mountain's history.

The Butterfly Traverse remains the closest call to death by hypothermia of my climbing career. Without the maps, we would never have found our way back to base camp. But without the maps, we would have turned back on the third or fourth day, leaving the dream of the perfect exploratory loop to wiser or luckier climbers in the future.

On August 2, the rest of our team—Rick and George Millikan and Art Davidson—flew in. During the rest of August, we made the first ascents of nine peaks, but the prize on which we had set our hearts— the Angel, spreading its perfect wings—eluded our grasp after five attempts, the last thwarting Matt and me only 750 feet short of the summit.

The weather stayed mostly atrocious during that month. Indeed, conditions in our newfound range were the worst I would encounter in thirteen expeditions to the Far North.

Partway through August, we realized that it was our right, as the first explorers, to name the range. We had already bestowed other names on the most daunting of the peaks that towered over us— Golgotha and Apocalypse, among them—that struck a mythic chord along with the Angel. On the trip I was reading the Bible, not in search of divine enlightenment but as part of my grad school education in literature. The book that matched the gloom and fury of our surroundings was Revelation, and I could not help reading passages out loud. Like the auditors of Saint John the Divine, the six of us craved "a woman clothed with the sun" and "silence in heaven about the space of half an hour."

It was George Millikan who suggested calling our mountains the Revelation Range. After the expedition, the name became official. The accounts I wrote for climbing journals about our storm-plagued ordeal seemed to scare off climbers for another three decades. But after the turn of the twenty-first century, coteries of ambitious young alpinists, led by the indefatigable Clint Helander, descended upon the Revelations, putting up routes that we could only have dreamed of. As of 2017, the range still abounds in unclimbed challenges as extreme as anything in Alaska, and aspirants from as far away as Europe are drawn to this frontier of exploratory mountaineering.

In 1967, because there were no more blanks on the map, I felt that I had been born too late. By 2017, fifty years had elapsed since the expedition the six of us shared in that magical range—twenty more years than had yawned between me and Shipton's ramble across the Karakoram. Today, there are climbers who wonder aloud what it must have been like to have had a whole virgin range to explore, let alone to have basked in the privilege of giving it the name by which it would be known to posterity.

––––––––

By mid-July, Shipton's team had gotten all their loads ferried down to the "base camp" at Suget Jangal. But one group of Balti porters after another demanded to be paid off and allowed to return to Askole. In the end, only four Baltis remained—the same loyal four that the team had first recruited in Srinagar.

The men were dead set on exploring the Aghil Range, which they could see looming in the northeast. But to do so would require fording the Shaksgam, the biggest river the team had faced since the Indus. And of course there was no wooden barge here in the wilderness to facilitate the crossing. Shipton decided to limit the Aghil recon to three weeks, for there was no doubt the Shaksgam would run even higher as the summer wore on and the glaciers that fed it melted.

Wading across rivers is an art at which climbers are far from proficient. Nor, to this day, is there any consensus as to how best to proceed at that dicey business. More than one expedition—like the French who made the first ascent of Fitz Roy in Patagonia in 1952—has had a member drown before the team even came to grips with its mountain objective. On July 19, Shipton and the Sherpa Ang Tensing edged nervously into the churning, ice-cold river. In his usual vein of understatement, Shipton records the near disaster that ensued: "Angtensing and I led the way across the stream, holding on to each other for mutual support. We very nearly came to grief. Angtensing was swept off his feet and I had great difficulty in holding him up until he had recovered enough to struggle ashore. . . . After this, we humbly followed the lead of the Baltis, who knew far more about this hazardous business than any of us, and faced the torrents with surprising nonchalance." Unfortunately, Shipton gives no indication as to just what technique the canny Baltis employed.

Only a day later, the team crested one of the main divides in the range, which they called simply Aghil Pass. To maximize the discoveries they might make, they split into three sub-parties, as Shipton and Tilman sent Auden and Spender off on separate missions, each fortified by four Sherpas and a single Balti, with plans to reunite in twelve days.

For the first time on the expedition, Shipton and Tilman climbed a peak. Gauging the route to be an easy scramble, the two mountaineers did not even bother to bring a rope. The climb, however, turned into a minor epic, as one man had to chip the ice off hand- and footholds before using them, sometimes while standing on the head of his partner's upraised ice axe. "After an exciting climb," Shipton deadpans, the pair stood on the peak's 20,200-foot summit.

The climb had been undertaken not to bag a first ascent, but to reach a vantage point from which to sort out the unknown topography. "The view was magnificent," Shipton writes, but "too vast to comprehend. . . . I tried to memorize the form of the country to the east, which we had come to see, but it was far too complicated, and I could not disentangle its intricacies."

On the third day in the Aghil Range, as they descended a valley on the far side of the pass, Shipton and Tilman made another startling discovery of human presence. This was not a collection of ancient ruins, but rather a "shepherd's encampment" in current use. "The Sherpas were very excited at our discovery, and evidently felt themselves to be approaching the luxury of a civilized metropolis." On the other hand, "the Baltis were not enthusiastic at the idea of meeting anyone. They said that the people on this side of the range were a race of giants and were not friendly toward intruders."

The weeks that followed amounted to a frenzy of exploration, as each bend revealed a new side valley leading to a previously unglimpsed cluster of nameless peaks. At night the men usually slept without tents, their sleeping bags laid out on beds of grass or sand. Shipton was in ecstasy. "How satisfying it was to be travelling with such simplicity. I lay watching the constellations swing across the sky. Did I sleep that night—or was I caught up for a moment into the ceaseless rhythm of space?"

It might seem that exploration of the sort the men undertook in the Aghil Range was largely devoid of the hazards of technical ascent. Yet during their four months in the Karakoram, the men regularly braved hardships ranging from waterless camps to treacherous icefalls to stones falling from high cliffs as they wended their way through tight valleys. No obstacles were more menacing than the river crossings. Near the end of June, as Shipton's party tried to ford a river called the Zug Shaksgam (*zug* meaning "false" in Uzbek), they survived their closest call of the whole expedition.

> *Tilman started across and very soon got into difficulties. When he had nearly reached the far side he was swept off his feet, and was carried, load and all, about ten yards down before he could haul himself on to the bank. His leg was bleeding freely and he had lost his ice axe. But in spite of this I did not take the river very seriously. . . . I threw a rope across to Tilman, and together we held it taut across the torrent. Lobsang and Angtharkay waded out into the stream, hanging on to the rope. In a moment Angtharkay was knocked over. Lobsang made a desperate effort to hold on to him, but Angtharkay was wrenched from his grasp by the force of water and was carried down, battered against the rocks in midstream as he went. . . . It was horrible to stand there watching Angtharkay being pounded to death without being able to do anything to help him. Each time he was flung against a rock I thought he would be stunned, and every*

*moment I expected to see his head disappear for the last time. He
was approaching a steeper drop in the river bed, when, by an amazing chance he was caught up on a large rock sticking out of the water.*

After running down the bank, Shipton and the Balti porters were able
to help Ang Tharkay to shore. The Sherpa was completely exhausted
and bruised all over, but not seriously hurt.

"I was acutely aware that my own stupidity had very nearly caused
his death," Shipton confessed. As it was, the fiasco forced the divided
party to bivouac for the night on opposite sides of the river.

After three weeks in the Aghil Range, the men reunited near the
banks of the Shaksgam, each sub-party regaling the others with their
adventures. On July 9 they returned to Suget Jangal. The expedition was
only half over, but already the various contingents had sorted out the
convoluted topography of a half-dozen unknown glaciers and scores of
peaks. The return to base camp occasioned another outpouring of grat-
ified contentment from Shipton.

*Suget Jangal was a perfect resting-place, for it had the quality of
serene peace, rare in this country of stern severity. Some tall shrubs
which grew beside the shallow blue pools were now covered with
pink blossoms. The song of small birds, the splash of a brook which
welled from a crystal spring, the young hares running shyly across
the meadows all welcomed us, and we lay on glades of soft green
grass, half hidden in shady caverns of willow branches.*

Yet even on his last day in the Aghil Range, as he prepared to return
to the main Karakoram, Shipton felt the sting of regret: "I had become
very attached to this place, and was most reluctant to leave. But one
day I shall go back there, prepared for a long stay, to gain a real knowledge of the range."

From Suget Jangal, the team now set out to explore the northern approaches to K2. No part of the Karakoram is wilder or more difficult to penetrate. Pushing up the K2 Glacier, as the men had named the ice flow that drains the great mountain on the north, Shipton and Tilman ran into a labyrinth of crevasses and *nieves penitentes*—weird ice pedestals as tall as 150 feet. At last, on July 14, the men stood at the base of the stupendous north face of the world's second highest mountain. The summit of K2 would first be reached by an Italian team in 1954, but no climbers would solve the much more daunting north face and north ridge until 1982, when a Japanese team, after a massive logistical buildup, put three men on top (one of whom died on the descent).

Shipton recorded his awe as his eye swept the 12,000 vertical feet from glacier to summit. "The sight was beyond my comprehension, and I sat gazing at it, with a kind of timid fascination, watching wreaths of mist creep in and out of corries utterly remote. I saw ice avalanches, weighing perhaps hundreds of tons, break off from a hanging glacier, nearly two miles above my head; the ice was ground to a fine powder and drifted away in the breeze long before it reached the foot of the precipice, nor did any sound reach my ears."

After the Aghil Range and the northern approach to K2, there still remained a huge tract of unmapped land to the west for the team to explore. One could retell each triumph in this four-month campaign of geographic success, but to do so would amount to a poor substitute for the vivid account Shipton has left in *Blank on the Map*. Instead, it may suffice to touch on a few of the high (and low) points of that summer of discovery.

In early August, on one more unnamed glacier, Shipton and Ang Tharkay suffered another close call—one that Shipton again unhesitatingly blamed on his own "stupidity." Well after dark, roped together with Shipton in the lead, the men came to a badly crevassed section.

Worn out after a very long day, almost within sight of camp, Shipton let down his guard.

> *Suddenly I felt the ground give way from under my feet and found myself falling through space. It seemed an age before a tug came from the rope, and I had time to wonder whether it was really tied around my waist! But at length my fall was checked with a sudden jerk; it felt as if the rope had nearly cut me in two. It was difficult to judge how far I had fallen. The ragged patch of starlit sky, at the top of the hole through which I had dropped, looked very far above me.*

The "stupidity" consisted of traveling across a dangerous glacier after dark, and going as a rope of only two, for in Shipton's present predicament it was impossible for the much lighter Ang Tharkay to haul him to the surface. Shipton managed to start chimneying between the walls of the crevasse, but he soon thrust his foot against an icicle that broke loose, and he fell back into the depths, this time landing in a moat of glacial water. "I tried to find some purchase below the surface of the water," Shipton recalled, "but could find nothing but loose bits of ice floating about. I was becoming very cold, and there was not much time to waste before numbness would make action impossible."

As usual, Shipton underplays the superhuman effort it took to get an arm hooked over a bollard of ice protruding from one wall of the crevasse, and, with a strenuous tug on the rope from Ang Tharkay, pull himself out of the water. Shipton then managed to chimney the rest of the way to the surface. "I sat gasping on the ice while Angtharkay banged and rubbed my limbs, which had lost all feeling," Shipton later wrote. "I was lucky to have got off so lightly."

On August 10, to maximize their discoveries, the team once more broke into three sub-parties. So autonomous were the men by now that Auden would reunite with his teammates only weeks later, in Sri-

nagar. Tilman took two Sherpas and set off with twenty-three days'
food to explore to the west and south. If the men felt gloomy on parting, Shipton's narrative never lets on. Instead, he covers the farewell in
a single jaunty sentence: "At the upper camp we said good-bye to
Auden and Tilman, whom we did not expect to see again until we got
back to England."

During those twenty-three days, Tilman performed a tour de force
of reconnaissance, crossing five high passes and traversing six unknown
glaciers. To recount that accomplishment, he contributes a single chapter, titled "Legends," to *Blank on the Map*. The contrast in styles between
Shipton and Tilman leaps from the page. Shipton's wit, on the whole, is
drier, his flights of joy more lyrical. Tilman keeps his tongue firmly in
cheek and confesses to the pleasures of discovery only in the most reti-
cent of passages.

As his party traversed a ridge between two of those glaciers, they
came upon a set of strange footprints in the snow. Tilman deadpans:
"we saw in the snow the tracks of an Abominable Snowman. They were
eight inches in diameter, eighteen inches apart, almost circular, without sign of toe or heel. They were three or four days old, so melting must
have altered the outline.... We followed them for a mile, when they disappeared on some rock. The tracks came from a glacier pool where the
animal had evidently drunk..."

From the 1930s well into the 1990s, a great debate about the possible existence of the Abominable Snowman, or Yeti, raged among
Himalayan travelers. No less an authority than Reinhold Messner
would later declare his unflinching faith in the existence of the fugitive
beast. But according to Jim Perrin, in *Shipton and Tilman: The Great
Decade of Himalayan Exploration*, the existence of the Yeti was for these
two best friends "a standing joke between them that was perpetuated
for over fifteen years at least."

In "Legends," with his Swiftian penchant for spinning a virtuosic fantasia out of a satiric conceit, Tilman uses his Sherpa companions as foils: "The Sherpas judged [the tracks] to belong to the smaller type of Snowman, or Yeti, as they call them, of which there are two varieties: the smaller, whose spoor we were following, which feeds on men, while his larger brother confines himself to a diet of yaks. My remark that no one had been here for thirty years and that he must be devilish hungry did not amuse the Sherpas as much as I expected!"

Back in England, Shipton and Tilman's Everest companion Frank Smythe had waged a vociferous newspaper campaign against the Yeti, which according to Perrin annoyed Tilman by its sanctimoniousness. Now Tilman pretends to take the side of the believers.

> *I have no explanation to offer, and, if I had, respect for ancient tradition would keep me silent. They were not the tracks of one of the many species of bears which seem to haunt the Himalaya, either Isabillinus, Pruinosis or "Bruinosus".... A one-legged, carnivorous bird, weighing perhaps a ton, might make similar tracks, but it seems unnecessary to search for a new species when we have a perfectly satisfactory one at hand in the form of the Abominable Snowman.... [W]hen the dust had settled, the Abominable Snowman remained to continue his evasive, mysterious, terrifying existence, unruffled as the snows he treads, unmoved as the mountains amongst which he dwells, uncaught, unspecified, and not unhonoured.*

Tilman delighted in the role of debunker. Among his cardinal achievements during that August romp through the western reaches of the Karakoram was to settle a geographical controversy that was a quarter-century old. From a distant ridge in 1912, another pair of exploratory pioneers, Fanny Bullock Workman and William Hunter Workman, had reported that the Cornice Glacier, nestled between sharp ridges in one of the most obscure corners of the range, had no outlet. If this were true, it would be the only known case in the world of such an anomaly.

A lifelong bachelor, Tilman was something of a misogynist, and Fanny Bullock Workman had built a reputation for overhyping her exploits in the Himalaya as well as lacing her written accounts with the kind of strident feminism that a skeptic such as Tilman could not abide. In "Legends," however, Tilman slyly camouflages his motives by pretending that throughout the 1937 expedition, the team had argued about the Cornice Glacier, with Shipton and Spender pooh-poohing the Workmans' claim while Auden and he defended it.

On August 22, after solving several technical puzzles, Tilman's small party reached the Cornice Glacier, then followed it downhill until they discovered the gushing stream that drained it toward the lowlands. Writes Tilman, "In a drab world it would be refreshing to report the discovery of a glacier flowing uphill or even of one that did not flow at all. It gives me no pleasure, therefore, to have to affirm that this glacier behaved as others do. . . . I can honestly say that to tramp down the Cornice glacier, hoping every moment to reach an impasse and finding none, was as sorry a business as any that has fallen to my lot."

Meanwhile, Shipton and Spender spent the rest of August pushing far into the northwest corner of the greater Karakoram. As they did so, they traveled the length of the Braldu Glacier, the last of all the great ice streams in the Karakoram to be explored. Pushing beyond the glacier into the lowlands, on September 3 the men stumbled into a startling encounter.

Coming round the corner of a willow thicket, we saw a horseman riding away from our camp. The idea crossed my mind that the camp had been raided, but when the man saw us he dismounted, came over to us, and shook us cordially by the hand. He was the first human being outside our party whom we had seen for nearly three and a half months. It was at once evident that we had no common language. Angtharkay tried Tibetan and Nepali, which were as useless as my Hindustani and English.

Despite his friendly greeting, the horseman had been freaked out by the meeting and tried to flee, but the Sherpa Lhakpa convinced him that the explorers "had no evil designs."

Below the snout of the Braldu Glacier lived the little-known natives of Shimshal. There followed several days of awkward but eager interchange, conducted in sign language and pantomime, enlivened by shared feasts in which each party was astonished by the other's cuisine.

With his canny instinct for mountain topography Shipton worked out the arduous route from Shimshal back to Askole, fording rivers and winding through gloomy canyons much of the way. There still remained the long trek all the way back to Srinagar. By now the men's boots were falling apart and they were exhausted by their four months of toil, but Shipton treats the three-week march to Srinagar as a lark.

Only when they reached that outpost of British colonial sway did the men learn what had gone on in the world during their absence. The news was dark: the Spanish Civil War showed no signs of terminating, the Sino-Japanese War "was a new horror," and storm clouds gathering over Europe portended World War II. Writes Shipton, "The world seemed an even blacker and madder place than when we had left it."

The great Karakoram reconnaissance ended as a colossal success. No small band of explorers had ever covered more unknown and difficult terrain in a single season. Better yet, for all their close calls, the team had lost not a single porter.

True to form, Shipton's envoi—the last line of *Blank on the Map*—hews to his penchant for modesty and understatement: "Distance has no need to lend enchantment, although it seems to lessen the difficulties and soften the hardships; for the supreme value of the expedition centered in an experience of real freedom rounded off with the peace and content of an arduous job of work completed and enjoyed."

In his autobiography, *That Untravelled World*, published in 1969, Shipton only slightly amplifies his claim for what, in retrospect, must have seemed as charmed a campaign as he had ever waged in the mountains.

Never before had I seen anything like the wild grandeur of those desert mountains, their stark simplicity and their boundless range. Every phase, every step of the way, whether in known or unknown country, had opened another door upon a new aspect and fuller understanding of that fantastic world; yet such was its scope that the more familiar it became, the more powerful was its impact upon the imagination. To have captured so much of it in a single season, and yet to feel we had won but a bare acquaintance, was at once tantalising and deeply satisfying.

In the summer of 1966, I got a job in Anchorage, teaching college-level English courses to GIs on Elmendorf Air Force Base from 6:30 to 10:30 PM four nights a week. The pay was good, and I counted on the nest egg I saved to fund another climbing expedition in September, my fourth in Alaska. With new friends from the local mountaineering club, I took off on weekends to bag peaks in the Chugach Range just east of the city.

One day the club got the electrifying news that Eric Shipton was coming through town. On his first trip to Alaska, Shipton was joining Adams Carter and Bob Bates—veterans two generations my senior whom I knew through the Harvard Mountaineering Club—to attempt a new route on 11,670-foot Mount Russell in the Alaska Range.

We arranged to meet Shipton at the airport and throw a makeshift reception for him (beer and pretzels, as I recall). Shipton and Tilman were already heroes of mine, not so much through their writings as for their legendary championing of the fast-and-light alpine style that we tried to bring to our own expeditions.

In *That Untravelled World*, Shipton recalls flying nonstop from Copenhagen to Anchorage, only to be whisked from the airport to a reception by us club members: "the programme included a talk by me. Already a little punch-drunk, I gave a performance of slapstick buffoonery, quite out of character, which brought down the house." That summer Shipton was fifty-eight, while I was twenty-three. (Bates was fifty-five, Carter fifty-two. Carter had been with Tilman on the first ascent of Nanda Devi in 1936, Bates on two American K2 expeditions in 1938 and 1953.) We were all struck by Shipton's aquiline good looks and his dignified bearing, and I remember noticing especially the tufts of white hair that sprouted from his ears. I don't recall in detail the impromptu talk Shipton gave—I think we were all too awed simply by his presence. But it was obvious that the poor man was jet-lagged to the very edge of exhaustion.

In our awkward way, we wished the three famous mountaineers the best of luck on Russell. I knew I'd see Carter and Bates again at Harvard, but I was sure that those few hours had amounted to the only encounter I would ever be granted with a man who had been on five Everest expeditions and had unlocked the mystery of the greater Karakoram.

But Shipton arranged to meet with the club members the next morning, before his team took off for Talkeetna and the flight in to Russell. In the interim, somehow he had done his homework. Now he singled us out, congratulating Art Davidson for his first ascent of Mount Seattle, Dave Johnston for his traverse of Denali, me for the west face of Mount Huntington. We were thunderstruck.

A two-week storm that destroyed the team's tents thwarted our elders' attempt on Russell. The men were lucky to escape with their lives. But Shipton continued to explore remote places all over the globe, and in 1973, at the age of sixty-five, made the first ascent of Monte Burney in Chilean Patagonia. He died in 1977.

In the last line of the penultimate chapter of *That Untravelled World*, Shipton wrote, "My visit to Alaska left me with a vivid impression of its vast mountaineering potential, and of a dynamic group of young climbers revelling in their splendid heritage and eager to share it with a stranger." Fifty years after our meeting, I cherish Shipton's gallant gesture in acknowledging our youthful ascents. And for decades after 1966, whenever I set off on a wilderness journey of my own, I felt him looking over my shoulder, silently teaching me how exploration should be done.

THREE

PREHISTORIC
5.10

The idea that wilderness is beautiful, and that exploits performed there—climbing mountains, running rivers, backpacking long distances—are rewarding, even inspirational, is so entrenched in our culture that casual students of history are shocked to learn that throughout most of the span of Western civilization quite the opposite view prevailed. The linkage of wildness with the sublime has actually held sway only during the last 250 years, since the end of the eighteenth century. Far more characteristic in Western history is the complaint of an early traveler who braved the forests to reach the castle of Fontainebleau, the swanky royal hunting lodge southeast of Paris, built in 1137. "We had to go four leagues with nothing to eat or drink," the man averred, "and to console us we had nothing before our eyes but frightening and horrible mountains full of gross rocks, piled one on top of another." Those gross rocks are the sandstone boulders on which France's best rock climbers now cavort.

When I taught at Hampshire College in the 1970s, I liked to expose my students to such passages, just to rub their noses in their cultural parochialism. My iconoclastic nudges failed: the hippies and nature lovers who filled my classrooms remained incredulous that those benighted travelers could get the wilderness so wrong.

The radical shift in Western attitudes toward nature launched by the Enlightenment and the Romantic revolution has been analyzed by many cultural historians, none more perceptive than Marjorie Hope Nicolson, whose *Mountain Gloom and Mountain Glory* (1959) fixes the long legacy of regarding raw nature as ugly and monstrous in the Judeo-Christian tradition of viewing the material world as sinful and corrupt.

Nicolson bases her exegesis on a principle that I had tried to impress upon my students: "What men see in Nature is a result of what they have been taught to see—lessons they have learned in school, doctrines they have heard in church, books they have read." She traces the tradition of fear and abhorrence in the face of wilderness back to the Greeks and especially the Romans, but sees it solidified in the New Testament. Mountains, in particular, inspired distaste and horror. *Mountain Gloom and Mountain Glory* serves, among other uses, as a rich anthology of passages in English literature that equate the peaks of the Alps and even the hills of Britain to "Earth's Dugs, Risings, Tumors, Blisters, Warts." The connection between these "monstrous excrescences" and Original Sin became explicit in such poems as Henry Vaughan's "Corruption," in which Adam, exiled from Eden, "drew the Curse upon the world, / And Crackt the whole frame with his fall."

All this changed dramatically after the middle of the eighteenth century. In western Europe, a new interest in climbing mountains was awakened by the competition to make the first ascent of Mont Blanc. Attempts beginning in 1762 culminated in the triumph of Jacques Balmat and Michel Paccard on August 8, 1786. The birth of modern mountaineering is conventionally attributed to the race to reach the highest summit in the Alps.

Before the second half of the eighteenth century, ascents of mountains anywhere in Europe or North America were few and far between.

Yet a single exception stands out, a cultural and historical anomaly that is still wreathed in mystery more than five hundred years later.

―――――

Mont Aiguille is a limestone peak in the massif of the Vercors in southeastern France. At 6,841 feet above sea level, it is not even the highest point in the range, whose Grand Veymont towers 800 feet higher. The Vercors itself is dwarfed by the Chamonix Alps 80 miles farther east. Yet Mont Aiguille stands in striking isolation, like a western satellite of the north–south chain of the Vercors, its mesa-like summit surrounded by steep cliffs that rise a thousand feet on all sides.

In 1489 Charles VIII, king of France, on a pilgrimage to the medieval cathedral of Notre-Dame d'Embrun, was forcefully struck by the silhouette of the peak (then known as Mont Inaccessible). His curiosity was further whetted by local rumors that angels had been seen floating around the summit. A year later, Charles incorporated the peak in his royal seal, with the motto *Supereminet Invius* ("It stands, inaccessible"). And in 1492, he ordered his chamberlain, Antoine de Ville, to climb it.

A chamberlain's duties were to manage the household of the royal personage who hired him. Why the king thought de Ville was the man for the job is one of the lost details of this unprecedented campaign. In any event, de Ville put together a team, of which the indispensable member was Reynaud Jubié, official ladderman to the king. Rounding out the party were a professor of theology, an almoner (a cleric charged with dispensing alms to unfortunates in hospitals), a carpenter, and four others.

Only four concise, legalistic documents survive as primary sources for the extraordinary siege of Mont Aiguille that de Ville's team undertook. Most vexing for the modern observer is that the climbers left only the sketchiest account of how they tackled the peak. A curt phrase in de Ville's *procès-verbal* (a kind of legal deposition) alludes to the "*subtilz engins"* the team deployed, and a single sentence in the quaint French of the day evokes the terror of the climb, which was *"le plus horrible et expovantable passage que je viz james"* ("the most horrible and appalling passage that I have ever seen"). It's clear that Jubié brought his special craft to the game, as an official letter penned by the almoner states that "One has to climb for half a league by means of ladders, and for a league by a path which is terrible to look at, and is still more terrible to descend than to ascend."

The climb took the team three days. At last the men reached the summit plateau. To their astonishment, after battling precipitous lime-stone, they discovered a lush meadow "which it would take forty men or more to mow." The meadow was "a quarter of a league in length, and a bow shot, or cross-bow shot, in width." (In the fifteenth century, the French *lieue*, or league, was about two and a half miles. Incredulity played its trick on the men's judgment, as their measurements consid-erably exceed the reality of Mont Aiguille.) The team also found crows and sparrows of kinds they had never seen before, and "a great quantity of flowers of various colors and various fragrant scents, and, more par-ticularly, lilies."

If the men detected the presence of angels near the top, they kept the news to themselves. But there was other evidence of the divine, for installed in the meadow was "a beautiful herd of chamois, which will never be able to get away." On the spot, de Ville changed the peak's name from Mont Inaccessible to Mont Aiguille (*aiguille* means "needle").

Having expended such an effort to climb the mountain, the team was reluctant to close up shop and go home. Using the route they had established as a thoroughfare, they hauled enough material to the sum-mit to build a small hut. De Ville also directed the clerics in the team to erect three crosses on the highest points of the meadow, in honor of the Trinity, as well as to celebrate a mass and sing the "Te Deum" and "Salve Regina."

At the time, about a thousand miles to the southwest, in the harbor of Palos de la Frontera in Spain, a little-known mariner named Cristóbal Colón was loading his three ships with cargo in preparation for a voyage across the Atlantic into the unknown.

De Ville and company were all too aware that their bold ascent might later be regarded as suspect, so they sent messengers to the Parliament of Dauphiné in Grenoble announcing their deed. The letters indeed prompted an investigation, as the parliament sent its usher to check out the story. That fellow got to the base of Mont Aiguille, saw the ladders propped up against the lower cliffs, and promptly lost his nerve. "He was unwilling to expose himself," the subsequent report explained, "by reason of the danger that there was of perishing there ... [and] for fear lest he should seem to tempt the Lord, since at the mere sight of this mountain everyone was terrified." The witness did manage to spot de Ville and several others frolicking on the summit, as well as the three crosses, whose location had been chosen for visibility from the surrounding plains. As de Ville had hoped, the usher confirmed to his bosses that the protagonists of the adventure "ate, drank, and slept on the said mountain."

In 1984, with my longtime friend Matt Hale, I climbed Mont Aiguille by what, as far as we could tell, was de Ville's route. There was a small horde of other aspirants tackling what had become the most popular line in the Vercors, all of them roped up, placing protection, and belaying carefully. Matt and I chose to solo the route, on which we found no moves harder than 5.2 (on the decimal scale ranging from 5.0 to 5.15), but we had to be on constant guard against stones knocked loose by climbers flailing away above us. During our ascent, we politely asked one team after another, *"Est-ce que nous pouvons passer?"* By the time we topped out, we had overtaken some thirty fellow travelers. All the way up, I tried to imagine the plunge into the unknown that de Ville and his comrades had braved 492 years before us, *subtilz engins* or no.

In 1878, the French Alpine Club hung thick metal cables on the route to safeguard the more exposed passages (they were gone by 1984). As late as 1899 the climb was still earmarked in the guidebooks as "for experts only." The second recorded ascent had taken place only in 1834, although Peter Hansen, in his erudite *The Summits of Modern Man*, cites an obscure French source from 1729 that supposedly argues that the peak "had been climbed frequently by local shepherds in the 1530s." That source, however, is so thirdhand, with an axe to grind against previous authorities, that it is itself suspect. It hinges on the absurd claim that the 1530 peasants discovered an easy "secret" route that no subsequent suitors could find, A walk around the base of Mont Aiguille quickly dispels such a fancy.

That second documented ascent was an epic in its own right. It was undertaken by locals—"peasants," according to historians—who filed their own *procès-verbal* to certify the deed. The route they tackled was apparently a different one from de Ville's. The team of five, wielding "ropes, ladders, and a mason's hammer," failed on two attempts to get higher than a quarter of the way up the thousand-foot redoubt, whereupon the party's daredevil, twenty-six-year-old Jean Liotard, pushed on solo. Unhappy with his nailed boots, Liotard took them off to climb barefoot "with remarkable strength and hardiness." Zigzagging up and down and right and left, Liotard disappeared from sight of the anxious watchers below, only to re-emerge just below the summit. Celebrating his triumph from the rim of the meadow, he bellowed in a "thunderous voice" as he pushed off big rocks whose chute produced "a horrible noise."

On top, Liotard found no chamois, but detected "some debris very much resembling the remains of a stone wall"—possibly the ruins of de Ville's hut. Before starting his descent, Liotard prayed to God to give him confidence. "Tortured by the most painful anxiety," his friends watched him "now hanging on the face of precipices, now going off in a wrong direction, and presently recovering his original track." At last Liotard reached the base of the cliff, not without having abandoned his waistcoat, "which he had lost among the rocks by trying to use it to help him to grip hold of the sharp edges of the stones" (a technique hard for the modern climber to imagine).

Climbing historians hail the 1492 ascent of Mont Aiguille as a pivotal landmark. As Andrew Finkelstein writes, "Prehistoric man surely engaged in some low fifth class to reach a sacred summit or hunting vantage.... [But] really it was in 1492 ... that technical climbing began."

Yet de Ville's daring exploit inspired no immediate imitators, made no dent in Western culture's abhorrence of wilderness, which would span another two and a half centuries. It stands rather as a truly anomalous deed, inspired by quixotic motivations. In the last sentence of his *procès-verbal*, however, de Ville himself strikes a modern note, as he claims that Mont Aiguille "is the most beautiful place that I have ever visited."

═══

"It was in 1492 that technical climbing began." Such blanket statements proliferate in books that discuss the ever-changing relationship between man and nature (as critics framed the subject before the rubric "man" was deemed sexist). Like Marjorie Nicolson, these cultural historians plumbed references not only in English literature dating back to *Beowulf,* but in biblical texts from Genesis to Revelation. Few if any of these scholars acknowledged that their inquiries might be bound by a focus on the Western tradition, to the exclusion of the rest of human history.

In what is today southeastern Utah, more than 250 years before de Ville concocted his bold ascent, men and women, climbing in yucca sandals or barefoot, routinely scaled sandstone cliffs far more difficult than Mont Aiguille. The fact that we know not a scrap about the identities of these pioneers in no way diminishes the brilliance of their achievement.

As a kid growing up in Colorado, I visited Mesa Verde on a family vacation. Traipsing through the long-abandoned mud-and-stone villages of Cliff Palace and Spruce Tree House, I was captivated by the idiosyncratic architecture of the ancients, with their rectangular dwellings up to four stories tall and their circular underground kivas. My brother Alan and I climbed down a modern ladder through the roofhole of one reconstructed kiva, then hunkered in the gloom as we pretended we were sorcerers or spies.

The National Park Service saluted the vanished residents of these towns as the Cliff Dwellers. Later I would learn to call them by their archaeological tag, Anasazi. Laminated placards and ranger spiels explained that the settlements had been built inside deep natural alcoves in the cliffs for defense against an unknown enemy. But I had grown up playing at war in the vacant lot, where the neighbor kids and I threw rocks at one another and took cover in the lee of dirt piles, and Spruce Tree House, whose approach trail was navigated by oldsters hobbling along with canes, struck me as pitifully easy to attack. It was not surprising, then, to learn that the defensive strategy must have failed, for all the residents had fled for good by the year 1300.

The Cliff Dwellers stayed on my back burner for decades. In my twenties and thirties, as the pursuit of first ascents and new routes in Alaska became an all-consuming passion, the Southwest as a region registered only dimly among my *loci desiderabiles*. After all, I thought, there were no "real" mountains there, and how could a canyon hike, with no definite goal, compare to the quest for a summit?

But in 1987 I took a three-day backpack trip into Bullet Canyon, a tributary of Grand Gulch in southeast Utah. What I was looking for, I cannot remember. The ruins called Perfect Kiva and Jailhouse, I discovered, possessed a blithe, airy grace. What stunned me, however, was to find corn cobs and potsherds strewn in the dirt inside the small, dark rooms, left there since the thirteenth century. *So this is what Cliff Palace looked like*, I mused, *before the Park Service rebuilt and sterilized everything.* And both nights, as I camped under piñon trees in a canyon bend, I watched the stars wheel overhead as I conjured up the ancients, and marveled at the realization that I drank from the same spring that had sustained them seven hundred years before.

To reach the second level at Jailhouse, you had to crawl on your belly along a tight ledge with a certain exposure. That the Anasazi had chosen that ledge to adorn with a blank mortared wall looming over the void, and with a pair of spooky white shield- or facelike pictographs (Polly Schaafsma, the leading expert on Anasazi rock art, would surmise that the images were "hex" signs left to curse intruders), hinted at ancient terrors. As I had not on Mesa Verde, I got a visceral sense of lives shaped by defense against a lurking enemy.

Later I would return to Jailhouse ruin with friends who quailed at the crawl along the second-story ledge. But for a climber, it was child's play. Nor did I doubt that for the Anasazi—even their children and grandparents—a visit to that ledge amounted to a task in the daily routine.

That excursion into Bullet set some kind of hook. During the next few years, I headed off on other trips into the canyon country. At first, I sought out ruins indicated by marks on maps or recommended by rangers, but I soon found that it was more rewarding to push down a canyon with no *a priori* idea of what was there. Hiking from bend to bend, I learned to spot from afar the "signature" stamp of an Anasazi refuge (often an alcove facing south), or the kind of sandstone cliff that was likely to bear petroglyphs or pictographs; but the ancients frequently fooled and surprised me. Each find, no matter how mundane, provoked a spasm of delight, and of something deeper—awe at the strangeness of the site, laced with the unquenchable itch to fathom the unknown.

The rock art especially beguiled me. What had those chimerical figures once meant? The humanoids with what looked like ducks for heads, the spirals that turned into snakes, the beasts (apparently bighorn sheep) with conjoined bodies or double heads . . . ?

On my second or third trip, I discovered ruins that, without a rope or a partner, I couldn't get to. Some lay on ledges as high as a hundred feet above the foot of the cliff. Standing below several, I could see how smaller ledges at different intervals offered possible routes of access, and here and there gatherings of stones hinted at "platforms" where the butt-ends of log ladders must have been propped. But to imagine trusting such devices on nearly vertical passages far off the deck was scarifying. (Later, in more remote canyons, I came across several of these wooden ladders in place, small niches carved in the sides, leaning against the walls. They looked too spindly for humans.)

But the truly inaccessible ruins were inside alcoves enclosing small granaries in which the Anasazi stored corn and beans and squash, staples of their spartan diet. Some of those were 200 or 300 feet above the ground, and almost as far below the canyon rims. When I finally got to some of these eyries, sometimes by rappelling (a technique almost certainly not in the Anasazi arsenal), I was dumbfounded. In almost every case, the granaries were empty. Either the inhabitants had taken all the precious grain with them when they left, or later visitors had pillaged the stuff.

At first, in the face of these prehistoric wonders, I was preoccupied with the question of *how*. As a climber, I was confronted with the sheer technical improbability of the Anasazi achievement. Simply to get to the more difficult alcoves must have required a countless succession of life-risking ascents; to build granaries made of heavy stone and wet mud in them, then to fill those storage chambers with the precious grain and retrieve it when necessary, seemed mind-boggling. The question of whether the ancients used rope, and for what, has been woefully underposed by archaeologists. In 2003, I would lead a mini-forum published in *National Geographic* to kick the question around.

We hired an expert to fabricate some "Anasazi rope" out of narrow-leaf yucca, the most likely material. The process was messy, strenuous, and time-consuming, and by the end the man had produced two short sections of rope whose breaking strength was a fraction of that of modern nylon lines. Meanwhile, I canvassed archaeologists to ask them about the question and to probe for the largest and longest artifactual specimens they remembered seeing. Most were surprised that they had never before considered the question.

The verdict was ambiguous. I ended up skeptical, because so few viable pieces of rope had ended up in collections or excavations. My friend Greg Child, who was equally involved in the forum, ridiculed my doubts: how could they have done it *without* ropes, he parried?

Long before our rope debate, when I had first been struck by the severity of the climbing it took to get to the inaccessible alcoves, I had thought, *The archaeologists must have an explanation for this.* But when I ransacked the professional literature I found precious little discussion of this topic. Already I had found many examples of carved hand-and-toe trails that breached nearly vertical cliffs. The climber in me was stunned to find out how difficult these were to follow today, and more than once I backed off rather than risk my life. To my astonishment, I couldn't find a single published paper about hand-and-toe trails (or Moqui steps, as the cowboys called them). When I asked several archaeologists to direct me to the relevant literature, they misunderstood, citing analyses of trail networks like the Chacoan road system instead. One paper, by the great pioneering scholar Samuel Guernsey, shocked me with a photograph of the author using a metal axe to enlarge Ana-

sazi hand- and footholds so that he could climb to some ruin. Evidently
the same man who set new standards in the preservation of dwellings
and artifacts regarded Moqui steps as of no interest whatsoever!

When I asked some of today's leading experts about the vertigi-
nous ruins I had discovered, they tended to dismiss the challenge these
locations had posed for the ancients. "Most likely the access ramps
have collapsed during the last several hundred years," one would say, or,
"The only reason the hand-and-toe trails are scary today is because the
rock has eroded so much." Well, I silently countered, that's just plain
nonsense. Often my fingertips had found the hollows that had been
precisely carved to receive each digit within a handhold. And more
than once, a ruin a hundred feet up a featureless cliff loomed straight
above a contemporary structure at its base, proof that no collapsing
ramp had turned the access from a piece of cake into a perilous climb.

The better I got to know these archaeologists, who were only too
glad to entertain my curiosity, the more I realized that because they
were not climbers they completely underestimated the difficulty and
danger these prehistoric refuges embodied. Not coincidentally, they
also tended to dismiss the "cliff dwellings" as utterly marginal to Anasazi culture, freakish aberrations in an otherwise orderly civilization.

All the while I puzzled over the *how,* the *why* was peering over my
shoulder. There was no indication that the Anasazi were interested in
summits: the tops of buttes and pinnacles were more often than not
devoid of human remains. In this respect, there seemed to be no common ground between the Western climbers who began exploring the
Alps in the 1830s and the inhabitants of the canyons of the Southwest
before 1300. The motives of the Anasazi seemed primarily utilitarian—
to get to ledges and nooks in the sandstone where they could build
dwellings and granaries that would be fiendishly difficult for others
(enemies, invaders) to approach. Although the Anasazi were first celebrated by Anglo-American explorers as the Cliff Dwellers, only a small

fraction of their settlements over some two thousand years of human occupation were lodged in cliffs. By far the majority of Anasazi villages were built on open plains and plateaus, like Lowry Ruin, Yellowjacket, and Yucca House in southwestern Colorado.

Once tree-ring dating allowed archaeologists to locate Anasazi structures precisely in time, it became evident that nearly all the cliff-hung redoubts were built between 1150 and 1300. On the Colorado Plateau (where most of the cliff dwellings are located), those years spanned a desperate era of famine, drought, and environmental deterioration. And after 1300, the ancients abandoned those settlements en masse, never to return. The obvious conclusion—that the dwellings and granaries lodged high in the cliffs were defensive—became scientific orthodoxy, though a handful of scholars held out with ingenious counterexplanations.

To me, as a climber, the beauty and daring of the Anasazi achievement in the cliffs posed a beguiling conundrum. It is a perilous business to project motivation upon vanished peoples who left no written record, but it seemed completely unlikely that the Old Ones had been driven by the aesthetic passions of the men who made the first ascents of the Matterhorn, the Eiger, and the Chamonix aiguilles. Instead, it was survival that drove the Anasazi to such extremes.

For me, almost from the first time I stared up at a distant granary, wondering how to get to it, the challenge gave birth to a maxim that would become a personal touchstone whenever I prowled through the canyon country: *Fear is the mother of beauty.* I knew, of course, that my own notions of beauty were entirely culture-bound, but I doubted that fear was equally subjective across the ages.

We Westerners tend to measure our lives in terms of deeds that leave their lasting marks upon posterity. Edward Whymper, making the first ascent of the Matterhorn in 1865, believed that his triumph would be celebrated long after his death—as indeed it is. The novelist and the poet expend their deepest thoughts and feelings on combinations of words that they hope will achieve a certain immortality. (The mournful epitaph that Keats assigned himself betrays that hopeless desire: *Here lies one whose name was writ in water.*) The painters of the Renaissance believed their masterpieces would hang in palaces and churches long after they died. The composer's immortality lies not on the written page, but in the strophes and antistrophes that linger in the ear centuries after musicians have packed up their instruments.

This Western ambition harks back all the way to the Egyptians and their pyramids, those grandiose monuments to the purported immortality of the pharaohs. It is the same vain boast that speaks in Ozymandias's proclamation from the desert sands in Shelley's poem: "My name is Ozymandias, King of Kings; / Look on my Works, ye Mighty, and despair!"

After the summer of 2015, when cancer became the central reality in my life, I too began to wonder whether anything I had created in the previous fifty years would last. How long might my books be read, and by whom? Although rationally I could look askance at the vanity of my wishes, the terror of the abyss loomed larger than it had before. What if no one remembered anything I had done? What if no one cared?

Did the Anasazi cherish kindred ambitions? There is no way to know. Yet their works have lasted. In 2005, with Greg Child and archaeologist Renee Barlow, I explored the wildest of all the granaries in the Southwest I had ever been able to get to. The ruin—actually a substantial double granary, whose storage capacity Barlow later calculated at an extraordinary fifty-seven bushels of corn, which would weigh a ton and a half—was perched on a tiny ledge 70 feet up a nearly vertical wall, with 90 feet of overhanging precipice arching above it. Incredibly well preserved, its rooftop door slabs still in place, the double granary looked inaccessible even to top modern climbers. Only an incipient crack split the otherwise featureless sandstone wall beneath it. On first glance,

Greg blurted out in climber's jargon, "It's gotta be at least 5.11, on crumbly rock." Yet a rickety, 25-foot Douglas fir ladder still leaned against the bottom of the cliff.

After one failed attempt, we were able to get to the granary, thanks to Greg's ingenious rigging of an overhanging rappel from the brow of the cliff above. As I had so often before, I found myself thinking, *It would be hard enough for the Old Ones just to climb to the ledge. How the hell did they build those massive storage chambers on the skimpy ledge, then haul all the grain to fill them?*

Whether or not they meant to do so, the ancients had built here a lasting monument to their fugitive civilization. From a single piece of wood, Barlow was later able to retrieve a radiocarbon date. The stunning double granary, it turns out, was built before Shakespeare lived, before Giotto painted, before church choirs intoned their plainsong. The wood sample gave a date of around 1000 AD.

If any of their works was devised to outlive the centuries, it might have been the hallucinatory petroglyphs and pictographs the Anasazi carved and painted all over the Southwest. What else might the art have been for? Yet there are good reasons to doubt such an apparently reasonable conclusion. Aboriginal rock art from northern Australia abounds in layers of images superimposed one upon the next. Such wanton obliteration of many a masterly frieze seems to hint at a nihilistic revisionism—"our art is so much better than that of the old guys who preceded us." Yet living informants who stood at the tail end of the Aboriginal legacy told scholars that the art was meant not to be seen, only performed. Though not so pervasively as in Australia, the rock art of the Southwest teems with superimposition.

Under glass in a museum in Arizona, one of the finest specimens of a widespread ancient artifactual tradition resides. The object is called a split-twig figurine. To create it, the craftsman took a single slender willow branch, sliced it from end to end, and wove the twin pieces into a striking effigy of a bighorn sheep. If the museum figurine were unique, scholars today would regard it as the creation of a single inspired genius. Yet hundreds of split-twig figurines, all of them woven from a single piece of wood and nearly all of them shaped to conjure up bighorn sheep, have been found across the Southwest.

It is hard today not to see the museum figurine as an objet d'art. Yet it was left by the culture that crafted it in one of the most obscure nooks of the Grand Canyon. Once again, radiocarbon wizardry unlocks its age. The figurine is far older than Shakespeare and Giotto. It was shaped by a loving hand before the ancient Romans rose and fell. It was already centuries old by the time the anonymous oral bards concocted the *Iliad* and the *Odyssey*. It dates from somewhere around 1500 BC.

Nor was it left on display. It was discovered in the twentieth century deep inside a gloomy alcove in the Redwall limestone band of cliffs—the hardest of all the Grand Canyon bands to climb. And as if that were not concealment enough, the figurine had been placed under a flat rock.

No, it was not meant to be seen. It was hidden away to perform its arcane task, whatever that may have been (hunting magic?), as far from human eyes as its keepers could place it. The figurine communed not with human posterity, but with the invisible forces than ran the universe.

———

Once I had fully embraced the virtuosic strangeness of Anasazi climbing, I began to wonder: Was it unique? Or were there other examples of non-Western, preliterate peoples pulling out all the stops of radical ascent around the world, and if so, what were they all about?

One day in the 1980s, as I was reading *Danseuse de Roc*, the autobiography of France's top female climber, Catherine Destivelle, I came across a photo that left me speechless. It showed an alcove high in a steep sandstone cliff that was filled nearly to the roof with human bones—the utterly jumbled remains, I later learned, of three thousand individuals. The burial cave was in the West African country of Mali. The cliff was called the Bandiagara Escarpment. It stretches 150 miles from east to west at the edge of a desert 150 miles south of Tombouctou. The vertical precipice ranges up to 500 feet high. The inhabitants of the region today are the Dogon, but the necropolis was the work of a vanished prehistoric people called the Tellem. Destivelle gave only the faintest clues as to who the Tellem were. I was afire to find out more.

The Tellem, it turned out, were little understood. Only a single Dutch team of archaeologists had ever studied them. From radiocarbon and tree-ring dating, the Dutch determined that the Tellem had flourished from the eleventh to the fifteenth centuries AD. Several months after I had found the photo, I landed my first assignment for *National Geographic* magazine.

In November 1988, four of us (a photographer, myself, and a climbing partner each) flew to Bamako, the capital of Mali, rented two vehicles, hired a pair of savvy guide/drivers, and drove to the Dogon country, where we hired a local man as interpreter. We spent a month pushing our way across sand dunes along the Bandiagara. To this day, that month remains one of the truly enchanted episodes of my life.

On our first day along the Bandiagara, we decided to explore the cave of jumbled human bones. The Toloy Couloir, in which the alcove lies, is an overhanging precipice the summit of which can be easily gained by hiking up a series of ramps. On the rim just above the cave, we set up a belay, and I downclimbed and traversed to the right—climbing on solid rock that was about 5.6 in difficulty—and stepped inside the gloomy mausoleum. The chaos of bones filled the orifice almost to the roof, with only a narrow ramp across which I could tread without clambering over the human remains. Even so, I winced as I felt an ancient femur snap underfoot. I rationalized my profanation by remembering that the Dutch had spent days inside the alcove measuring and cataloguing the debris. As my eyes adjusted to the dim light, I saw dozens of skulls randomly strewn across a branchwork of ribs and fibulas. There were animal bones mixed with human, dusty pieces of cloth, and knotted skeins of rope scattered among the disarticulated skeletons. A musty, acrid odor fouled the air. After two hours inside the cave, I reattached my harness to the rope, swung back outside the entrance to the chamber, and was lowered by my partner 100 feet to the base of the cliff, the last 80 feet of it dangling in midair.

The Dutch archaeologists, not being climbers, had invented their own bizarre contraption to gain access to the cave. They had brought to Mali a spherical aluminum cage, inside which one or two researchers huddled while teammates hauled the thing up the precipice, with helpers on the ground using trailing ropes to pull the "bathysphere" (as I had nicknamed it) tight against the overhanging wall. For two decades they had used this ingenious but anachronistic device to get to the more inaccessible alcoves they studied, which amounted to only a small fraction of the Tellem graveyards that dotted the cliffs up and down the Bandiagara. Because of this, they had no conception of how the ancients had first gotten to those eyries, nor how they had hauled their dead up the cliffs. In an offhand remark in their official monograph, the Dutch had insisted that none of the Tellem lairs would have posed a serious challenge to an expert rock climber today. This assertion, as we discovered day after day, was complete nonsense.

Still, what was that talus pile of human bones all about? The Dutch speculated that in using the graveyard one generation after another, the Tellem had run out of space, and so had tossed aside the older dead to make room for the new. In my mind I added my own speculation: perhaps, like the ancient Egyptians and many another vanished civilization, one "dynasty" of Tellem after another had desecrated and graverobbed its predecessors.

A few days later, farther down the Toloy Couloir, we spent an exhausting sixteen hours concocting our own way to access alcoves the Dutch had never touched. From a bolted anchor, with three 160-foot ropes tied together end to end, I was lowered to a series of ledges, on each of which lay a Tellem necropolis. Here the cliff stretched an imposing 400 feet from top to bottom, relentlessly overhanging. Earlier we had spotted through binoculars from an opposite vantage point an assortment of Tellem structures on a ledge 100 feet below the rim. To reach it now, I made use of a clever contraption of our own manufacture—a long wooden stick with a metal hook taped onto the end. With this I was barely able to snag a bush and pull myself in to the ledge. I spent another two hours scrambling carefully from one struc-ture to another. Here I found orderly graveyards, rows of skeletons wrapped in faded, decorated cloth shrouds, undisturbed during the previous five hundred years. Several of the structures, however, lay on a smaller ledge 20 feet above me. I could see no way to bridge the gap without risking a fatal fall, so I left those tantalizing biers unvisited. As my partners at the top of the cliff lowered me the rest of the way to the base, I came in view of one Tellem burial site after another. Several had clusters of intact ceramic pots neatly placed beside the orderly dead. By now I dangled so far out in space that there was no hope of landing on these lower ledges, even with the aid of my grappling hook. All I could do was gaze in astonishment.

The Dutch had not tried to get to these alcoves farther down the Toloy Couloir. Nor had they deployed their "bathysphere" to visit any of the scores of really inaccessible gravesites that we discovered all along the Bandiagara during the subsequent weeks. The few that we our-selves were able to investigate up close, we reached only by rappelling.

All during the month, as the four of us lingered over campfires in the sand dunes, we debated Tellem climbing technique. The *why* of the phenomenon seemed evident: the caves were the places the Tellem chose to house their dead. The Dutch agreed, adding the speculative corollary that perhaps the alcoves had also served as defensive refuges when the people were under attack. Who the attackers might have been is lost to history.

During our nightly seminars, we agreed that the key piece of Tellem gear had been rope. Everywhere we looked, we found skeins and segments of inch-thick rope woven out of baobab bark. The other obviously crucial component of the ancients' craft was an object the likes of which I had never seen anywhere else, and which had no affinity with Anasazi climbing. From the floor of nearly every alcove, a black stick made of ironwood (one of the heavier species of wood found in sub-Saharan Africa) protruded two or three feet out of the entrance over the void, cocked at an angle about twenty degrees from the horizontal. The other end of the stick was anchored under heavy stones mortared in place. The Dutch, whose scholarly papers were written in French, called these sticks *boulins*, a word that has no good English translation. Many of the *boulins* were deeply scored by rope grooves.

It was clear, then, that ropes and *boulins* were the key to the Tellem achievement. A *boulin* served as a sort of yardarm by which materials of all kinds were raised to such a great height, including human bodies. This explanation, however, begged the question of how the initial climbers had gotten to the alcove. For various reasons, we concluded that the Tellem had not used their baobab ropes to rappel from the top of the cliff.

The modern-day Dogon are expert climbers. Over the span of time since their advent in the Bandiagara in the sixteenth century, they had been able to get to many of the Tellem alcoves. One day a jovial fellow named Amadomion, the virtuoso of the village of Pégué, told us how he did it. From a lower ledge, he tied a piece of wood as ballast to the end of a very thin rope of his own manufacture, then repeatedly tossed the rope until it looped over the *boulin* above. With both ends of rope on the ledge, he then tied one end of his thin cord to a much stouter rope. Once he had hauled the heavy rope over the *boulin* and anchored it in place, he simply shinnied up the rope like a kid in a gym class. I asked, "But how did the Tellem get the *boulin* up there to begin with?"

Amadomion shrugged and smiled. "They had a very strong magic."

The motive for the Dogon ascent was not to bury their own dead, nor to rob the graves of their predecessors. It was to gather the pigeon dung that coated the remote ledges, for that smelly stuff was a fertilizer without peer.

In village after village, through our interpreter, Oumar, who translated from the native language into French, I asked the Dogon about the Tellem. We were usually told that the Tellem were dwarfs who lived in the high alcoves. When we asked what had happened to them, the Dogon often said that they had migrated to the Congo or Gabon, where they lived today as pygmies. The Dutch, however, demonstrated by measuring the skeletons that the Tellem were of normal African height, about the same stature as the Dogon. Nor did the Dutch find any evidence that the alcoves had been used for habitation. The Tellem buried their dead in them, and also built granaries to house their precious grain—chiefly millet. One of the team's most valuable discoveries, obtained through DNA comparisons, was that the Tellem were related to no living peoples. They had in the truest sense died out.

Tellem is a Dogon word meaning "we found them." But when we asked our Dogon informants about their people's first contact with their predecessors, the answers varied radically from village to village. Like the Tellem, the Dogon bury their dead in caves in the cliffs. It was tantalizing to learn that the Dogon often appropriated alcoves that had already served as Tellem cemeteries. We would have given anything to visit one of these graveyards, but they were strictly off limits to outsiders. To gain permission to visit even the purely Tellem alcoves, we had had to arrange a meeting with the village *hogon*, its chief official. This required an elaborate séance with Oumar as our go-between. It would have been the height of rudeness simply to pop the question; instead, the decorum required a tedious roundabout palaver, in which we solicitously inquired as to the *hogon*'s health, the welfare of the village, and the progress of that season's harvest. Only after we offered a small "contribution" to the community in the form of Malian francs would the *hogon* grant us permission to visit the Tellem alcoves.

After weeks of such negotiations, one day Oumar, my climbing partner Matt Hale, and I approached an alcove low in a cliff. We were 30 or 40 miles from Oumar's home village, in country with which he was unfamiliar. From the look of the alcove, Oumar declared that it was a Tellem burial site. As far as we could tell, no Dogon village lay nearby. I urged our guide to shortcut the tedious ceremony of seeking out the nearest *hogon*, and we started hiking through tall grasses toward the foot of the cliff. All of a sudden, we heard shouts from the top of the cliff. A moment later, big stones started exploding all around us. A hasty glance revealed human hands launching these missiles from 300 feet above us, evidently with the intent to kill us. We turned and ran for our lives, until we were safely out of range.

My heart pumping with adrenaline, I begged that we regain our rented Land Cruiser and flee. But Oumar had lost face among his people, and now he demanded that we circle around the cliff and hike up to the village of the bombardiers, which turned out to be named Yawa. Half an hour later, as we entered the outskirts of the town, we met several Dogon men lounging on the rocks. They showed no trace of hostility. We shook hands with the men, while Oumar engaged in a long conversation.

"What was that all about?" I asked Oumar as we left.

"They said, yes, it was we who yelled at you, but it was the boys who threw the rocks."

"Why?"

"They said they have to guard their tombs." Apparently we had mistaken a Dogon cemetery for a Tellem one. "They have spies looking for them."

"But who are the spies?" I wondered.

"Us," said Oumar.

Gradually over the month, we elicited bits and pieces of the Dogon take on the Tellem. There were many theories about the strong "magic" that had enabled the earlier inhabitants of the Bandiagara to get to alcoves as high as 200 feet up overhanging cliffs. As translated by Oumar, "The Tellem could climb a single thread. And they had a way of making the thread go up there and attach itself." Some swore that the Tellem could fly, or that they could change themselves to giants, take a single step up to the caves, and change themselves back into dwarfs to live there. Some even swore that the Tellem were such powerful orators that they could talk themselves up to the caves.

The dwarfs-to-giants story explained the Dogon belief that the Tellem lived on as the pygmies of the Congo and Gabon. The assertion that the Tellem lived in the alcoves may have arisen from the fact that were no signs elsewhere of Tellem habitations. Indeed, in twenty years of research, the Dutch had found no traces of even the most rudimentary Tellem village. The team hypothesized that all the Tellem villages lay underneath today's Dogon towns. But it would have been the gravest transgression to dig a sample trench in even an abandoned Dogon village.

The other Dogon theories about how the Tellem had reached the high alcoves arose from some deep knowledge of magic that we Westerners would never penetrate.

Near the end of our journey, in a town called Tireli Sud, Matt and I were granted our deepest insight into the oral tradition that embodied the Dogon grasp of their vanished predecessors. Walking through the narrow alleyways of the town, we came to its central courtyard, where four ancient elders lounged in the sun. One was blind, another held up a left hand that shook with palsy, and a third had a look of perpetual outrage on his fierce face.

It took a while for us to break the ice. When we first asked these dignified oldsters what had happened to the Tellem, the blind man rejoined, "How do I know? I wasn't here." But slowly the men warmed to the inquiry. One of them teased another, "Tell them what you really know. Don't go making up stories." During long silences, the men spat in the dirt and shooed away noisy children.

At last we were allowed to enter the outer chamber of their long-pondered knowledge of the ancient past. All four agreed that when the Dogon came, the Tellem had already departed from the cliff. They also agreed that the Tellem had lived in the alcoves: they were hunter-gatherers, not growers, and they knew how to find water in some of the caves. I asked how the ancients had gotten to the dizzying ledges that hung above Tireli Sud (craning our necks, we could turn our gaze from the courtyard to the Tellem alcoves that hovered almost directly above us). At first the elders said only that they had no idea how the Tellem had done it, but that magic was the key to their exploit. I played devil's advocate: hadn't the Dogon actually driven the Tellem away? A scornful sneer came over the blind man's face. "How," he said sternly, "could we have driven out people who had such powerful magic?"

They had heard stories told by the sages of previous generations that the Tellem could ride horses straight up and down the cliff. They could even ride on the wind itself. Later the *hogon* of Tireli Sud pointed to a pair of *boulins* wedged in a crack above 40 feet of dead-vertical sandstone. Those, he said, were hitching posts the Tellem had used to tie off their horses.

At the end of our meeting with the elders in the courtyard, they seemed abashed at how much they had told us. The man with the palsied hand said, "You can only talk about your own village. You can't talk about another village." In the more touristic towns toward the center of the Bandiagara, European antiquaries had spawned a black market by persuading the Dogon to sell Tellem artifacts they had discovered in the shared burial caves. And the Dutch teams had brought back their own Tellem grave goods to serve as museum pieces. On a visit to Utrecht before my trip to Mali, I had beheld these strange objects, left by the Tellem to accompany the dead into eternity: not only the ceramic pots I had seen from my rope as my partners dangled me down the cliff, but finger bells made of copper, bracelets of iron, and necklaces made of hexagonal carnelian beads. Beside the skeletons, the ancients had laid bows, quivers, and hoes that had been broken in half to "retire" them from functional use. The most exquisite of the grave relics were beautifully carved wooden headrests, which remain the oldest man-made wooden artifacts yet found in sub-Saharan Africa (alas, on the European black market, the headrests fetch hefty prices).

At the time of my visit, the illegal trade in antiquities had not yet spread its tentacles to Tireli Sud. Curiously, in that village the Dogon never used Tellem caves for their own burials, seeking out instead untouched alcoves relatively low in the cliff. The elders in the courtyard had seen Tellem antiquities, but they had no interest in collecting them, much less selling them to foreigners. Waving his hand at the precipice above the village, the man with the outraged visage said that no Dogon had ever been to those higher ledges, indicating the distant alcoves from whose mouths we could glimpse protruding *boulins*. But yes, they were sure to be full of Tellem graves and Tellem grave goods.

I left the Bandiagara after my month of exploration with more questions nagging at my brain than answers. The main reason that in subsequent years I would doubt that the Anasazi had used ropes as crucial tools in reaching their own alcoves was that thick baobab ropes were so obviously central to the Tellem achievement. Not only was every *boulin* scored with deep rope grooves, but all over the Bandiagara we found long hanks of rope that were discarded in the ruins or still hanging in place. Something like the same time gap had yawned between the Tellem disappearance and the present day as stretched back to the Anasazi abandonment of the Colorado Plateau. Yet even the earliest archaeologists had found precious little rope in Anasazi ruins, and at its strongest it would have been too thin and fragile to hold a human body.

Western climbers tend to assume that the only way to ascend difficult cliffs is by some variant of a technique perfected over the last two centuries, starting in the Alps. The essence of that modus operandi is a rope connecting two climbers, one of whom stands attached to the cliff and belays his partner as he leads above, placing "protection" (pitons, nuts, spring-loaded cams, and occasionally expansion bolts) to shorten his potential fall. Gradually, however, I had sketched out my hunch of a very different Anasazi climbing technique. The key to prehistoric ascents in the Southwest, I believe, was log ladders notched with hand- and footholds and leaned against the cliff from one ledge to a higher one. Often the ladder on the higher ledge would be placed not directly above the lower one, but 50 or even 100 feet to the right or left, where the cliff yielded a subtle weakness. If the Anasazi were virtuosi of any technique, it would have been scaling scary ladders and traversing wildly exposed ledges.

No such theory fit Tellem ascents. I caught a glimpse of a possible vestige of the lost art in a few places where a vertical crack sported a series of sticks jammed tight, one above the next. These were not *boulins*. I guessed that they might have served like pitons, as points of protection for a roped leader or (more likely) for "aid," holds from which to hang, pull oneself up, then stand. But these sequences of jammed sticks were far too rare to account for access to all the hundreds of Tellem alcoves, the most inaccessible of which loomed above blank overhangs without a vertical crack in sight.

Anasazi climbing was a dazzling performance, no matter how it was accomplished, manifestly far more daring than what Antoine de Ville and his cronies had pulled off on Mont Aiguille in 1492. But Tellem ascent was in a league of its own, its most remote alcoves harder to get to than any Anasazi granary. Twenty-nine years after my visit to Mali, no Westerner has been able to explain it.

———

After my in-depth encounters with the Anasazi and the Tellem, I wondered how many other preliterate cultures around the world might have harbored serious climbers. The most valuable thing the Anasazi and the Tellem taught me was that climbing for all the reasons Western culture holds sacrosanct (and that I myself had felt)—the glory of putting up a new route or reaching a summit, the thrill of exploring new land no matter how tightly defined, the challenge of overcoming difficult obstacles and warding off danger, the joy of the perfect partnership—had nothing to do with the reasons that the Anasazi and Tellem climbed. If we can judge from appearances, the Anasazi climbed to hide their precious grain away from invaders in hard times. They left behind their ruins, their astonishing rock art, and such enigmatic artifacts as the split-twig figurines. But they cared so little for their dead that the most common burial site was the midden—the trash pile directly below the settlement.

The Tellem, on the other hand, devoted all their energy and skill to trying to ensure the immortality of their dead, or at least to preventing their bodies from being vandalized by enemies. Those burial alcoves and the grave goods left inside them are virtually all that remains today of Tellem culture.

In Western civilization, we go to our own considerable lengths to enshrine the dead. We lay out cemeteries in which to bury our loved ones, cover their coffins with dirt and grass, and erect headstones inscribed with the names, dates, and a word or two or a favorite quotation to mark the passing of an irreplaceable person. Or we cremate the body, scatter the ashes in a special place, and vow to return to connect with the lost one's spirit.

But the tombstones fade and erode until the inscriptions are reduced to unreadable "dog-biscuits" (Maya epigraphers' slang for weathered hieroglyphs), and the ashes are gone with the wind, or into the soil. No, we cannot keep the dead with us as the Tellem did.

I knew of three or four cultures elsewhere in the world that practiced what looked like serious climbing in the cliffs. They dwelt in very difficult places to get to. It would take a monumental investment of time and money and preparation to explore them, or a generous assignment of the kind that magazines were no longer dishing out in the 2000s. Still, I hoped to get there, "but knowing how way leads on to way," and ruing how little time there is in a single lifetime . . .

The Chachopoya flourished in the rain forest near the headwaters of the Amazon in northern Peru from about the year 800 to the end of the fifteenth century, when they were conquered by the Inca. Until recently, they have been little-known and even less studied. In several places the Chachopoya built wildly teetering and substantial edifices in nearly vertical cliffs made of loose limestone, apparently placing their highest structures as far as 200 feet off the ground.

Like the Tellem, some of the Chachopoya resorted to the cliffs to house their dead. But these Andeans mummified the bodies, through an elaborate process of removing the innards, drying the corpses, then wrapping them in cloth and installing them in the fetal position. According to Keith Muscutt, whose *Warriors of the Clouds* offers an excellent survey of what little is known about the Chachopoya, many of the skulls show fracture signs, ambiguously pointing either to battle wounds or to ritual execution. Many of the skulls also exhibit scars from trepanning, the practice of deliberately boring a hole in the cranium. These could be stigmata from desperate attempts to save the victims' lives, or they could further testify to some macabre rite of sacrifice.

Muscutt speculates that because some of the cantilevered buildings, parts of whose floors hang in thin air over the void, also have fronting platforms attached to them, the Chachopoya may have regularly displayed the mummies, or aired them out to dry between rains. A few rows of the dead have received special attention by being interred standing up in *chullpas*—anthropomorphic coffins, with painted ornaments and elongated heads, looking something like the Easter Island statues. These eerie reminders of mortality loom ominously over the misty valley below. Such special treatment would seem to argue for a reverence for dead ancestors, but some cultures, including the Inca, also conferred sacred display on their sacrificial victims.

No trained climber has yet visited the cliffs of La Petaca or its companion, Diablo Huasi, where the hanging tombs are clustered, to gauge the true difficulty of climbing up to them. A handful of archaeologists and journalists have reached them by rappelling from the tops of the cliffs; but on rappel, it's very hard to rate a move, let alone a pitch. Muscutt reports that many of the holds low on the cliff have been polished smooth. Such polishing, nearly unique to limestone, results from scores or hundreds of climbers grasping and standing on the holds. Does this clue reveal the secret of Chachopoya ascent? Probably not, as it could merely reflect the ceremonial passage of latter-day worshipers.

No matter what, the same puzzle that afflicted me as I explored the Anasazi leaps out in Peru. It is one thing to climb a steep cliff to reach a high ledge or alcove. It is quite another to build an elaborate structure there, much less to raise mummies to it and install them therein.

On the opposite side of the globe from Peru, in the South Sulawesi province of Indonesia, a people called the Toraja also use cliffs to enshrine the dead. These natives are in one sense an archaeologist's dream, for they continue to practice a burial ritual that is at least seven hundred years old. Not only can they be observed carrying out their customs, but (with the usual anthropological caveats) they can be asked why and how they are performing them.

Like the Chachopoya refuges, the Toraja graves are installed in limestone precipices. The rock is soft enough to be shaped with the vigorous use of metal hammers and spikes. Access seems uniformly to be by means of scaffolding and ladders made out of soft bamboo, and thus the installations being crafted today are for the most part not that high off the ground.

Ledges and niches to receive the dead are prepared months or even years beforehand. The funeral ceremony is a festive occasion, lasting several days, gathering hundreds. For the most part, the dead are laid not in the rock niches themselves, but in wooden biers and coffins that protrude from the cliff, propped in place with strong wooden beams (whence the epithet "hanging graves of Sulawesi"). Painted effigies sometimes accompany the dead, arranged in galleries like spectators in theater boxes. Babies are interred in hollowed-out trees.

The Toraja are animists who worship their ancestors, but there is evidence that the religion (and no doubt the burial rites) were modified by the advent of the Dutch in the seventeenth century, with the pressure to convert to Christianity. Today's practice does not usually involve real climbing. But tantalizing myths from the past hint at a more vertical ceremony. There is the legend of Pala' Toke' ("arm of a gecko"), a place where either a single genius or a whole class of virtuosi could climb the cliffs like geckos, with palms that stuck to the rock. Their job was to get noblemen's coffins to higher perches than scaffolding could reach.

Height off the ground is supposed to be proportional to rank in life, so the most exalted dead need coffins hanging from quite lofty eminences. At the Londa site, a few graves are reported to lie as high as 150 feet above the foot of the cliff. It is hard to imagine scaffolding sturdy enough to reach such ledges. Once more, the phenomenon is wreathed in mystery.

Mustang is a formerly independent kingdom near the headwaters of the Kali Gandaki and Muktinath river systems high on the Tibetan plateau. It was annexed by Nepal in the eighteenth century, but it remains ethnically Tibetan. Here a vast array of caves (as many as ten thousand) ranges across high cliffs overlooking desolate valleys. The rock is a conglomerate so soft that it can be easily carved with wooden tools. Like the cavates of Bandelier National Monument in New Mexico, carved out of soft tufa by many generations of the Anasazi, the caves of Mustang are mostly manmade.

Archaeologists have identified six successive periods of occupation of the caves, dating back to 1200 BC. Each era seems to have found different purposes for the grottos. The caves from the first three periods— spanning nearly two millennia, from 1200 BC to 700 AD—were used almost entirely for burial purposes. With the introduction of Buddhism around 700 AD, caves, sometimes very difficult to get to, became hermitages or meditation chambers. From that date through present times, the caves also cradled dwellings and, during the last four hundred years, storage chambers.

Sorting out the tangled history of these caves is thus an immensely complicated business. In 2011, a team from *NOVA* and the National Geographic Society descended on Mustang to make a film called *Cave People of the Himalaya*. The narrative arc seems to have been inspired by Indiana Jones, so a potentially ruinous campaign of access and salvage passes for the heroic rescue of threatened treasure. The climbers hack away at the cliff with drills, ice axes, and crampons, carving a passage in the fragile rock that no ancient could be presumed to have used, since bolt guns and ice axes were in short supply in 500 BC. Once inside the chambers, the rescue team shoves ancient manuscripts into duffel bags like so many groceries, then lowers them to the ground, where "helpers" beat the fragile sheaves on the rocks to get the dirt out. The cameras frame this ludicrous and destructive enterprise as responsible archaeology.

It is much more likely that ladders and scaffolding launched from ledges that intersect the cliffs were the key to reaching and carving the grottos. Some of the cave systems involve elaborate tunnels connecting chambers on many different levels. In one such site, human mummies were found in the seventh story of a manmade complex of interlinked rooms. To reach that arcane mausoleum, other modern discoverers used climbing gear, which, again, the ancients did not have and therefore could not have used.

Needless to say, the rich history of this extensive series of troglodytic settlements has only begun to be illuminated. The kinds of climbing it took to reach and carve out these strange vertical creations remain an enigma. There is little evidence that rope played a major role in the prehistoric ascent of the Mustang cliffs. And there is no doubt that danger of the highest order haunted every aspect of the centuries of worship and retreat that took place here.

In 1998, on assignment for *Men's Journal*, I visited Petra and the Wadi Rum in Jordan. My companions were two good rock climbers, and one of our goals was to explore the limitless climbing possibilities of the jebels in the Wadi Rum—massively convoluted, multihued buttes of sandstone rising as much as 2,500 feet above the desert floor. After 1984, these domes had become a favorite arena for European climbers putting up long, serious routes on cliffs that vary from solid to loose and crumbly.

We had no guides to direct our wanderings in the Wadi Rum, but I knew that this spectacular wilderness had been a favorite haunt of

Bedouins for at least the last two thousand years. On my second or third day there, intrigued by the challenge of finding any route to the summits of the complex jebels, I stumbled upon the first of several ancient Bedouin routes that wove in and out of buttresses and chasms as they made their way toward the highest reaches of the domes. Leaving my partners to prospect short, hard routes on the lower reaches of the jebels, I took up the challenge of following the old Bedouin trails. Doing so became a game not without risk, since in order to plumb the weaknesses of the jebels, the Bedouin had mastered intricate strategies involving zigzags, traverses, short downclimbs, and small overhangs. I came to recognize Bedouin markers that defined these routes: one-stone cairns, short pieces of wood jammed in cracks for aid, stones wedged like climbers' nuts and cams in cracks to use as handholds and footholds. It would have been quite easy to get lost along the way, in which case a solo descent would have been extremely dangerous. Rather than build my own cairns to mark the twists and turns in these itineraries, I decided to play the game by Bedouin rules, relying only on their subtle markers to indicate the way.

From locals in the nearest village, I learned that the purpose of these Bedouin routes was a simple one: to hunt for the ibex that cavorted in the upper realms of the jebels. It seemed mind-blowing to imagine these crafty hunters stalking and slaying the ibex with bow and arrow, then downclimbing the routes, overhangs and all, with dead prey slung over their shoulders. Later I would read the accounts of the Englishman Tony Howard, who opened the Wadi Rum to climbing after 1984 and made a minor study of these Bedouin routes. Howard rated the hardest moves on these ancient passages at Very Severe, or 5.7 to 5.8. Of one route on a dome called the Rijm Assaf, Howard wrote, "Its crux was a bold pull over an overhang from a tottering Bedouin cairn balanced on the edge of space." Howard also claimed that one route on Jebel Rum bore the signatures in Thamudic script of hunters named Kharajat and

Jahfal. That script was in use only from 200 BC to 300 AD. Thus Howard concluded that the Bedouin climb had taken place as long as two thousand years ago. He went so far as to speculate that it might have been the oldest known rock climb in the world.

Among the Anasazi, the Tellem, the Chachopoya, the Toraja, the cave diggers of Mustang, and the Bedouin of the Wadi Rum, prehistoric climbing of a high technical level evidently served various purposes, ranging from storing precious grain to commemorating the dead to seeking refuges for meditation to hunting ibex. None of the motives of those cultures bore any resemblance to the Western passion for climbing to achieve personal and aesthetic goals. Yet the severity of the climbing testifies to a commitment to needs both utilitarian and spiritual every bit as intense as the passions that drove Whymper up the Matterhorn or Hillary to the top of Everest.

For me, the awe and wonder that these ancient climbs evoked, along with the sheer alienness of the cultures in which they were embedded, made an impact that was at once humbling and inspirational. There were more things in those heavens and earths than were dreamt of in my climbing philosophy.

INTERLUDE

THE QUEST
for the OTHER

For about twenty years, from age seventeen to thirty-seven, climbing was the most important thing in my life. During that stretch, I went on expeditions to Alaska or the Yukon for thirteen straight years. For me, the ultimate prize in mountaineering was the first ascent of an unclimbed peak or a difficult new route on a mountain that had been climbed only a few times. The seasons were geared almost manically to next summer's expedition. During those decades, I was successively a college student, a graduate student, and a teacher at Hampshire College, but I conceived my real identity to be that of a mountaineer. Each September brought a huge letdown, with nothing to look forward to during another school year before I could once again chase my destiny in the remote ranges.

By the age of thirty-seven, however, I no longer felt that the mountains furnished an all-consuming purpose in life. It was, I suppose, partly a matter of simply getting older, of realizing that I had passed my climbing prime. I also felt that I was lucky still to be alive, and sometimes late at night, when sleep wouldn't come, I counted the close calls I had survived, rating them from fairly threatening to truly serious. I wish that I could have bowed out with some major accomplishment capping a worthwhile career, but it became instead a matter of choosing less and less ambitious goals. The list of mountaineers who quit cold after some stellar deed is indeed a short one—the great Italian alpinist Walter Bonatti being the exemplar.

Instead of a sense of fulfillment, at age thirty-seven I felt only a dull sense of loss. Nothing in my life, not even the writing career I was beginning in earnest, took the place of the yearly round geared to a climactic adventure each summer. What was missing in my life, in fact, was just that: adventure.

It was not as though I deliberately set out to find a new passion to take the place of mountaineering. Surviving the transition from college professor to freelance writer was scary and uncertain enough. I don't remember even framing my dilemma in coherent words. There was just a certain emptiness that seemed to settle upon my spirit.

In my early forties, I gradually drifted into a fascination with the Anasazi. The family visits during my childhood to Mesa Verde and Bandelier National Monument had failed to light the spark. It was only after I started hiking down canyons in southeastern Utah and stumbling upon ruins and rock art that were on no map nor in any guidebook that my curiosity bloomed into a nagging passion. My first several outings involving the Anasazi came in the guise of magazine assignments, but soon I was saving my own time to hike and backpack into more and more remote canyons. By 1990, I had solidified a habit of spending at least several weeks each spring and fall in the Southwest, almost all of it in pursuit of little-known Anasazi wonders.

At no point did I consciously tell myself, *This is what takes the place of climbing,* but by the early 1990s I realized that those journeys had begun to shape my year every bit as meaningfully as the old climbing cycle had once done. I was aware of the irony of comparing my two passions. Climbing had always been for keeps, an ultimate game of life and death with the ecstatic joy of success on a difficult mountain as the reward. Canyon prowling, in contrast, was not very dangerous, while the camping and hiking were infinitely more pleasant than bivouacking in storms in Alaska. But soon there was no denying that my fixation with the Anasazi was as all-consuming as Alaskan expeditions had been. I started reading archaeological journals with the same fervor that I once had lavished on climbing magazines. The thrill of turning a canyon bend and discovering an unrecorded ruin or rock art panel came close to matching what I had once felt when putting up a new route. And because the Anasazi were themselves such gifted climbers, my explorations took on a certain tinge of dangerous discovery. More than a few of the high granaries and dwellings that I came across, I was quite sure that I was the first person to explore in at least seven hundred years.

The essential difference between the two passions that successively centered my life was one that only slowly dawned on me. However dramatic or exciting, climbing was in a certain sense a sterile pursuit. The deed of a new route or a first ascent was of interest only to oneself, and perhaps to a small fraternity of fellow devotees. Climbing was not heroic, nor did it do anyone except its practitioners any good, nor did it really stretch the mind. But each time I found a new Anasazi site in the backcountry, the pride of discovery was subsumed in a larger concern: *What was it all about? What were they doing here?*

Those forays into the backcountry, either solo or with one or two like-minded companions, felt adventurous. Sometimes the canyon itself wouldn't "go," when a sudden pour-over declared a dead end. Or it would go only with tricky, exposed scrambling to find a route through the scrub oak and manzanita that clung to nearly vertical cliffs. Sometimes a whole day of exploring came up empty, not a single potsherd or squiggly petroglyph in miles of what looked like a perfect canyon for the Anasazi. But the rewards were proportionate to the effort. More than once it was only when I wrenched my gaze upward from the rocky

ground in front of me that I saw, hundreds of feet above, granaries peeping into sight on almost imperceptible ledges.

What I was doing, of course, was not archaeology. Some might
sneer at my pursuit as a kind of dilettantism, skimming the surface of
prehistoric sites without having to commit to the drudgery of proper
survey and excavation. From what little I saw in action in the Southwest, toward the end of the twentieth century field archaeology had
lost any semblance of the adventurous. The major sites that were still
being dug, like Sand Canyon Pueblo or the villages salvaged in the Dolo-
res Archaeological Program before they could be swallowed by the
McPhee Reservoir, were rows of room blocks laid out in relatively flat
landscapes to which the excavators could drive on county roads. There
was indeed a kind of adventure attached to these inquiries in the soil,
but it was of a purely intellectual nature.

What saved my canyon wanderings from the shallow stamp of hob-
byism was the fact that the archaeologists had so turned their backs on
the hard-to-get-to canyons with their soaring cliffs. As mentioned
above, when I searched the professional literature for any discussion of
hand-and-toe trails, I couldn't find a single paper. Yet the Moqui steps
that I tried to follow, often with my heart in my throat, raised genuine
archaeological questions. How did the ancient craftsmen, with only
quartzite pounding stones for tools, create them? Some were plainly
staircases to distant ruins, but others seemed to go nowhere. What
were those about? Inside alcoves, I often found short sequences of tiny
steps. Were these practice tracks for Anasazi youngsters? A few of the
scarier trails seem to be booby-trapped, as, far off the ground, the steps
suddenly went haywire: three awkwardly placed right-foot steps in a
row, for instance. Were these, as my friend Joe Pachak speculated, death
gauntlets laid to seduce overcurious visitors?

Beyond a vague general agreement that the dwellings and granaries in the cliffs were defensive, the archaeologists seemed unwilling to

face the obvious questions they raised. It was hard enough to figure out how the boldest of the Anasazi climbers had gotten to those airy refuges in the first place. It was much harder to discern how the ancients had hauled all the mud and stone and water up to them to build dwellings and granaries that had outlasted the centuries.

Many high room blocks were fronted with blank walls of stone and adobe that the Anasazi had pierced with six or eight or a dozen "loopholes." To me their purpose was obvious: they were tunnels pointed at all the crucial vantage points so that hidden residents could spy on invaders approaching from below. Yet what literature I could find on the question drifted into (to my mind) fanciful explanations. They were watching tubes, some argued, through which hidden dignitaries could observe ritual dances in the village plaza, by analogy with the Shalako ceremony at historic Zuni Pueblo.

There were a few aspects of the canyon ruins that I like to think I might have been among the first to note. One was a fiendish construction that I called the "stopper wall." Many of the inaccessible dwellings could be reached only by scuttling and even crawling on one's belly along lengthy exposed ledges. Often, just before I could get to the dwelling, right where the ledge was the narrowest and most dangerous, the ancients had mortared a triangular wall blocking my way. Any unwanted visitor slinking along the ledge could be apprehended as he struggled to bypass the stopper wall. A thrown stone or two or even a vigorous push would suffice to send the intruder on a long fall to certain death.

It was only after I had spent several years indulging my Anasazi passion that I recognized its essential difference from the mountaineering that had driven me to the remote ranges in my twenties and thirties. However thrilling my canyon play, however ingenious the passages I worked out, the game was not about *me*. It was about *them*.

Were I inclined to be dogmatic, I might frame my realization thus:

A quest in the wilderness to probe the mysteries of a lost or little-known
culture is ultimately more rewarding than a quest to claim a trophy such
as a new route or first ascent. But retrospective self-congratulation of
this sort is the province of the aging adventurer. Instead, I will say only
that such quests have given my life, after the age of forty, as much grati-
fication and fulfillment as the boldest mountaineering ever did.

———

In March 2016, I ventured out on the first trip of any kind I'd undertaken since my cancer diagnosis the previous July. With my friends
Matt Hale and Sarah Keyes tagging along as personal custodians, I flew
to Charlotte, North Carolina, and drove to Boone for Appalachian State
University's annual celebration of the Banff Mountain Film and Book
Festival traveling exhibition. Months earlier, Alex Honnold and I had
been invited as keynote speakers, but I had held off on accepting until
just weeks before the event.

During the four days in North Carolina, I felt constantly weak, and
finding food I could eat posed a challenge for Sarah and Matt. But Alex
and I spoke at a pair of events, and we signed 250 copies (my personal
record) of the book we had cowritten, *Alone on the Wall*. At the Saturday
evening film screening, as I introduced the program and shared a little
bit of my personal ordeal, I was stunned to receive a standing ovation
from the 1,800 people in attendance.

The event in Boone went a long way toward making up for missing
the launch of *Alone on the Wall* at Banff the previous November. On one
morning, we went climbing at a small crag infelicitously named the
Dump. With Sarah leading (and Alex chiming in with encouragement),
I seconded a pair of easy routes. It was the first outdoor climbing I had
done in seven months.

The next week, I got my feeding tube removed after six months of
being harnessed to the grotesque contraption. My diet had expanded

to include poached eggs on toast, turkey chili, and the occasional beer. I dared to hope that I had finally found a path that led to the promised road to recovery.

Sharon and I planned a three-week trip to my beloved Southwest at the end of April. For most of the year I had been longing for Cedar Mesa, for one more brush with Anasazi mysteries. There was still, however, the business of the pesky nodules in my chest. But when another CT scan proved inconclusive—the nodules seemed to have enlarged a bit, though they were still too small to biopsy—I was freed to attempt my Southwest escape.

Hiking again on real trails, I was mortified by how weak I felt, by how little stamina I had. But slowly I gained a vestige of fitness, and at the end of our trip Sharon and I joined Matt Hale and Ed Ward for a week on Cedar Mesa. We punctuated six days of hiking with three nights of car camping in cherished sites affording views to the southern and western horizons. We limited our outings to ruins and rock art panels I'd visited before, though all the country was new to Ed, and one or two of the hikes took Matt and Sharon to places they had never seen. The weather was perfect. None of our forays covered more than five miles round trip, but I was overjoyed to be able to accomplish that much.

When I got home from Utah, I felt such an acute longing to travel that within a few hours I had plotted trips to Montreal in late June and to Paris in August, with a far more ambitious return to the Southwest for September and October.

But the nodules . . . On June 6, I had another CT scan. The verdict was the worst I could have imagined. Several of the nodules had significantly grown. My oncologist, who had seen too many similar cases, could not hide his pessimism. In all likelihood, despite the intense chemo and radiation I had absorbed the previous fall, the throat cancer had metastasized to my lungs.

To be sure, I needed a biopsy. And now matters took another bad turn. The surgeon who had performed scores of similar biopsies turned over my job to an inexperienced resident—who promptly botched the biopsy. Not only did she fail to retrieve a viable sample, she punctured my lung in the process. For the first time in months I was readmitted to Brigham and Women's Hospital.

When I got out of the hospital I felt more exhausted than I had since January. The collapsed lung was the immediate cause, but I couldn't shake the thought that cancer might be attacking me anew. Still, Sharon and I went ahead with our plans to drive to Montreal, though only at the last minute were we freed to head north to New Hampshire. My sodium level had dropped to an alarming 123 (normal being 135 to 145). My oncologist grudgingly endorsed the road trip only after I took 3,000 mg of salt tablets per day and raised the level to 125—still disturbingly low.

Montreal gave us a few good days, as we played golf on a pricey course, toured the botanical gardens, and hung out in a lively neighborhood on the Mont Royal Plateau. There were a dozen restaurants within three blocks of our apartment, but I was finding it harder to eat than it had been in months. The temperature hovered near 90 degrees Fahrenheit during the day, and as we strolled from roses to bonsai in the botanical gardens, I had to sit down and rest on every other park bench.

On the way home, we stopped in Quechee, Vermont, to visit a friend, who had arranged a golf game on an exquisite private course the following morning. But at dinnertime I collapsed, vomiting and nearly fainting, and for the first time since October I felt my mental grasp on the world start to dissolve. We rushed to the emergency room at Dartmouth–Hitchcock Hospital, where I would spend the next four days.

In the ER, my sodium level measured 115. Coma and even death lurk not far below that number. Within a few days, the doctors at Dartmouth–Hitchcock came up with a new diagnosis. I was suffering from SIADH—syndrome of inappropriate anti-diuretic hormone secretion. Somehow my body was retaining too much water while it allowed the sodium level to get far too low. Chances were that SIADH was a side effect of metastasized cancer. The only treatment was to keep downing big doses of salt tablets while limiting all my liquid to 1,500 ml a day. That's about a quart and a half. As the doctors prescribed the new regimen, I succumbed to despair. How could I hike or play golf if I could drink only a quart and a half of water a day?

The clincher came in early July, when a competent surgeon performed a bronchoscopy, snaking a tube down my throat to snip a hunk of chest nodule (I was out cold during the procedure, thanks to a general anesthetic). The sample proved the case: the enlarged nodules were cancerous, having metastasized from the cells in my throat. Cure was no longer possible, only palliative treatment to keep me alive. All my hopes for the future seemed to vanish like a soap bubble.

Just when I thought things could not get worse, in late August I was dealt another nasty blow. A quick visit to the hospital for low blood pressure and trouble swallowing led to a six-day incarceration, starting in the ICU. My sodium level was so low I was put on an IV super-saline drip.

In the middle of my stay, I took a swallowing test. In February I'd passed my previous test with flying colors, which gave the technicians the go-ahead to remove my feeding tube. Now, six months later, I failed the test completely. Apparently I was aspirating part of every mouthful of food I tried to swallow, sending it down the wrong tube and into the lungs. If that error persisted, I would develop aspiration pneumonia, which is often fatal and not a good way to die.

Another oncologist gave me the ultimatum: a new feeding tube, with no guarantee I'd ever get rid of it. No assurance that I would ever eat or drink normally again. At first I refused, claiming petulantly that I'd rather take my chances with aspiration pneumonia. My first feeding tube had symbolized for me the nadir of invalidism. I could not bear the thought of going back to that humiliating apparatus, and to the indignity it wreaked on my daily life.

By the end of September 2016, however, I was once again siphoning six cans per day of mud-brown gunk (Osmolite, rather than Ensure) down the new tube—and still restricting the liquid, now to 900 ml per day, also flushed down the tube. All day and night, I took mouthfuls of water to relieve my parched, saliva-less mouth, swished, and spat it out.

The only bright spot in my second autumn of housebound misery was that I was being infused every three weeks with Pembrolizumab, a drug that tries to stimulate the immune system to attack the cancer cells. This new frontier of immunotherapy had shown good results with melanoma and lung cancer, but it was virtually untried with throat cancer. Preliminary findings gave only a 20–40 percent chance that it would have any effect at all. Yet a CT scan after three Pembro infusions revealed that the nodules had stopped growing. It was no proof that the Pembro was working, but it gave me hope.

Not hope of curing cancer—for the rest of my life, however long or short, I must live with the mindless proliferating cells that have made my body their home—but hope that I might forestall the brutal end.

Hope that someday, with or without a feeding tube or a cap on my liquid intake, I might hike again, and camp out under the changeless stars, and even climb easy routes. Hope that I still have months or years to write, to reassess what the first seventy-three years of my life have meant, and to squeeze new meanings from all that I had and had not done, before it was too late to remember or even know.

FOUR

FIRST DESCENT

On November 14, 2015, Henry Worsley set off on an attempt to traverse Antarctica solo, with no resupply airdrops and no devices such as sails to boost his progress. As he launched his expedition from Berkner Island, near the Ronne Ice Shelf, he was man-hauling a sledge that weighed more than 300 pounds. In attempting this record journey, Worsley hoped to fulfill the dream of his hero, Sir Ernest Shackleton, whose own attempt to traverse Antarctica in 1914–17 ended in disaster followed by heroic survival, after the expedition ship, the *Endurance*, was crushed and sunk in sea ice before even reaching the continent. Worsley was a distant relative of Frank Worsley, whose miraculous navigating on the open-boat journey from Elephant Island to South Georgia Island saved the entire team.

In 2008–09, with two companions, Worsley had retraced Shackleton's attempt to reach the South Pole on the *Nimrod* expedition of 1908–09. The four men in the polar party reached a point 97 miles short of the pole, where Shackleton confessed to his diary, "We have shot our bolt."

In January 2016, seventy-one days after launching his traverse, having crossed 913 miles of the polar plateau, exhausted and ill, Worsley had to give up his attempt. He was camped only 30 miles from the finish line on the Ross Ice Shelf. After lingering in his camp for several days, unable "to slide one ski in front of the other," he sent out his message of resignation via sat phone. Echoing his hero, he announced, "I too have shot my bolt." Only a few days later, on January 24, he died.

The outpouring of tributes to Worsley spanned the globe. *Outside* magazine hailed him as "one of the world's great polar explorers." It could be argued, however, that Worsley's feat of endurance had nothing to do with exploration. And in the universal outpouring of sympathy and acclaim in the wake of Worsley's death at age fifty-five, the profound differences between his deed and that of his hero a century earlier were glossed over by the media and polar enthusiasts alike.

During his seventy-one days on the ice, Worsley was in constant contact, via radio and sat phone, with his support team. He recorded daily dispatches about his progress that were broadcast to a wide public, and answered questions that were sent in by his listeners. Every foot of the frozen continent that he traversed had been mapped and photographed from the air, and his GPS device precluded any chance of getting lost or even off-route.

Most importantly, when Worsley collapsed only 30 miles short of his goal, his support team sprang to his rescue. On January 22, a plane landed near his camp, loaded the invalid aboard, and flew him to Punta Arenas, Chile. Worsley died not in a tent but in a hospital, after doctors were unable to reverse a case of severe peritonitis.

In 2008–09, as he retraced Shackleton's pioneering attempt on the South Pole, Worsley counted on a similar network of contact, support, and rescue capability. In 1909, when Shackleton turned back, he and his three companions faced a desperate return voyage to the base camp hut at Cape Royds. The only rescue team was themselves.

In 2009, rather than stopping 97 miles from the pole, Worsley's team pushed on to 90° S. Instead of having to retrace the arduous trek from the coast, the three men were flown by airplane from the pole back to civilization. In his expedition book, *In Shackleton's Footsteps,* Worsley rather cavalierly glosses over the huge safety margin that technology had wrought since Shackleton's day.

Yes, Worsley died in the effort to set a polar record. But compared to the paragons of the golden age of Antarctic exploration—Scott, Shackleton, Amundsen, Mawson, and their men—Worsley and his rivals in the modern polar game are not playing for keeps. The technological progress of the century has reduced what were once the last unknown places on earth to arenas in which modern adventurers compete for increasingly arcane records (the fastest trek from A to B, the longest unsupported journey across C), always with one foot firmly anchored in the bailout zone of rescue by air.

It is tempting to see the state of exploration today as a played-out endeavor, a stage on which latter-day impostors try to emulate the heroes of yesteryear by manufacturing artificial challenges that grab headlines but add little or nothing to terrestrial discovery. (Worsley, no impostor, must have known how far his feats fell short of Shackleton's.) Indeed, the thrust of this book, in the preceding chapters, might seem to support such a pessimistic view. If we can no longer push into the unknown North, like Nansen, or reconnoiter a vast uncharted tract of the Karakoram, like Shipton, what is there left to discover?

My take on this dilemma, however, is in the end an optimistic one. As I hope to show in the following chapters, there are still plenty of regions on earth where no one has ever set foot. And there are legions of young explorers who devote their lives to getting to those places and finding out what's there. They do so, for the most part, far from the media spotlight, which for perverse reasons focuses on today's record-questers, all but ignoring the true explorers.

Even before Jon Krakauer, in *Into Thin Air,* laid out in all its sordid detail the scene Mount Everest has become, with dilettantes who can scarcely put on their crampons forking out big bucks to get dragged up the world's highest mountain, serious climbers tended to turn their backs on Everest. From 1999 to 2009, I was the go-to chronicler of mountaineering for *National Geographic Adventure* magazine. In vain I beseeched the editors to let me write about Cerro Torre in Patagonia, or Mount Edgar in western China, or the Devils Thumb on the Alaska–Canada border. Each spring (and several falls) I churned out a feature story about the doings on Everest. It was, swore the editors, what the readers wanted. Along with chronicling the follies perpetrated by guided clients, I half-heartedly saluted the record-setters: those who climbed the mountain in the fastest time, or who were the youngest or oldest to succeed, or who tagged the summit the most times.

By 2016, nearly all the highest peaks on all the continents had been "conquered," to use the verb in currency until the late 1960s. But there are still today scores of unclimbed peaks in the lesser-known ranges—in Alaska, in Greenland, in corners of the Himalaya outside Nepal. The 2016 *American Alpine Journal* featured an essay on the Neacola Range, a low-altitude wilderness tucked into an obscure bend where the Alaska Range abuts the Aleutians. The Neacolas abound in small glaciers and sharp peaks rising as high as 3,000 feet above their bases. The first recorded ascent of any of the mountains took place in 1965, but more than fifty years later, according to climbing historian Steve Gruhn, 90 percent of the peaks in the range remain unclimbed.

———

Throughout history, rivers have been far more central to human existence than mountains. Towns and cities inevitably sprang up on the banks of great waterways such as the Nile, the Yangtze, the Danube, while before the nineteenth century only rustic hamlets dared to creep into the foothills of the Alps. Because hundreds of miles of the world's greatest rivers proved navigable, they became thoroughfares long before highways or train tracks scored the landscape.

Even so, throughout the ages rivers retained a powerful aura of mystery. When René-Robert Cavelier, Sieur de La Salle, succeeded in descending the Mississippi River all the way from present-day Illinois to the Gulf of Mexico in 1680–82, he believed he had laid the blueprint for a campaign to claim all of North America for the French. By the 1860s, the upper and lower reaches of the Colorado River were familiar ground to mountain men and government explorers, but some 500 miles of its midsection, as it plunged through one canyon after another, were unknown to Anglos and only hazily comprehended by Native American tribes in what are now Utah and Arizona. John Wesley Powell's perilous 1869 descent of the Colorado from Green River, Utah, to the end of the Grand Canyon stands as one of the epic voyages of American discovery.

Rivers tantalized the human imagination before mountains did. The source of the Nile had puzzled geographers from the second century BC onward, but the quest to reach it on foot climaxed only in the 1850s, with the bitter rivalry between John Hanning Speke and Richard Burton. This despite the fact that the source of any river is an ill-defined, nondescript place in some upland valley, far less dramatic or obvious as a goal than the summit of a mountain.

By the 1850s, the competition to make the first ascents of the highest and hardest peaks in the Alps was in full swing. More than a century would pass before a comparable rivalry to make the first descents of wilderness rivers took hold. By the late 1930s, the challenge of running the scores of rapids on the Colorado River through the Grand Canyon had not only inspired a handful of descents in emulation of Powell, but had given birth to a fledgling industry offering guided trips to paying clients. Still, by 1949 fewer than a hundred people had floated the length of the Grand Canyon. Along with the Colorado, pioneering explorations of the Snake and Salmon rivers had started to make white-water rafting an adventure game with cadres of devotees. But the quest to seek out first descents of dangerous rivers all over the globe emerged only in the 1970s.

A landmark achievement came in 1968, after Ethiopia's Emperor Haile Selassie invited a British Army colonel, John Blashford-Snell, to organize a descent of the Blue Nile from its source in Lake Tana to the Sudanese border. The massive expedition that Blashford-Snell led comprised no fewer than sixty novice river runners, scientists, and support crew from both Ethiopia and Great Britain. Although one team member drowned on the journey, the flamboyant Blashford-Snell trumpeted his first descent, claiming "to have invented whitewater rafting by accident."

Motivated in part by the Blue Nile descent, in 1973 a young Colorado river guide named Richard Bangs gathered a few cronies and arrived in Ethiopia to attempt the first descent of the Awash, a major river that flows from the highlands northeast to its terminus in the Danakil Depression. Bangs's team ran a bare-bones trip, the opposite of the massively funded Blue Nile extravaganza, but the men knew what they were doing and pulled off the first descent without a serious mishap.

Ravenous for more of the same, Bangs's party turned to the Omo River, another of Ethiopia's great waterways, which they ran as smoothly as they had the Awash. In December 1973, Bangs returned to Ethiopia to attempt the Baro, a river that runs west toward South Sudan before emptying into the White Nile.

On the first day on the Baro, disaster struck, as Bangs's raft overturned in a monstrous rapid. Bangs and teammate Karen Greenwald managed to swim to shore (not before Bangs was tossed through a few more rapids and nearly drowned), but the inexperienced Angus Macleod disappeared. Gathering themselves on the bank, the shaken team realized that it had lost two of its three rafts and much of its food and gear. Half the party hiked out to the nearest road the same day, while Bangs and four teammates scouted downriver in their only remaining raft for three days before hiking out themselves. Neither their probe nor two others launched in subsequent months ever found any signs of Macleod. In 1984, Bangs recalled his life-changing catastrophe in a moving essay for *Outside* magazine called "First Bend on the Baro."

Despite the tragedy, Bangs and friends were hooked on exploratory rafting. They incorporated themselves as Sobek, the name borrowed from the Egyptian crocodile god, because a chief hazard of the rivers of Ethiopia was the hordes of crocs that make the rivers their home. By offering guided commercial expeditions on some of the tamer rivers they had pioneered, as well as on the most popular whitewater runs Stateside, Sobek became a profitable business. (Today it flourishes as Mountain Travel/Sobek.)

The raison d'être of incorporation, of course, was to provide a means for Bangs and his impassioned partners to chase first descents all over the world. There followed landmark Sobek "exploratories" on such daunting rivers as the Bio-Bio in Chile, the Zambezi in Zimbabwe, and the Tambopata in Peru.

I got to know Richard Bangs in the early 1980s. Realizing at once that we were kindred spirits with kindred passions for the wilderness, we began a friendship that is now in its fourth decade. And in 1983, and again in 1996, Richard invited me to join him as a journalist on Sobek attempts to make the first descents of major rivers in Papua New Guinea and Ethiopia.

It was not as though I had any expertise in whitewater rafting, or even the rudest skills as a boater of any kind. In fact, having never learned to swim, I was a confirmed aquaphobe. But a peculiar aspect of rafting, unlike mountaineering, is that complete beginners can accompany experts on significant expeditions. (The passive role of a passenger in a raft is the key to the quick transformation of breakthrough descents of little-known rivers to "adventure travel" junkets for paying clients.)

Still, I had my qualms before signing on to the New Guinea adventure. Richard blithely reassured me, "Don't worry, David, anything you don't like the looks of you can walk around." This turned out to be so far from the truth that I would later realize how smoothly Richard had sandbagged me. My qualms would intensify when, in August 1983, I first boarded my raft on the Tua River, just upstream of a frothing cauldron of rapids. I asked my captain, Mike Boyle, what my duties were. "Shut up and hang on," he answered.

———

In the early 1970s, the Sobek pioneers scrimped and saved to afford their trips. And in those days, there was no GPS to fix an explorer's latitude and longitude, no sat phone with which to call for a handy rescue. For the take-out on the Omo, Bangs's team had to locate the right tributary stream among the dozens on the lower river, hike up it 25 miles, and find an airstrip indicated on the unreliable map, where once a week a C-47 landed to supply a primitive game park. The team had no viable second option.

But rafting trips on inaccessible rivers in far-off countries are expensive undertakings. In the decade since the Awash and the Omo, Bangs had nursed a talent almost as impressive as his expertise on the river—that of the entrepreneur. Through sheer trial and error, he had discovered how to sweet-talk dubious sponsors into funding expeditions to the far corners of the earth.

The river on which Bangs and his 1983 teammates had focused their wanderlust was one of the great waterways in Southeast Asia. It begins in the relatively civilized New Guinea highlands as a gentle

stream known to the locals as the Wahgi. Flowing south, it gathers vol-
ume as it plunges into the highland fringe, where deep rain forest shel-
ters a handful of unacculturated tribes, changing its name to the Tua.
Even farther south, it becomes the Purari, a powerful torrent that ultimately discharges its fury in the Gulf of Papua. No boatmen had ever
attempted the Wahgi/Tua/Purari.

Bangs had managed to talk a BBC crew into making a film about
our exploratory, as part of its ongoing series *Great River Journeys*. The
partnership turned into a bargain with the devil, as the BBC director,
Clive Syddall, assumed that controlling the purse strings should allow
him to dictate the action.

A true source-to-sea descent would have had us launch on the highland stream and float all 400 miles to the ocean. But that was beyond
the budget and the patience of the BBC. Instead, after a few one-day
rides on the Wahgi to get our feet wet, Bangs and Syddall agreed to start
the drama near the head of the Tua, by helicoptering to a put-in in a
clearing in the jungle reconnoitered beforehand by air.

At age forty, I had never been in a rain forest of any kind. I had
always thought that the jungle would be for me a nightmare landscape,
full of creepy-crawlies and claustrophobic tangles of vegetation. I
stepped out of the chopper into a searing heat: cicadas whining in the
treetops, black rocks too hot to walk on, a mud-colored maelstrom of
river seething through the valley. Yet within an hour I had begun to love
the place.

While the rest of the crew assembled camp, and Richard pow-
wowed with Clive Syddall to sketch out the first day's filming, I started
hiking alone down the left bank of the mighty river. I had gone only
about a mile when I was stunned to discover a classic Burma bridge
spanning the torrent—one strand to walk on, two for handrails. Full of
a reckless passion to explore, I started across the bridge. From the far

side, I heard voices, then glimpsed in the shadowy underbrush a small group of natives, mostly women, who were in the process of fleeing from my intrusion. As I started back, I heard a single call. A young man had appeared at the far end of the bridge and seemed to be gesturing for me to come on across. For the first time, I felt fear. I tried to make signs for him to come my way, even as I retreated further to the safety of my bank.

At last the man scampered across the bridge. As he came closer, I wondered whether I should run back to camp, but the stranger looked unarmed. I reached out a hand to shake; instead, he half-knelt and rubbed his head against my T-shirted stomach.

I was not, I guessed, the first white person he had ever seen. By the 1980s, there was little chance of making true first contact with natives anywhere in the world. Probably the man's village had been visited by aid workers or missionaries. Yet the wonder and edgy apprehension of the meeting hung in the sweltering air.

I tried to signal to my new acquaintance to come back to the Sobek camp with me. But he was signaling something else—a "wait a minute" plea, as far as I could tell. Suddenly he started scrambling up the steep slope at our backs, deftly slithering through vines and over tree roots.

I waited for about ten minutes, still jittery with unease. For all I knew, the man was fetching warrior kin to deal with the white intruder. But then he reappeared. In his hands, he held a gift. It was a giant yam. He had apparently known just where he had to climb to harvest the tuber in all its glory. (I had read that 73 percent of the native diet of New Guinea consisted of yams.)

I lugged the precious object back to the gang setting up camp. My new friend, however, had judged the risk of joining me too great a chance to take. I never saw him again.

That first night on the Tua, the BBC crew camped out with us, and an amicable feeling held sway in our clearing in the wilderness. But the filmmakers had already confessed that they were too spooked to ride the rafts with us. All the footage would have to be captured by cameras on shore or from a hovering helicopter.

In the morning, all of us were itching to head downstream. We were up by 6 AM but didn't launch until noon, because Syddall couldn't figure out how to script the day's float. As we lounged in the heat, with sweat bees clinging to our shirts, the natives started to arrive, no doubt from the same village as the women I had scared away on the other end of the Burma bridge. They hunkered upstream, a good fifty yards from us, and simply stared.

The Sobek veterans were used to such scenes, and they did their best to ignore our audience. We had already been admonished not to offer the locals so much as a stick of chewing gum, should they turn out to be beggars. But I had never been part of such a strange cultural interchange, and I covertly stared back, wondering, *What are they thinking? Who do they think we are? Why do they think we've come?* Our arrival on the Tua had been so abrupt, so artificial, that none of us even knew which tribe the onlookers belonged to, let alone anything about their way of life.

At last we got underway, leaving a throng of staring locals behind. Not far below camp, the BBC set up their gear on shore and spent three and a half hours filming our rafts through the first sizeable rapid (one I had been happy to walk around).

By afternoon, the BBC had retreated to the helicopter, and we were free to career downstream. Every bend gave our sovereign wilderness a whole new look, and as the captains of our three rafts barked orders, I tried to imprint on my memory every scrap of landscape before it spooled out of sight. And now the Tua became serious.

Toward late afternoon, Skip Horner's boat flipped. Mike Boyle's raft, in which I rode, took up the chase. We hauled two of the castaways aboard; the other two splashed through another bad rapid clinging to their upside-down craft. At last Boyle rowed eight people and two boats to the blessed firmness of shore. He collapsed, exhausted. In the middle of this drama, we had become aware of the helicopter screaming overhead; even though we cursed its noise and the wind its rotors blasted us with, we hoped the BBC was getting their footage.

The helicopter landed; Richard disappeared with Syddall into a story conference. Later we learned that the director had decided that on the morrow we should heli-lift the boats back upstream and run through the thing again. Incredulity gave way to obscenity—though we kept our derision from Syddall's ears.

That evening the filmmakers, more spooked than ever, declined even to camp with us. For the rest of our brief expedition, the BBC crew commuted by helicopter from a hotel in Kundiawa, the highland town we had made our headquarters. This meant endless waits on perfectly good mornings before we could continue down the river. One day Syddall's team didn't arrive until early afternoon. I learned from the sound man that the delay had been caused by a hassle over changing rooms in the hotel.

On our third day, we were stopped cold by the Tua itself. A major rapid stretched, uninterrupted, for half a mile. The jungle was so thick it took two hours just to scout the rapid. By nightfall we were camped in drizzling rain in miserable semi-bivouacs among a mass of boulders.

The captains had been mulling over the nasty rapid. Skip Horner pointed out that it wasn't the individual moves that made it so tough; it was the lack of calm water between them in which to recover. John Kramer said, "You'd run it if it were the only way out of here. But it's a life-or-death proposition, not a sporting one."

Thanks to the fiendish vegetation, the portage would take at least two days. Guiltily, the guides reconciled themselves to the alternative.

The helicopter could be used to carry all our gear and boats past the half-mile rapid. The next morning, the heli-lift went like clockwork. Our crack Korean pilot got everything downstream in only two hours.

From the onset of the trip, I had been disturbed by the way the demands of the film crew adulterated our voyage. Here was the starkest example yet of how technology cheapened the adventure. Portaging is a time-honored gambit for river runners, who pay in backbreaking misery for their choice not to run a perilous rapid. But if a helicopter could leapfrog the whole expedition past the scary sections, did the claim of "first descent" still have meaning?

On our fifth day, we ran a solid 10 miles of the Tua. We were deep in the rain forest now, and the banks no longer bore signs of human habitation. Riding my raft, as I gazed at the intricacies of the jungle, I tried to recapture the transport I had first tasted on Denali in 1963—the sense that we might be exploring country no human beings had ever before seen. But the presence of the BBC—the chopper filming overhead, the twice-daily conferences between Bangs and Syddall as to how to shape the story—killed any inkling that we were pioneers.

And now another crisis arose. Syddall's fear of the river, along with his detachment as director, emboldened him to declare to Richard that he would allow one more river day before declaring our trip a wrap. Richard called his bluff, protesting vehemently that there was no way a chopper-aided float of less than half the Tua could be called a "great river journey."

As if the absurdity of our prepackaged adventure needed further underlining, Syddall now announced that the morrow, which happened to be Sunday, would be a day off. He claimed that regulations imposed by the film crew's union precluded working on the Sabbath. The BBC would linger in the Kundiawa hotel, while we could do whatever we pleased.

That Sunday saved the journey, though not, of course, the film.

While the BBC crew lingered in bed, we were on the river at dawn. By camp that evening, we had covered 45 miles—as long a jaunt as any of the Sobek guides had ever made on any river in a single day. The rapids relented and we found continuously swift current with only a few tricky spots. We passed out of the deep canyon we had started in and entered a zone of rolling jungle hills. The rock turned to basalt, then to a marbly conglomerate, and by nightfall we had glimpsed limestone that presaged the Purari. All day we watched lumbering black hornbills saw through the air, white cockatoos glide from limb to limb, and Brahminy kites loiter in airborne helixes. The terrain seemed virtually uninhabited.

In the euphoria of camp, the guides began to talk mutiny. Fuck the BBC, they said; instead of helicoptering out, we ought to go for it, take off downstream, run the Purari, and live on our resources. But the next morning, the BBC was back on the river. Before we could launch, however, we had to film Syddall's idea of a portage. Led by Richard, who slashed away at the foliage with a machete, we carried oars, water cans, and other miscellaneous gear—though none of the rafts, which, needless to say, are the most cumbersome and difficult part of any real portage operation.

By 1 PM we were headed downstream. The BBC crew helicoptered miles ahead to wait for us on a generous gravel bar. The river had grown to an immense size, and the current, Mike Boyle swore, was the strongest he'd ever rowed.

Late in the afternoon we stopped to scout a rapid. Once we had accommodated to the scale, it looked terrifying: a pair of savage drops separated by only thirty yards. I chose at once to walk, as did Richard, who simply didn't like the aura of the thing.

The first boat burst through in fine fashion, full of water but upright. Boyle's came second. He missed the line on the upper drop by only a few feet and slid stern-first into a gigantic hidden hole. Boyle was ripped from the oars and flung out of the boat, which danced for a few seconds, stood on its stern, then did a perfect "endo," or backward flip.

Boyle's two passengers managed to crawl to shore, not before thrashing through more rapids. Boyle had the good luck to pop up right beside the third boat, rowed by John Kramer, and was instantly hauled aboard. They barely made it through the lower drop, then set off in pursuit of the runaway raft. Meanwhile, the helicopter pilot, a Vietnam vet, had been hovering to watch the action. Tired of playing taxi driver to the BBC, when he saw the overturned raft heading downstream, he swooped to the left bank and motioned to Richard to jump in. Like cowboys in a corny western, they set off after the raft. Kramer's boat seemed hardly to be gaining, and so, without much thought, Richard performed a stunt that may never before have been attempted: he leaped out of the helicopter onto the upside-down raft.

Richard slowed the runaway enough so that Kramer and crew could catch up to it, but it took four men and half a mile to fight the thing into submission. Once they had it captured, Kramer lay in the bilge of his raft and gasped for breath.

That night, our last on the Tua, we celebrated, but in a chastened mood. There was no further talk of turning our backs on the BBC and bombing down the Purari to the seacoast. A reconnaissance just below camp revealed more of the same whitewater, and then much worse, including an unportageable canyon that Richard was sure would have been certain death. The next morning we flew out.

Back in Kundiawa, as we packed up to head home, I tried to digest the experience we had all shared. In the end, I wrote a sardonic account of our journey for *Outside* magazine, under the title "Rafting with the BBC." Not surprisingly, Syddall responded with a letter to the editor asserting the integrity of his production. When Syddall's contribution to *Great River Journeys* appeared on TV, I watched it. The film turned out to be deft, dramatic, and every bit as far from our New Guinea reality as I had feared.

The attempted first descent of a great wilderness river ought to be an immersion in true discovery. Thanks to Richard's bargain with the cinematic devil, our trip instead landed in the limbo between the blatant artifice of a simulated voyage and the genuine risk and excitement of the real thing.

Thirty-four years later, I vividly remember the best moments of our nine days on the Tua. Foremost in my mind, when I drift back to that star-crossed adventure, are the alienness of the rain forest stretching to unknown horizons beyond our camps and the terrifying power of the river itself.

If our 1983 expedition had sought the first ascent of some striking peak in the Himalaya, you can be sure that by 2017 that mountain would have been climbed. But in the decades since Sobek descended on New Guinea, the Wahgi/Tua/Purari remains untamed, a challenge for the next generation or the generation after that. Thanks to the daunting logistics of that convoluted wilderness and to the fury of the river itself, no subsequent team has even attempted the first descent.

In this sense, the art of running the most difficult rivers on earth remains a work in progress. By 2017, all the highest and nearly all the hardest mountains in the world have been climbed. But the hardest rivers are still virgin. Among the forms of terrestrial exploration that still promise the allure and challenge that Powell's men found on the Colorado in 1869, the quest for first descents stands high.

———

Thirteen years after our New Guinea adventure, Richard invited me on another river journey. This time the objective was the Tekeze (pronounced "TALK-ah-zay"), one of Ethiopia's great rivers and the last major tributary of the Nile to be explored. The Tekeze had been high on the wish list of the Sobek pioneers in the 1970s, but before they could get to it, the 1974 revolution that overthrew Emperor Haile Selassie burst upon the country.

Under the brutal Communist dictatorship of Mengistu Haile Mariam, between five hundred thousand and two million Ethiopians were murdered during the next seventeen years. Tourism of any kind ground to a halt, as an endless civil war pitted the ruling junta against rebels from various ethnic groups, most notably the Tigrayans in the northern part of the country. In 1991, the government collapsed and Mengistu fled the country.

It took Richard five more years to organize his assault on the Tekeze. The take-out location was self-evident: a bridge carrying the highway between the ancient cities of Gondar and Axum, which had been bombed and rebuilt during the civil war. But the headwaters were a mystery. After several aerial reconnaissances, Richard homed in on the highland town of Lalibela, a center of Ethiopian Orthodox Christianity since the twelfth century, where cruciform churches carved out of bedrock paid a stunning tribute to a faith that had been cut off from Rome for centuries. The rivulets that converge to form the Tekeze spring from foothills only a few miles west of Lalibela.

No matter what compromises and disappointments the wedding of our expedition to the BBC had inflicted in New Guinea, Richard remained a firm believer in the conjoining of filmmaking with river-running. This time he had snagged the sponsorship of Turner Original Productions. But Richard's plan to package our adventure didn't end there. In 1995, he had been lured away from Sobek by an offer from Microsoft to create an online adventure travel magazine. The appeal of covering a wilderness exploit "in real time" via dispatches, photos, and film clips sent from remote campsites to personal computers all over the world seemed to Richard to promise an unmitigated boon. As he would later write in *The Lost River*, a memoir focused on our Tekeze journey, "Why not take the power of the World Wide Web into the field and allow virtual travelers to join an expedition, follow it and participate from the portals of their computer screens, be they at offices, schools, or homes?" The ambitious "magazine" Richard created bore the name Mungo Park, after the great Scottish explorer (1771–1806) who lost his life on the Niger River in West Africa.

Microsoft was not the only outfit toying with new technology that would bring adventure instantaneously to the living rooms of an armchair audience worldwide. In December 1995, I had been hired by Discovery Channel to report from Argentina on the seventh annual running of the Raid Gauloises, an adventure race that drew teams from all over the globe. Instead of attending the event and writing about it when I got home, as I had done during my previous fifteen years of magazine journalism, I was asked by Discovery to write dispatches on my laptop each day and send them to Washington, DC, where techies would edit and format the pieces and put them up on the Web within hours. In addition, I was given one of the first prototype digital cameras to fire off snapshots, download them to my computer, and send them to Discovery headquarters to accompany my writing.

Since I was (and am) an irredeemable Luddite when it comes to technical gadgetry, my editors gave me a crash course in downloading and sending before I went to Argentina. Even so, they were as nervous as I was about whether the whole show would crash before reaching any of Discovery's hordes of enthusiastic browsers. The camera was so crude, they warned me, that I shouldn't try to photograph any subjects from farther away than six feet.

I arrived in Bariloche full of misgivings, not only about my technical duties but about adventure racing itself. By turning the stunning peaks, rivers, and deserts of northern Patagonia into a racecourse, with forty-eight five-person teams careening their way on foot, by horse, and in rafts through a 250-mile gauntlet, supported and refereed by hundreds of company staff and reported by scores of journalists (mostly French), the Raid threatened, I thought, to desecrate the wilderness. Aside from the sheer human impact, racing against competitors seemed to me a perversion of the contemplative mind-set with which men and women had explored the natural world for centuries.

It took only a couple of days for my skepticism to give way to total involvement. I rented a car to get around, since I needed to seize upon one of the few cyber cafes in Bariloche every evening to download and send. The rest of the time, I drove recklessly along a sketchy network of roads, studied the maps, and hiked as fast as I could into the wilderness to intercept and interview teams strung many miles apart along the intricate and challenging course. My grasp of the language helped me to communicate with the French teams, several of which ended up in a breakneck dash for first place.

The Raid offered helicopter rides to the journalists to help them solve the complexity of the circuit, but the fawning and begging it took to snag a ride offended my pride. I resolved to cover the race only by car and by foot, and I took great joy in outsmarting the other journalists to find a given team deep in the forest or high on an alpine ridge.

The French photographers, from *Paris-Match* and *Figaro* and *L'Equipe*, sneered at my point-and-shoot digital camera. But at a checkpoint during a lull in the action, one of these veterans, cigarette dangling from his mouth, asked to look at my toy. He turned it over disdainfully in his hands, but when he handed it back to me, he said, "That fucking thing is going to put us all out of business."

When the race was finished, I was exhausted. But there was a giddy relief in the thought that I didn't have to go home and write my story—and when I caught up to my own dispatches and snapshots on the Internet, I felt a burst of pride at what I had hammered out under such diabolical time pressure.

Later I covered the Eco-Challenge, America's answer to the Raid

Gauloises, for Discovery Channel. This time the race unfolded in the glacier-hung mountains of British Columbia, with the *gemütlich* town of Whistler as its base. Here my competitive juices really started flowing. The Eco-Challenge was concocted by Mark Burnett, the media entrepreneur who would later create *Survivor* and *The Apprentice*. But in the media headquarters in Whistler, he was a man overwhelmed by his own production. Snafus and minor disasters were cropping up hourly, radioed in to headquarters by the referees and safety personnel in the field, and Burnett's addled response was to make whimsical changes to the rules of the race in midstream.

After a couple of my dispatches critical of Burnett went up online, he banished me from the media room. That snub only redoubled my drive to scoop the competition, so I dashed in and out of the wilderness and caught the leading teams in full charge even more skillfully than I had in Argentina.

So in 1996, when Richard Bangs unveiled his plans for the Tekeze expedition, I was gung-ho from the start. Yet the challenge of filing words and pictures from a canyon deep in the Ethiopian wilderness was far dicier than that of reporting from cyber cafes in Bariloche or Whistler. All of us on the Mungo Park team met beforehand at the Microsoft headquarters in Redmond, Washington, to work out the glitches—and to come up with a plan to fake our way through the potential disaster we had nicknamed "the seventeen-day blackout."

Twenty-three years after their first descent of the Awash, Richard had talked four out of the other five surviving Sobek pioneers into attempting the Tekeze. Pledged to the first descent of the last unrun major tributary of the Nile were John Yost, Jim Slade, Bart Henderson, and George Fuller. Only John Kramer, the stalwart of our Tua expedition, was unable to make it. To give the film a narrative focus, Richard and Turner director Bill Anderson decided to focus on the reunion of the five old hands, back in Ethiopia where Sobek had launched its far-flung mission. The footage would try to capture the old gang reminiscing by night and navigating by day down 250 miles of *aqua incognita*.

By the time we reached the Tekeze in September 1996, our team numbered twenty-two, an even larger entourage than the one with which we had attacked the Tua. In Bariloche, I had served as a one-man Internet crew, charged with writing, photographing, downloading, and sending everything to Discovery's offices. The Mungo Park tech team numbered five. Richard would also write daily dispatches, covering different angles from mine; a professional photographer would snag the digital pictures; another fellow would capture video clips and audio bites; and a British techno-whiz would ensure that our laptops and satellite links, all powered by a portable generator, succeeded in sending masses of text and film to Redmond every evening.

The Turner crew added another eight souls, while the roster was rounded out by junior guides. At the last minute we secured the services of Daniel Mehari, an interpreter who would translate between English and Amharic in the event that we ran into natives living near the river.

By 1996, Richard was forty-six years old, and I was fifty-three. Neither of us was quite as willing to take crazy risks as we had been in our youth, but on the aerial recon Richard had judged that the rapids along the Tekeze would present far fewer rafting challenges than the furious Tua had sprung upon us. This time my misgivings were not so much about flipped boats as about the media circus we were carrying down the river.

The Raid Gauloises and the Eco-Challenge had turned semi-wilderness into an engineered race track. But the 220-mile-long Tekeze flowed through genuine wilderness, unknown to white men and women. Our journey was not a race, but, if all went as planned, a true exploratory voyage. To adulterate it not only with filmmaking but with real-time broadcasts gave me qualms that the sheer joy of penetrating the unknown never assuaged. During several spells of downtime on the Tekeze, Richard and I sat on rock benches away from camp and debated the ethics and aesthetics of our venture.

Although he never let on during the trip, Richard had been briefly assailed by qualms similar to mine. In *The Lost River*, he confesses to an impulse that seized him in October 1995, as with a small scouting team he finally found a stretch of canyon that would serve as our put-in on the Tekeze. Rather than wait another year to organize the Sobek–Turner–Mungo Park assault,

> *Suddenly I had a plan: "Pasquale... Conrad has got rafts. What do you say we hike out, fetch a raft, come back and run this thing, guerrilla style. The four of us. We could bag it now."...*
>
> *Then I had second thoughts and put on the brakes. "You know, I'd like nothing better than to do this alpine style, quick, simple, light, the way we used to, but we can't. We have no defenses against shifta [bandits], no safety support for big rapids, no backup if a croc chomps our raft. Besides, we have an obligation to Turner." Sanity prevailed, not, though, without regrets.*

In New Guinea, the abrupt transition by helicopter from our highland hotel to a gravel bar on the Tua deep in the jungle had been vaguely disturbing. In Ethiopia, after a couple of days spent admiring the rock-cut churches of Lalibela, we hiked 13 miles across rolling hills ablaze with yellow daisies, greeted in Amharic by herders and farmers. The transition was gentle and bucolic, even though we were lugging so much gear and food that it took a mob of porters and three trips by Russian MI-8 chopper to deliver all our goods to the riverbank.

Richard had decided that September, on the cusp between the rainy and dry seasons, was the only feasible month to attempt the

Tekeze, whose current varies from a trickle to a raging flood. On September 9, when we finally started down the river, the water was so low the rafts scraped bottom. But as each small tributary added its flow, the Tekeze slowly took on the power of a massive stream. The only drawback was the equatorial heat, which reached 100 degrees Fahrenheit most days. During the searing midday, from eleven to four, we tasted relief only by pouring buckets of river water over ourselves. In camp each evening, the bugs, including a dozen species I had never before swatted, made life frantic.

Bill Anderson, the Turner director, was a different sort of cineaste from Clive Syddall. As we floated from one basalt canyon to the next, the film crew was content to let our journey script their story. Their only qualm was that, so far, none of the rapids had been serious enough to scare even a novice. The Sobek veterans were surprised, for the gradient of the Tekeze from put-in to take-out averaged twelve feet per mile, half again as steep as the Colorado in the Grand Canyon.

The first night, the Mungo Park team set up shop under a huge tarp supported by oars: five laptops, a sat phone, power strips and cords galore, all laid out on folding card tables and fired by our gas-powered generator. To everyone's relief, the media center was up and running with the first passage overhead of a geosynchronous satellite. Within minutes we were connected at the speed of light to the Microsoft offices in Redmond.

I thought I had prepared myself beforehand for the technological overkill of the expedition, but even as I relished hammering out my dispatches—no second drafts for the Internet—I found the strangeness of our situation unsettling. It was a malaise I never shook during the following weeks.

I wasn't the only skeptic in our team. John Yost, Richard's pal since high school and the cofounder of Sobek, had taken one look at our pile of equipment after the last helicopter cargo load had arrived and griped, "On the Baro, we only had five black bags. Maybe one percent of what we've got here."

Yost continued, focusing on me as his auditor, "It's not just overkill. It's a serious safety issue. When a boat's overloaded, in high water it's very hard to navigate. Your momentum builds up, and it's very hard to change direction. And if we have to portage, forget it! We'd have to hire a whole village as porters."

Yet the first three days on the Tekeze passed in a lazy, floating trance. Troops of Gelada baboons, with bright red splotches on chest and rump, ran barking up the hillsides away from our boats. Verreaux's eagle owls and hammerkop water birds stared gloomily from dead branches. Colonies of yellow weavers flitted in and out of softball-sized nests that hung from willow branches over the river. On the third evening, however, George Fuller, one of the Sobek pioneers and the only doctor on our team, fell ill with a raging fever. By morning his temperature had risen to 105. Delirious, throwing up every half hour, shaking uncontrollably, he was too sick to travel, so we lingered on our sandbar as the day turned sweltering. Thanks to our sat phone, we had the option of calling for a helicopter to pick Fuller up and fly him to an Addis Ababa hospital. His friends whispered in Fuller's ear, "George, do you want to fly out?" At last Fuller mumbled, "No, it'll pass"—then chucked up another stream of yellow-green bile.

As I had sat at my laptop the previous evening, I faced a dilemma that had never before presented itself to me in the wilderness. Should I write about Fuller's illness? If so, his wife and closest friends would learn that he was facing a potentially life-threatening predicament before we could do anything about it. But if I kept his fever secret, wasn't I sabotaging the immediacy of Internet reporting that Richard passionately claimed would transform expeditionary adventure?

On the fourth morning, as we lingered on the sandbar, a group of men suddenly arrived, wading the river toward our camp—the first natives we had seen since launching on September 8. They looked agitated, and they were carrying AK-47s. We had not so much as a pistol among the twenty-two of us. Could these be the notorious *shiftas*—bandits the Sobek veterans had run foul of on other Ethiopian rivers?

Fortunately, shouting from a distance of 50 feet, Daniel Mehari was able to talk to the men in Amharic before they took action. It turned out that they feared that *we* were *shiftas*, or even worse—soldiers left over from the Mengistu regime, who during the worst of the civil war had invaded remote villages in this part of rebellious Tigray and had slaughtered civilians, sparing neither women nor children.

Once we convinced these scouts that we were harmless, they invited us to come and stay in their village. The only trouble was that it lay seven hours away. The warriors, tipped off by furtive sightings of our armada, had hiked all night to intercept us.

During our long day of inaction on the sandbar, our visitors conveyed their curiosity about what we were doing through Daniel. The three basic questions they asked would be repeated by every group of natives we ran into during the expedition. *Where did you come from? Where are you going? Why are you doing this?* To use a device such as a raft to cross the Tekeze made perfect sense to these men. What seemed incomprehensible was the notion of employing a raft to go *down* the river.

When Fuller's temperature dropped to 99, we piled onto the boats and headed onward. That day we saw our first crocodile, in a shallow eddy near the right bank. Each day thereafter the crocs got bigger, more numerous, and more aggressive. It took me a while to get the hang of spotting them, as they lurked a few feet off shore, only bug eyes and scaly upper head above water, but Jim Slade, in our lead boat, routinely racked up counts of thirty a day—more than any of the Sobek veterans had ever seen on a river.

By the next day, the occasional croc was charging a boat. Our response was to load up the rafts with baseball-size "croc rocks" that we winged at the beasts to discourage them. One day John Yost suddenly stood up in the bow of his boat and swung an oar viciously overhead, slamming the water just in front of an overcurious croc. Later, another feisty reptile swam straight at Richard's boat, unfazed by the stones plunking near him, and surfaced with a thump under Richard's feet before reappearing on the other side of the boat.

Each evening, we duly reported such incidents to Mungo Park. Thanks to the sat phone, we could even call our editors in Redmond and bitch about how they'd mangled our prose or cropped our photos. And we sent and received a nightly flurry of e-mail messages. I was amused to watch the outback-hardened Sobek guides, used to disappearing from the known world for a month at a time, line up outside the Mungo Park tent to plead for computer time so they could peck out their missives to wives and girlfriends.

Richard had made sure that our broadcasts were fully interactive by building in a feature called "Ask the Expedition," whereby fans at home could pose us questions in mid-voyage. One interlocutor mailed in a query as to whether on a trip such as this one it was still possible to know solitude and isolation. That query hit a nagging qualm of mine square on the head.

Because of the Turner crew's filming, there was plenty of downtime. One morning I took a two-hour hike up the side canyon near which we were camped. Hearing distant cries, I watched a solitary local jog along the skyline, no doubt alerting his neighbors to the stranger in their midst. Then I scared up a troop of some thirty or forty baboons. Scampering up the ridge above me, the babies rode their mothers' backs while the dominant males turned to threaten me with shrieking barks. When the baboons felt safe, they paused to groom one another and to swing upside down from tree limbs.

It was one of my best interludes so far on the expedition. As I pondered that fact, I realized it was also the first time on the trip that I had been alone.

A week into our trip, 95 miles down the river, we were puzzled by the fact that so far we had seen no evidence of natives living on its banks. Yet every evening, as word spread of our intrusion, a crowd would gather near our campsite to stare at us. A few men got up the nerve to approach and talk with Daniel Mehari. At first we assumed it was the crocodiles that scared the natives away. Indeed, we heard many a dolorous tale of croc death, such as the one related by a young man whose brother had recently perished when he crossed the Tekeze to visit his fiancée. Said another informant, "When a crocodile eats you, he eats every part except the soles of your feet." But it was George Fuller who, still recovering from his fever, nailed the right explanation. "Malaria," he croaked. "It's malaria."

Sure enough, the next day a native explained that his people could live with the crocodiles, but had learned that to inhabit the banks of the Tekeze was to invite certain death from the shaking sickness. As we pushed farther north, we talked to many locals whose villages, perched on high mesas, were waterless seven months each year during the dry season. Every day women with large jars on their heads hiked as much as 2,000 feet down to the Tekeze and back just to fetch the life-sustaining water.

Gradually we passed out of the region of basalt into a sandstone landscape. As the canyon deepened, I was reminded often of the American Southwest, with pinnacles and blank walls looming on either side, a climber's paradise for the second half of the twenty-first century. The Tekeze carved its way from west to north around the Simien Plateau, a striking upland whose highest peak, Ras Dashen, reached 14,928 feet above sea level. Eventually we stared up at precipices that soared 7,000 feet above the river, as we entered the deepest canyon in Africa.

For me, the best times on the expedition came when we were

camped and I was free to explore the side canyons and hike up the enclosing slopes. On one such foray, hundreds of feet above the river, I discovered a swath of petroglyphs carved on a buttress of orange slate—humans hung upside down, crisscrossed torsos surmounted by upside-down heads, fierce visages caught in the O-mouthed terror of mid-scream. It was impossible to tell whether the macabre panel was recent or centuries old.

On another day, as we floated lazily downstream, one of the junior guides spotted a hidden set of cliff dwellings high on a right-bank cliff. We parked the boats while several of us scrambled up to the site. Homely furnishings—a stool, a flywhisk, a gourd full of grain—testified to current use. But on the walls there were charcoal drawings of winged creatures and writing in a script that Daniel identified as ancient Ge'ez. In the dim recesses of the troglodyte alcove I saw what looked like sealed-shut tombs.

Later, downriver, two young natives told us that the place we had visited was called Hassena. It was a hermitage for the ill, and those who failed to recover were indeed buried within the holy site. The shrine was guarded, the men said, by a resident monk who had made himself invisible as he observed our trespass.

As the trip progressed, the Turner team grew increasingly worried that the rapids weren't living up to Richard's pre-expedition hype: the "Terrible Tekeze," he had proclaimed, "the Last Great First." At every gentle class II rapid we spent hours filming the Sobek five as they splashed through the waves, straining grim-faced at the oars as the camera shot telephoto footage from inches above the sandbars. Toward the end of the journey there was even talk of trucking our four tons of gear from the takeout hundreds of miles over to the Awash, just to bounce through some photogenic rapids the veterans had first conquered twenty-three years before.

Personally, I was quite pleased that the river dealt us no hairy runs, much less flipping boats as the Tua had in 1983. The landscape grew more and more stunning as we coasted beside the Simien Plateau. Here, we encountered natives who spoke almost no Amharic. They were Agaw, impoverished herders of goats, sheep, and cattle, sneered at by the Amhara upriver. Once they learned that we meant them no harm, they asked their own questions through halting exchanges with Daniel. One young man, we learned, had hiked two hours to greet us. Certain that we must be starving, he offered to find a friend who would sell us a goat. He confirmed that he had spent his whole life within a corridor of land only seven miles long beside the Tekeze.

Gradually we realized that these Agaw were living on the very edge of survival. During the wet season just before our arrival, not a drop of rain had fallen. Twice we saw men plowing the dusty river bank with yoked oxen, desperately hoping to plant sorghum in sand sprinkled with alluvium from the far-off highlands. At one stop, several men begged us to let them ride our boats so they could go somewhere else— anywhere else, out of their hopeless lives on the margin of famine.

Several times during our trip, I sought out Richard to argue about how the filmmaking and especially our Mungo Park connectedness transformed what should have been a true wilderness journey. On my Alaskan expeditions in the 1960s and 1970s, the absolute separation of "in" from "out" had cast its spell on me and my teammates. On Mount Deborah in 1964, for forty-two days Don Jensen and I had had no contact with the outside world, not even a bush pilot flyover checkup. At first the transition was cruel, as I longed for the easy habits of newspaper and telephone and friends dropping by. But once my psyche adjusted to "in," a spell of magical grace came over my life. For six weeks, Don and I became our own society. If we got in trouble (as we did in spades), we had to get ourselves out of it. But once adjusted to our wilderness, all the half-formed worries and nuisances of "out" simply fell away.

On the Tekeze, I never felt fully "in." It was not just that a problem such as George Fuller's delirious fever could be solved by sat phone and helicopter. The nightly communication with our Mungo Park editors halfway around the world rendered the river experience weirdly secondhand. I noticed, for instance, how the whole team began to focus not on the raw encounter with a charging crocodile, but on how the croc footage looked when we downloaded it in camp, then sent it off to our live "audience."

Richard was unmoved by my purism. "I think," he said, "that in the future we're going to see more and more vicarious exploration. There'll be communities of armchair travelers who care passionately about a river in Ethiopia without ever hoping to go there. I actually think that sharing our experience with all the folks who call up Mungo Park is less selfish than just making the first descent of the Tekeze by ourselves." The nightmare scenario for river runners is dam-building. Already Richard had seen the magnificent Bio-Bio in Chile, of which he had made the first descent, ruined by a dam. Shortly before our visit to Ethiopia, an Italian company had proposed a dam on the Tekeze. Vicarious adventure of the sort we were offering, Richard believed, could build an environmental constituency that would help save wild rivers.

We agreed to disagree. Three years after our journey, in the pages of *The Lost River*, he reaffirmed his credo. "Would the Tekeze expedition have been a 'purer' experience without laptops and digital cameras?" he wrote. "In my mind, no ... it just would have been simpler."

Yet twenty years after our Tekeze expedition, I still wonder how much deeper the adventure would have been had we run the river "alpine style," as Richard had characterized the early Sobek exploratories on the Awash and the Omo. The dispatches, digital photos, and film clips we labored so diligently to produce have long since vanished into the void of cyberspace. Mungo Park itself folded only two years after launching. Whether we provided a vicarious adventure to the thousands of armchair fans Richard envisioned, there is no way of knowing today. Yet my old friend was ahead of his time: hardly an Everest expedition or a polar traverse such as Henry Worsley's takes the field nowadays without the gadgetry of daily reports on the Internet, or the promise that schoolkids back home can "participate" in the journey via interactive connection with their heroes in the field. The skeptic in me tends to see these media extravaganzas as gimmicks to raise funds for costly expeditions. As to whether almost three decades of hyperconnected adventure have built a public constituency to save the wilderness, I am also skeptical.

Yet in 2017, many of the most challenging rivers around the world still await their first descents. And a small band of latter-day explorers, some of whom choose to go without the comforts and safety nets of sat phones and helicopters, are pushing their rafts and kayaks down whitewater canyons that remain as little known as any places on earth.

Had John Wesley Powell been offered a GPS or sat phone in 1869, I have no doubt that he would have seized upon the technology to bolster his chances of getting down the Colorado River alive. The take-out for that pioneering push into the unknown was predetermined, for the 350 miles from the river's mouth in the Gulf of California upstream to the vicinity of today's Lake Mead had been tamed. It was, in fact, a paddle wheeler milk run. The challenge for Powell's crew was to traverse the gigantic blank of canyon country from Green River, Utah, to the end of the Grand Canyon—a distance of almost 500 river miles.

Very near the end of Powell's epic journey, three members of the team, having had more than enough of flipped and wrecked boats, decided to leave the expedition and try to hike out. Seneca Howland, Oramel Howland, and William Dunn parted from their comrades at a northern tributary named by the party Separation Canyon. They did not survive their attempt to escape. Powell later traveled to southwest Utah to try to ascertain his teammates' fate. Mormon settlers told him that the three men had been killed by Shivwits Paiute Indians. In more recent years, scholars have pointed the finger at the Mormons themselves, who on the very fringe of Brigham Young's breakaway empire feared encroachment on their hard-won land by Gentile "invaders."

Had Powell in 1869 had the option of calling for a helicopter pickup at Separation Canyon, as we did on the Tua, the Howlands and Dunn would have lived longer—perhaps even decades longer, for the men ranged in age from twenty-six to thirty-six.

Only recently in the history of adventure have its champions recognized the threat posed by technology to the integrity of their deeds. As late as 1953, the British team striving to make the first ascent of Mount Everest believed that any means they could throw into the effort were sporting and legitimate. In the quest for the South Pole in 1910–12, Robert Falcon Scott brought tractors to base camp in McMurdo Sound. Had they worked as planned, Scott would gladly have deployed the machines to carry loads and men as far up the Beardmore Glacier as possible. When Sir Edmund Shackleton's dream of traversing Antarctica was finally realized by Vivian Fuchs and Edmund Hillary in 1957–58, the men rode tractors across the ice.

Once mountain climbers realized that the use of pitons and expansion bolts could solve blank precipices that were otherwise unclimbable, purists began to argue for deliberate self-limitation. Led by the visionary Yosemite pioneer Yvon Chouinard, an ethos called "clean climbing" swept the coteries of alpinism. In part because drilling bolts and hammering pitons damaged the rock, but also because it tended to reduce the challenge to mere engineering, climbers vowed to use only nuts (and later spring-loaded cams) to safeguard and aid their ascents. The ultimate swing toward purism emerged in the vogue of free soloing, or climbing without a rope or any gear—just man or woman against the rock, with a slip any farther than 80 feet off the ground a death sentence. Beginning in 2007, and still in the vanguard ten years later, a young Californian, Alex Honnold, has pushed this ultimate form of adventure far beyond what was previously thought to be possible.

Ironically, purism has been a reactionary thread in climbing since the first decade of the twentieth century, when an Austrian idealist named Paul Preuss declared that even the use of a rope (let alone pitons) corrupted alpinism. He fell to his death from the Mandlkogel in 1913 at the age of twenty-seven. Preuss's aesthetic was considered so radical that he inspired very few imitators before the 1980s, when a handful of free soloists upped the ante on harder and harder routes.

Deliberate self-limitation has become the guiding principle in all kinds of adventure today, but in ways that fall far short of the purism of Paul Preuss. The trend is epitomized by the Antarctic traverse on which Henry Worsley set out in November 2015. Skiing solo, Worsley chose not to accept a single resupply, which meant that all the food and gear he needed for his nearly three-month-long journey had to be carried on the sledge he hauled behind him. Even at the South Pole, where the scientists manning the Amundsen–Scott Station heartily greeted him, he accepted not a bite of food or swig of drink from their hands. In 1996–97, the great Norwegian polar adventurer Børge Ousland had completed the Antarctic traverse in admirable style. His only mechanical aid was a kite he sometimes unfurled to use the wind to speed his passage.

In refusing to use a kite, Worsley felt justified in touting the exploit he attempted as "the first solo unsupported crossing of Antarctica"— sticking an asterisk on Ousland's deed. As noted above, Worsley's hero and historical mentor was Shackleton. Yet he never contemplated pushing the purism of his crossing to the extremes that Shackleton took for granted. No observers questioned Worsley's toughness or endurance. But only a few pointed out how vitally the man counted on his high-tech safety net. It was a compromise that made a mockery of all comparisons to Shackleton.

There are still rivers in the remote corners of the world that no one has explored. Four of the current generation's boldest river runners are Ben Stookesberry, Chris Korbulic, Pedro Oliva, and Ben Marr. In 2015 they descended the Beriman Gorge on the island of New Britain, part of the country of Papua New Guinea. Though only 30 miles long, the gorge is virtually inaccessible by foot, with sheer sandstone walls as tall as 4,000 feet guarding a gauntlet of rapids and waterfalls in the canyon depths. To get to their put-in, the team was dropped into the upper gorge by helicopter. Before their trip, the men had spent a week reconnoitering their objective by chopper.

On such tight, highly technical rivers, rafts are useless, so kayaks must be brought into play. Although cameramen filmed the team in action from a helicopter, they would have been powerless to effect a rescue or aid an escape from the gorge. The kayakers took thirteen days to make the first descent of the Beriman. Among the toughest tasks they faced were three portages around death-trap falls and rapids. One portage took two and a half days to complete, as the men drilled bolts and strung fixed ropes along the enclosing walls, then had to carve their way with machetes through the jungle to regain the river.

The descent of the Beriman combined the high-tech disciplines of canyoneering and whitewater kayaking. Stookesberry, who has notched 120 first descents spaced across thirty-two countries, swore that the journey "was like nothing I've done before."

A year earlier, on a very different sort of expedition, the same team had tackled what they called North America's most remote river, the Nachvak, which cuts its way through the Torngat Mountains of Labrador, in the Canadian Arctic. The journey unfolded across forty-one days and 500 miles of paddling. One of its most daunting aspects was a marathon jaunt along historic canoe routes on other rivers just to get to the headwaters of the Nachvak, a river that had never before been attempted. Of the final leg, Stookesberry later reported, "It was the first time in my expedition kayaking career that a first descent was made with no portages and at the same time had multiple drops approaching a hundred feet tall."

The small band of aficionados seeking out first descents all over the world keeps the roster of virgin rivers a closely guarded secret. But veterans such as Stookesberry have no fear of running out of prizes. One of the paramount challenges of recent decades was the first descent of the Tsangpo Gorge in Tibet, through the deepest canyon in the world, whose walls rise as much as 17,000 feet from river to rim. After numerous attempts costing several lives, a seven-man team successfully navigated the fierce upper gorge in 2002.

The lower gorge, even more chaotic and dangerous, remains untouched, a challenge for the best river runners of the next generation. But there are other canyons hidden all across our planet, through which run rivers that the boldest explorers have yet to confront. The feats to come may well transcend the wildest dreams of the Sobek pioneers who descended on Ethiopia in the 1970s, full of hope and ambition, as they slid their rafts into the Omo and Awash with no idea how their adventure would end.

FIVE

FIRST CONTACT

On my two expeditions to wilderness rivers with the Sobek veterans, the most memorable events included our contact with natives who had seen few white people before. On the Tua in New Guinea in 1983, the encounter was limited to my solitary meeting on the Burma bridge with the man who dashed up the jungle hillside to fetch me a giant yam, then later that day and into the next with a crowd that gathered near our campsite to stare at us for hours.

On the Tekeze in Ethiopia in 1996, the interplay with natives stretched through the eighteen days we were on the river, from the warrior-scouts toting AK-47s who hiked through the night to confront our intrusion to the Agaw who, living on the edge of starvation, found our mission unfathomable. Never before had I come face to face with men and women (mostly men) who were so unaware of the outside world. And though on the Tekeze, thanks to Daniel Mehari, we were able to craft the beginnings of a dialogue with the locals—to ask them a few questions and to answer a few of their own—our passage downriver had been so impetuous that the cultural exchange ended up fleeting and superficial.

In signing on to Richard Bangs's campaigns to make the first descents of two major wilderness rivers, all of us who rode Sobek rafts expected a unique adventure. If I came home from both trips disillusioned by the ways in which modern technology had tamed and diluted the adventure, still, those encounters with peoples living near the banks of the Tua and the Tekeze lingered long afterward in my imagination, charged with tantalizing hints of worldviews so alien from my own that they stretched my concept of humankind.

In their abbreviated fashion, those encounters echoed the shock and surprise that greeted explorers throughout history as they thrust into "unknown" lands and discovered people living there. The phenomenon that anthropologists call "first contact" is inevitably profound and all too often tragic, as men obsessed with gold and land and saving pagan souls failed again and again to comprehend how their coming tore asunder the cultures they invaded.

By the beginning of the twenty-first century, true first contact was no longer possible anywhere in the world. All the more reason now, I believe, for me to sift through the debris of history to understand what my own glancing interactions with natives in what we call remote regions have to say about the true nature of adventure.

In 1995, a year before my trip to Ethiopia, on assignment for *Smithsonian* magazine, I spent ten days among a people called the Suyá, who numbered only 180 men, women, and children, and who lived on an island deep in a mangrove swamp in Brazil's Mato Grosso. To reach the village required a four-day, 800-mile journey by VW bus, motorboat, and dugout canoe into a labyrinthine wilderness. My host and guide on that mini-expedition was the anthropologist Tony Seeger, nephew of folk singer Pete Seeger. In 1971–72, with his wife, Judy, Seeger had spent fifteen months with the Suyá, as they became the first two outsiders to master the tribe's language, while Seeger made the first (and still the only) comprehensive study of the people. To do so, the pair had to give themselves over completely to the Suyá way of life. If they did not contribute to the backbreaking labor of the tribe's very existence, they would go hungry. As Seeger later wrote, after fifteen months "I could paddle, fish and hunt about as well as a 12-year-old."

By 1995, the Suyá were far from acculturated, but they had acquired shorts and T-shirts, a radio and a few firearms. A thatched dwelling in the village had been converted into a school where the children were learning Portuguese. But not a single man or woman had yet left home to try to live in mainstream Brazil.

During that trip, I learned an uncomfortable truth about myself. As curious as I thought I was about peoples whose worldview was utterly different from mine, I was psychologically ill-equipped to make the passive surrender it takes to probe deeply into another way of being human (to borrow Gene Lisitzky's pithy phrase). I found it hard to adjust to the Suyá diet—95 percent of it manioc and fish. The tribal dances, for which the men stripped almost naked and painted their bodies in vivid colors, were spectacular and strange, but after four non-stop hours of monotonous singing and drumming, I grew bored. I was much happier joining the soccer games that sprang up in the dirt courtyard. It was tiresome to understand not a word anyone said, except when Seeger translated. Hardest of all for me was the absence of privacy. For the Suyá solitude is anathema, the resort of witches. When I retreated to my tent each evening, the people worried that I might be cold and lonely, though the temperature never dropped below 80 degrees Fahrenheit and there was not a moment of true silence. Craving escape, I declined the chief's offer to exchange my tent for a hammock in his hut.

As an adventurer and as a person, I now realize, I need to stay in motion, and I'm all too used to staying in charge of the agenda of my life. (I suspect this is a failing from which most mountaineers suffer, as, for example, in the Himalaya they dash through the lowlands, feigning fascination with native cultures, hiring porters but haranguing them when they go on strike, on the way to the real goal—the great peaks and glaciers where no one lives.) I realize that I could never have mustered the self-abnegation that Tony Seeger had accepted when he immersed himself in the Suyá existence. I could never have gone solo into the Trobriand Islands like Bronislaw Malinowski or Samoa like Margaret Mead.

Did my decades-long fascination with the Anasazi depend on their having disappeared from the Colorado Plateau? I could control my searches for their ruins and rock art as I could not control the schedule of daily activities among the Suyá. The Anasazi were more interesting to me than the Puebloans who were in some sense their descendants: the dwellers at Hopi, Acoma, Zuni, and Jemez. The fear that my cultural curiosity might partake of dilettantism has bothered me since the age of twelve, when I came across a cartoon in my parents' *New Yorker.* Well-dressed society matron entering a hogan-like dwelling in the American Southwest, to discover an Indian family eating dinner. Caption: "Oh, I *beg* your pardon! I thought you were extinct."

———

As late as 2017, claims of the accidental discovery of "uncontacted tribes" in the Amazon rain forest still occasionally splash the pages of newspapers. We seem to have a romantic need to believe that Rousseau's noble savage may flourish somewhere, untouched by the corruption and squalor of modern civilization. Yet even in remote corners of South America or Southeast Asia, marginalized tribes today are all too aware that "we" exist.

When the catastrophic tsunami swept the Indian Ocean in 2004, causing massive losses of life, many experts feared that the tidal wave might have wiped out the Sentinelese, inhabitants of one of the Andaman Islands—a people often labeled "the most isolated tribe in the world." But when a helicopter flew over the island to check, a Sentinelese man raised his bow and arrow, mutely signaling "Go away! Leave us alone!" A photo of that encounter went viral. The astonishing conclusion that anthropologists could not avoid was that during the sixty thousand years the people had lived on their island, they had learned from watching the water when a tsunami was coming, and had fled to higher ground to survive it. Theirs was a hard-won lore that nearly everyone else in the world had forgotten—including the tens of thousands of seacoast dwellers from Indonesia to Thailand who drowned in the flood.

Throughout history, true first contact brought devastation on a colossal scale: think of Cortés and the Aztecs, Pizarro and the Inca. In adolescence, I fantasized about being part of an exploring party that stumbled across natives previously unknown to the outside world. As an adult, when I read the classic narratives of first contact, including Bernal Díaz's *The Conquest of New Spain* and William H. Prescott's *A History of the Conquest of Peru*, I railed against the ethnocentrism of the European accounts. Why could we never know what the Aztecs really thought when the fair-skinned, bearded warriors marched toward Tenochtitlan from the east?

Thanks to accidents of history and logistics, and to the extraordinary work of a pair of Australian journalists, the last great pageant of first contact played out anywhere in the world can be witnessed and apprehended from both points of view. This unique cultural clash, which took place in the early 1930s, unfolded in the highland valleys of New Guinea.

The European discovery of New Guinea was made by Spanish and Portuguese sailors in the early sixteenth century. It is the second largest island in the world, after Greenland—though the distinction between an island and a continent such as Australia is ultimately an arbitrary one. By the turn of the twentieth century, the coast of New Guinea had long been settled, its native peoples pacified and indentured, as the Netherlands, Germany, and Great Britain fought over ownership of the island. Inland from the coast, dense jungles thwarted exploration, though entrepreneurs and missionaries had pushed their way up navigable rivers such as the Sepik and the Fly in search of resources to exploit and natives to convert. From vantage points on all sides, a towering, rugged mountain range could be seen in the distance, giving rise to the universal notion that the vast upland interior of New Guinea must be uninhabited.

By the 1920s, airplanes regularly serviced such coastal outposts as Port Moresby, Lae, and Rabaul on the nearby island of New Britain. Those Junkers and De Havillands were fully capable of flying across the interior of New Guinea, but so pervasive was the notion of an uninhabited highlands that no pilot bothered to make the reconnaissance. In 1926, prospectors found gold in copious quantities at Edie Creek, a small stream toward the eastern edge of New Guinea. So rough was the terrain that although the creek lay a mere 35 miles inland from the coastal town of Salamaua, the trek with porters took eight days via a roundabout circuit of faint trails in the rain forest. Undaunted by such hardships, scores of miners, mostly Australian, stampeded toward Edie Creek to stake their claims.

Among them was a tough, adventurous Aussie named Michael ("Mick") Leahy (pronounced "Lay"). Twenty-five years old when the gold rush began, a timber cutter from Queensland, Leahy was fit, ambitious, and a skilled outdoorsman. When he heard about Edie Creek, he dropped his axe and booked the first steamer from Queensland to New Guinea.

Although he pushed himself to the limit to beat all kinds of crazed rivals to the gold field, Leahy just missed out on the bonanza. His chances were not helped when he developed appendicitis and had to dash back to Australia for an operation. But the fever was in his veins. There must be other Edie Creeks farther inland, Leahy told himself, and all it should take to find them was pluck and endurance. So in May 1930, with another Aussie prospector, Michael Dwyer, and fifteen native porters, Leahy headed inland near the headwaters of the Ramu, a river that flows into the Bismarck Sea on New Guinea's north coast. Promising strikes had already been made on stretches of the Ramu, but the high massif of the Bismarck Range blocked access to the interior.

In the foothills of the Bismarcks, the trails blazed by natives living downstream petered out. Leahy, Dwyer, and their trusted lieutenant Ewunga, from the Waria tribe, forced a route through tangled forest up to a crest at 9,000 feet. Expecting only more timbered mountain slopes beyond, Leahy was surprised to see grassy valleys stretching into the distance. And that night in camp, the party was further startled and alarmed to spot a far-off pinprick of light. In the memoir he would write with American journalist Maurice Crain in 1937, *The Land That Time Forgot,* Leahy dramatized that moment of discovery:

> *"Take a look at that!" I called to Dwyer. As we watched, another dim point of light appeared, then another and another.*
>
> *"It's a village, all right," said Dwyer. "The kanakas* must have seen our fire by this time, and you can bet they are just as uneasy as we are. They're probably planning right now to pay us a surprise visit just before daylight. I've heard that is the fashionable hour for massacres in these parts."*

After an uncomfortable night in camp, Leahy and Dwyer watched as the natives approached at dawn.

> *We waved to them to come on, which they did cautiously, stopping every few yards to look us over. When a few of them finally got up*

---

* "Kanaka" was slang, with derogatory overtones, for natives living in what Aussies deemed to be a primitive state.

courage to approach, we could see that they were utterly thunder-
struck by our appearance.

When I took off my hat, those nearest me backed away in terror.
One old chap came forward gingerly, with open mouth, and touched
me to see if I were real. Then he knelt down and rubbed his hands
over my bare legs, possibly to find if they were painted, and grabbed
me around the knees and hugged them, rubbing his bushy head
against me. His hair was done in dozens of little plaits and stank ter-
ribly of rancid pig grease.

In that encounter in the Bismarck Range on May 26, 1930, Leahy
and Dwyer discovered the near edge of a vast highland population of
tribes with no knowledge that any other people but themselves existed
in the world. Their numbers approximated one million men, women,
and children. There is some evidence that German Lutheran missionaries had made contact with other highlanders even earlier, but if so, that
event was kept a secret.

Neither Ewunga nor any of the team's porters could understand a
word spoken by the tribe they had stumbled upon. Ewunga tried pidgin, the lingua franca of the coast, to no avail. In the normal course of
human affairs, the impasse between the prospectors and the highlanders would have gone down to posterity in terms no more enlightened
than the passage quoted above. But Mick Leahy carried a camera—a
Leica—and that made all the difference.

Between 1930 and 1935, Leahy led no fewer than eleven expeditions into the interior, always in quest of gold. He enlisted three of his
brothers, Pat, Jim, and Dan, to share his prospecting adventures. Taking photos, which began as a hobby, became a more and more serious
pursuit for Mick, and after the first trip he added a movie camera to his
documentary arsenal. Leahy had a real curiosity about the natives he

encountered on his wanderings, and he gradually came to recognize New Guinea's immensely complex pattern of warring tribes separated by mountain ridges only a few miles apart. That understanding was inevitably shaped, however, by the colonial assumptions of the day, which posited that the "kanakas" needed to be taught the white man's standards of right and wrong. If these lessons could be instilled, "savages" might reap the benefits of civilization.

Leahy also kept a diary on all his trips. A perfunctory log at the start, the record of his daily doings gradually became more thoughtful and introspective. Curated in the National Library of Australia in Canberra, the diaries have never been published.

Mick Leahy died in 1979, a cranky and embittered man who never found the bonanza he had chased all his life. He left behind some five thousand photographs and many reels of 16mm film from his expeditions. These documents, of which the man was justly proud, might well have vanished with his passing but for the intercession of Rob Connolly and Robin Anderson, photojournalists who first explored the New Guinea highlands in 1980. The pair befriended Leahy's surviving brothers Jim and Dan, and they were stunned to discover Mick's photographic record.

It occurred to Connolly and Anderson that there must be many natives still alive who had witnessed Leahy's *entrada* into the highland valleys in the 1930s. As they would modestly claim in 1987: "There is no great difficulty today in finding highlanders who participated in these events of fifty years ago. It is simply a matter of following Michael Leahy's line of march and talking to people along the way." So began a project lasting three years, as Connolly and Anderson tracked down elders all over the highlands who vividly recalled their tribes' first contact with the gold miners in the 1930s, compiling one hundred hours of interviews conducted in eight languages. In addition, the journalists showed the natives the photos of themselves that Mick Leahy had taken, and even managed to project some of the film footage in impromptu outdoor theaters in the locals' villages.

The film that Connolly and Anderson put together, titled simply *First Contact*, was nominated for an Academy Award. It remains, thirty-five years after I first viewed it, the most powerful documentary I have ever seen. Connolly and Anderson's book, *First Contact*, published in 1987, profoundly deepens the story.

In Leahy's photos, the "utterly thunderstruck" countenances of natives in village after village are preserved at the moment of discovery. Handicapped by the huge linguistic gulf and by his own cultural baggage, Leahy could only guess what the "kanakas" thought. Thanks to Connolly and Anderson, we have at last as deep an understanding of first contact from the victims' point of view as we are ever likely to get. We glimpse, as it were, what the Aztecs thought and feared when they first laid eyes on the conquistadors.

More than fifty years after Leahy and Dwyer saw those pinpoints of light from their campsite on the south side of the high mountain ridge, Connolly and Anderson recorded the reaction of Kirupana Eza'e, a young boy at the time, to the sudden advent of strange creatures in his valley:

> *"I was terrified. I couldn't think properly, and I cried uncontrollably. My father pulled me along by the hand and we hid behind some tall kunai grass. Then he stood up and peeped out at the white men.*
>
> *"Once they had gone the people sat down and developed stories. They knew nothing of white-skinned men. We had not seen far places. We knew only this side of the mountains. And we thought we were the only living people. We believed that when a person died, his skin changed to white and he went over the boundary to 'that place'—the place of the dead. So when the strangers came we said: 'Ah, these*

men do not belong to the earth. Let's not kill them—they are our own
relatives. Those who have died before have turned white and
come back.'"

Because they were prospectors rather than anthropologists, the
two Aussies were anxious to move on quickly from the first group of
natives they encountered in the highlands. But once the "kanakas"
encouraged them to visit their village, Leahy and Dwyer realized that
the well-tended gardens and the domesticated pigs that the highlanders kept promised a golden opportunity for resupply. So began a
pattern of trade that would persist through the next five years. In
exchange for yams, bananas, cucumbers, sugar cane, and the occasional pig, the gold miners offered glass beads. The natives seemed
overjoyed at the parley.

There was no ignoring the frenzy of wonderment that Leahy and
Dwyer's party sparked as they passed from one village to the next. Ever
wary of attack by the natives, who greatly outnumbered them, the
explorers decided to make a show of force. Camped in a clearing, they
apprehensively watched as an ever-growing throng of staring highlanders surrounded them. As Leahy would write in 1937:

To their way of thinking, our guns were no more than sticks and we
were otherwise unarmed. Dwyer thought it would be a good idea to
show them how our rifles worked.

"Come on, you baboons!" he shouted. "Pipe down and give
attention."

The chatter stopped immediately.

"That's right, folks, gather round," he continued. "Now I want you
to get this. It's going to scare the life out of you, but it's for your own
good. My young friend here," he waved to me, "is going to show you
something that has your lousy bows and arrows beat all hollow.

Hey—you over there—you big-mouthed ape with the shield—this is mainly for your benefit."

Leahy set up three wooden slabs against a nearby hillside, one in front of another, then loaded his rifle.

Dwyer herded the natives out of range and I blazed away, the high-powered bullet tearing through the slabs as if they hadn't been there. At the report of the gun, the kanakas simply fell over backward. Some of them ran away, others groveled on their bellies. I got them calmed down finally by taking the empty cartridge hull out of the gun and blowing across the end of it so it whistled.

For Leahy and Dwyer, the discovery of natives in an upland assumed to be uninhabited amounted to a serious threat to their prospecting. To add to the Aussies' frustration, stream after stream tested negative for gold. As the men moved southward, the string of villages left behind loomed as a nuisance, complicating the return journey. At first Leahy and Dwyer were perplexed to find how uneasy each batch of natives grew when they ventured only a few miles from home. It was the men's first inkling that the highlanders, far from comprising a uniform culture, were partitioned into a complex patchwork of tribes that spoke mutually unintelligible languages, cleaved to different myths and cosmologies, and warred upon one another.

The photographs Leahy took of these encounters strip the native people of the smug colonial assumptions that the Aussies carried from camp to camp. Their faces are screwed into agonies of terror and disbelief. In one memorable shot, a porter from the lowlands mugs for the camera in front of a row of women whose eyes are closed, their mouths agape with wails. Those faces seem to betoken grief, but thanks to the research of Connolly and Anderson, a more nuanced gloss explicates the moment: "The crying women are convinced Porte is their relative returned from the dead. They clutch onto him in tearful elation and try to prevent him from leaving."

Likewise, the direct testimony of the elders interviewed in the 1980s by the documentarians unravels the shock those men and women had undergone as children, as they lived through the most profound event of their lives. In the film *First Contact*, they speak directly (via subtitles) to the camera:

> *"The whiteman came from over there. We'd never seen such a thing. Did he come from the ground? Did he come from the sky? The water? We were confused."*

> *"We heard a strange story that the lightning had come. We thought these whitemen were lightning from the sky."*

> *"This is what the people said. They are not of the living. They must be our ancestors from the land of the dead. . . . We thought we were the only living people. We believed our dead went over there, turned white and came back as spirits. Our own dead had returned."*

Although Mick Leahy does not quite admit the fact in *The Land That Time Forgot,* by some point in June 1930 he and Mick Dwyer were effectively lost. As they followed a large river they assumed must flow into the Ramu (near whose headwaters they had climbed into the "blank on the map" in late May), they realized the topography was all wrong. Rather than try to retrace the bewildering path of their outward trek, they resolved to follow this new river downstream, reckoning that sooner or later it must reach the sea on some coast of New Guinea.

That decision could well have spelled disaster, but Leahy and Dwyer were tough, resourceful outdoorsmen, and despite the anxieties of their predicament, they welcomed the challenge. Passed on from one village to the next, repeating over and over again the drama of first contact, they wandered south on faint native trails or used machetes to cut their own through the forest. Before long they had eaten nearly all the food they had packed in from the upper Ramu, and they ran desperately short of trade goods. They had no choice but to march on.

As it turned out, the major river the party followed was the Tua–Purari—the same torrent whose first descent our Sobek team would attempt in 1983. So tangled and impenetrable were the hills and valleys through which the men forced their way that often they had to veer far away from the river, sometimes losing sight of it for days at a time. Guides from one village after another led the men on what seemed like profitless zigzags. Leahy carried a compass, but he could not figure out the lay of the land. He and Dwyer began to wonder if their guides were deliberately leading them into an ambush, or simply prolonging a wild goose chase to wear them into exhaustion. With no means of communication except sign language, mutual incomprehension ruled the day.

Then, in the middle of nowhere, the bedraggled team stumbled into what might well have been a fatal geographic trap. Blocking their path was a substantial tributary of the main river, flowing into it from the east, far too deep and swift to ford. The natives called the new river the Piu. By now Leahy and Dwyer were both afflicted with malaria, and the whole party was beginning to starve. Only the odd sago palm, which could be cut down, cored, and cooked, gave them a modicum of starchy food.

A steady rain soaked everything. That evening Leahy asked Ewunga, the foreman of the team of porters, what he thought about their chances. Ewunga answered in pidgin, "Bimeby bone belong me stink along bush." ("Soon my bones will be rotting in the forest.")

For days the men camped in the fork between the two uncrossable rivers. As the rain continued unabated, the rivers topped their banks, forcing a relocation of camp. Leahy and Dwyer decided they would try to build a dugout canoe to ferry the team and gear across the tributary. It took three days to build, and when launched, the canoe came close to swamping. But by ferrying three or four men at a time, the team succeeded in crossing the Piu.

By now the party had left the highlands and were deep in the densely jungled highland fringe. It was impossible to hike along the banks of the river, so the men resumed their endless zigzags up and down the steep ridges that cut across their southward march. The supply of food was almost gone. "A couple of spoonfuls of sago for breakfast," Leahy observed one morning, "and no immediate prospect of more."

Out of desperation, Leahy concocted a plan to build a raft to float the whole party down the river. Before the men could resort to that last-ditch expedient, Leahy set out on foot from camp to investigate a dull roar he heard in the distance.

> *A half-hour's travel brought us to the source of it. The stream had become much narrower and deeper, running between two steep mountains, and all at once the whole immense volume of it plunged down into a deep gorge, through a long series of rapids. If we had trusted ourselves to a raft, none of us could possibly have come out alive.*

The occasional natives the men encountered during these grim days in the jungle were far more frightened by the intruders than the highlanders had been. But one day Leahy spotted a "kanaka" wearing a *lap-lap*, the wraparound loincloth adopted by the coastal natives but unknown in the interior. It promised the nearness of the coast. Dwyer had developed a sore leg that threatened to incapacitate him—a "tropi-cal ulcer, the most pernicious of the ills with which New Guinea is cursed," Leahy wrote.

Nearly a week later, the men found a native who could count to ten in English, and the next day, another who managed to convey that there was a settlement called "Tawmillie" only a few miles ahead. The river by now had braided into many channels, the whole current several hundred yards across.

At 11 AM the following day, in early July, the exhausted party sud-denly came in sight of "a large frame building and several sheds, with new lumber all about." "Tawmillie" resolved itself into the native's attempt to pronounce "sawmill." From the building emerged a white man covered in sawdust. His name was Charles McKinnon, and he was astonished to learn about the journey the newly arrived team had completed.

> *"What is the name of this river we have come down?" was one of the first questions I asked.*
>
> *"The Purari," answered McKinnon. "You must have struck it a little south of the Papuan border. It's supposed to rise somewhere in that neighborhood."*

Leahy detailed the party's wanderings over the last few weeks. "Then the map is all cockeyed, and you've found a new river," said McKinnon. "Come on in and have some civilized food for a change."

An easy four-mile hike finally brought the whole team to the settle-ment of Port Romilly on the southern coast, where the Purari flows into the Gulf of Papua.

Leahy and Dwyer and their porters had completed an epic journey, making the first recorded traverse of New Guinea at its widest extent. Had the leaders and porters alike not been so good at living off the land, it is entirely possible the whole team might have perished. Hoping only for gold, Leahy and Dwyer had made the accidental discovery of a vast highland population of natives who until 1930 thought they were the only human beings in the world. Yet to Leahy and Dwyer, the voyage had been a failure, since they had found not a single stream bearing commercially viable traces of gold.

Despite the dramatic if understated account of the expedition that Leahy would publish in *The Land That Time Forgot* in 1937, his pioneering journey has been relegated to a historical footnote. In Gavin Souter's excellent chronicle of exploration in the world's second largest island, *New Guinea: The Last Unknown,* the monumental traverse accomplished by Leahy, Dwyer, and their fifteen Waria teammates occupies less than a page.

━━━━━━━

We who were born too late...Do we envy the luck of Leahy and Dwyer, who stumbled upon an unknown civilization? Do we wish we could have marched toward Tenochtitlan with Cortés?

As mentioned above, one of my adolescent fantasies was to be part of an expedition that made first contact with natives somewhere in an unexplored corner of the globe. As a pipe dream, that was not in the league with my desire to find a blank on the map—to reach the summit of a nameless mountain, to traverse an unknown desert. But in my ongoing scheme of a future life as an explorer, why not combine the two? Be the first to trade sign language with a tribe of people who had never seen humans with white skin, as I steered my course, in Kipling's words, toward "something lost behind the ranges"?

I doubt that many boys and girls growing up in the twenty-first century share the fantasy that was so real to me as an adolescent. (My role in that imagined scenario, of course, was a heroic one. I would have been the captain who persuaded Cortés to spare Moctezuma. In another daydream, an airplane on which I was a passenger crashed in the mountains, and I hiked solo out to the nearest road to summon the rescuers.)

Yet a hunger for the exotic stirs even the most jaded city dweller today. On a magazine assignment in the 1990s, I sailed aboard a cruise ship that embarked from the southern tip of South America on a three-week tour of the Antarctic peninsula. My fellow passengers, nearly all Americans in their sixties and seventies, had internalized the travel company's promise that they were launched on "the adventure of a lifetime." The exotica they trained their telephoto lenses on day after day turned out to be penguins rather than natives, but the fact that the strutting birds somehow resembled clumsy humans wearing tuxedos, and that my companions had never before seen a penguin outside of a zoo, fueled a yen not all that different from the dream of first contact.

Certain peoples living on the margins of mainstream society serve today as exemplars of "primitive" tribes that have resisted acculturation. Think of the Hopi in Arizona, the Inuit in Greenland, the Sherpas in Nepal. No lifeway in the world more neatly fills the niche of the "exotic" and the "unspoiled" than the Maasai of East Africa.

In 1982, on another magazine assignment, I joined a group run by a commercial adventure travel company touring the Serengeti and Ngorongoro Crater in northern Tanzania. The great draw for the clients, of course, was wildlife. The trip was, inevitably, billed as a safari, though the game we brought home was not lions hunted with guns but giraffes and wildebeest apprehended with long lenses. Several of the travelers had life lists of animals to tick off. Peter, our guide, told me how a client on a previous safari had complained that the whole trip was a waste of time because the company had failed to scare up a leopard, the most elusive of Serengeti beasts.

During our tour, for an "add-on" charge of four dollars a head, we spent an afternoon visiting a Maasai village. Inside the thorn fence that delineates the settlement, the four-foot-high dwellings in which the natives lived were clustered. Each *enkaji* is made of a framework of branches plastered over with cow dung. We were invited to crawl inside one of these hovels, then sit on the dirt floor as our eyes adjusted to the darkness. The smell, the closeness of women and goats lounging on straw pallets, the strange intimacy of the place seemed to overwhelm my companions, who were only too eager to escape. When our host, Samwell, offered us fresh milk in a calabash cleansed with cow urine, no one drank.

Ouside the *enkaji*, the clients tried to take photos of the "warriors," clad in red calico *shukas,* leaning on their spears, but the Maasai demanded a small fee for each snapshot. Later that day I overheard the patriarch of a family of four in our group lecture his fifteen-year-old son on the principles of bargaining with natives. His dicta included "Size up your opponent" and "Stand on your maximum."

My good friend Judi Wineland, cofounder of Thomson Safaris, runs package tours in Tanzania and many other countries. Back in 1978, she founded Overseas Adventure Travel, the first American outfit to bring clients to the Serengeti. Born with an itch to explore, Judi had taught high school anthropology before starting her company. She hoped to pass on to her clientele her passion for travel to exotic places. In the early 1990s, Judi led a group of American women to Tanzania on an idealistic if short-lived effort to experience the Maasai way of life firsthand.

"The idea," she says, "was to do all the things Maasai women have to do in their daily life. So we gathered firewood from far beyond the village, and fetched water, and even milked their cows. It's incredibly hard work. I wanted the group to build an *enkaji*. It went fine as we tied the poles together to make the skeletal structure. But then we had to collect the cow poop and smear it onto the framework.

"None of the women except me would touch the cow dung. I was gobsmacked.

"Then I asked the women to spend the night in the *enkaji*. They couldn't do it. They all went back to our tented camp. I decided to go ahead and sleep Maasai-style. It was very dark inside, and hotter than hell, with a fire going. There were other women sleeping in my bed, and baby cows inside, pooping and dropping all night. I couldn't sleep, and I couldn't breathe. I tried to lie with my mouth near one of the smoke holes poked in the walls. It was pretty intense."

Judi's experiment, needless to say, went nowhere. Yet still today, Thomson Safaris clients interact with the Maasai during their tours of Tanzania. "But it's really hard for tourists to buy into true cultural relativism," she says. "We had one guy who was determined to end the practice of clitoridectomy. 'It has to happen sooner, not later,' he insisted. 'These women are being mutilated. We need to start a revolution all over Africa.'

"Well, I'm sorry, but you can't just walk into another culture and walk out. You can't come in and tell the Maasai, 'We can fix this for you.' I told the guy that. He thought I was horrible.

"I'm not in favor of female genital mutilation in any form. But change has to be gradual, and the Maasai have to want change in order for change to happen. That's why we support education as a remedy, not a 'revolution.'"

In 2017 the Maasai continue to serve the need tourists seem to feel to expose themselves to a way of life utterly different from their own. But the "Maasai experience" comes packaged in a way that minimizes the squeamishness and indignation outsiders feel when they cede control of the encounter.

Olpopongi is a visitor center in northern Tanzania that calls itself a "Maasai cultural village and museum." Tourists stop for a day or an overnight stay in hopes of acquiring an in-depth understanding of these herders and hunters, despite the brevity of their visit. If you can believe their enthusiastic reports on such sites as TripAdvisor, this patently artificial replica of the Maasai way of life delivers the goods. One tourist raves about having had "the typical 'Chai' (tea) with the 'Bibi' (grandma) in a real Maasai hut." Another waxes rhapsodic about how clean the hut was, "with . . . full flushing toilets and running hot water showers." A third visitor comments that "it made the experience that much more authentic to sleep in the hut on a raised bed. Mosquito net included, of course." Another describes the village as "a truly unique part of east African culture without all the fake tourist packaging . . . the real thing."

The key words embedded in these trip reports are "real" and "authentic." If any of the clients recognized the corruption of Maasai culture crystallized in such sideshows as Olpopongi, they kept quiet about it. That dancing for tourists and hawking souvenirs had replaced hunting for game and gathering medicinal plants in the Maasai way of life, or that an "authentic" Maasai hut came equipped with flush toilets, showers, and mosquito netting, embodied an irony that was largely lost on the clients.

The Olpopongi formula is hardly a new one. In 1902, when the Fred Harvey company opened its Indian Building in Albuquerque, New Mexico, Navajos and Puebloans were hired to make pots and weave blankets in live dioramas for the edification of tourists. In 1905, architect Mary Colter designed Hopi House on the south rim of the Grand Canyon, in emulation of adobe buildings she had admired at such ancient villages as Walpi and Oraibi. Inside, Indian men and women crafted jewelry to sell to visitors in quest of authentic artifacts. (More than a century later, Hopi House serves as a gift shop offering everything from postcards to snack food.)

Lulled into the passive role that guided group tours prescribe, even the most earnest clients hungry for some talisman of the exotic and the authentic need the reassurance that such exposure comes in packages lasting no longer than a single overnight. The Maasai encounter becomes another shopping option, which inevitably disappoints some of the shoppers, including the visitor to Olpopongi who succinctly wrote, "Although village interesting and Maasai male dance interesting it [was] not worth $20 per person."

The ambivalence I felt during my ten days with the Suyá in 1995—fascination at odds with the fear of surrendering control—gets boiled down by the group tour to a manageable taste of an alien way of life. Even as the customer relishes his or her immersion in the "authentic," the outfitter promises that the group will soon move on—toward a wildlife ramble in Ngorongoro Crater, for example, where the gazelles and zebras have little say in the structuring of the cultural exchange.

At its most one-sided, the display of native pageantry for the benefit of paying clients degenerates into the obscene. In 1990 I came across the stunning work of a German photographer named Michael Friedel, who had embarked on a project to document what he called "homo turisticus." Friedel's images froze smug and entitled Westerners posing for their companions' cameras in ludicrous and tawdry vignettes with performing natives: a cigar-chomping, overweight tourist lying athwart the laps of a row of bare-breasted maidens in Cameroon, an outrigger canoe full of clients in Hawaii transfixed as a man wearing a lei and a grass skirt pretended to throw a spear at them.

I interviewed Friedel for *American Photo*. How, I wondered, had the man been able to get model releases from the boobs who made such a travesty of the Third World encounter? "In fact," he said, "most of them are pleased with my pictures, because after publication all their friends can see that they've traveled far."

Friedel believed that the vogue of traveling in tour groups, which took off in the 1970s, unleashed the kinds of behavior he documented. "I should say right away that I think travel is good for people. . . . But modern travel—spending a single week or even a weekend somewhere being taken from place to place on a bus—teaches you very little. It breeds a contemptible attitude. In a big tour group the traveler feels safe, freed of all inhibitions."

Friedel discovered a Maasai showplace akin to Olpopongi. In his photo, a woman in a sheath dress and tennis shoes, clutching her purse and handbag, and her male partner in golf shirt and pants stand flanking a teenage Maasai girl sitting on the dirt. The couple beams at their companion, who crouches as he takes the snapshot. "This wasn't a real village," said Friedel. "It had been built just off a big highway in the bush, and buses would stop there.... The Maasai did not live there; they only posed there.

"The strangest sight I've ever seen was in Nepal, at a hospital for lepers. This place was on a tour as an example of life in the Third World! Groups of tourists were pushing visiting relatives out of the way to get pictures of the sick and dying. I actually heard one of the tourists ask, 'When is this man going to die? We have to see his cremation but we still have two more temples to visit before sunset.'"

According to Friedel, the brevity of the visit had everything to do with the crude behavior of its European participants. "Gauguin needed six months to get to Tahiti; now you can get there in a weekend. We need to think about how we are going to act when we arrive."

———

Despite the desperate journey Mick Leahy and Mick Dwyer had survived in June and July 1930, as they staggered down the banks of the Purari River to the coast, both men could not wait to head back into the interior. From Salamaua, in November of the same year, they made their way back to the headwaters of the Ramu and crossed the same high mountain ridge, but this time veered westward into the Goroka and Asaro valleys. From their first trip, the men had learned that glass beads and bolts of calico cloth were far less valuable in the natives' eyes than seashells. All kind of shells were prized by the highlanders, but the gold-lipped mother-of-pearl shells (known as *kina* shells in pidgin) represented unfathomable wealth.

Shells, of course, were utterly commonplace along the coasts of New Guinea. Leahy and Dwyer could buy a pound of the tiny giri giri shells for sixpence—three hundred shells to the pound. It is a measure of just how cut off the highlands were from the coast that the rare traded shell that had found its way inland in pre-contact times became the most precious item in the highlanders' world. In the 1980s, Rob Connolly and Robin Anderson recorded an elder's rhapsodic memory of the wealth that Leahy and Dwyer brought with them in 1930: "We held them in our hands so carefully, and then we would wrap them up in leaves and put them in a house. And then we would have to go and have a look at them so we'd unwrap them again and look at them. We couldn't believe how wonderful they were." Eventually, Leahy's importation of shells en masse would completely transform the highland economy.

In each new valley that the prospectors entered, the drama of first contact played out anew. The belief that the white men were ancestors come back from the dead, though widespread, was by no means universal. It was inevitable that familiarity with the intruders would breed a certain disenchantment. In the film *First Contact*, Connolly and Anderson hear a man from the Seigu valley recall a crucial turning point in the interaction between his people and the strangers. "One of us hid one day and watched the whiteman excrete. 'That man from heaven has just excreted,' he told us. As soon as the whiteman had gone away everyone went to look. Their skin is different, they said, but their shit smells just like ours."

Leahy and Dwyer's second foray into the New Guinea upland in 1930 ended up as fruitless, in terms of gold, as their first. But when one village after another greeted the prospectors with awe and astonishment but not hostility, they began to relax the guard that had initially kept them vigilant through every campsite. They even professed a certain concern for the welfare of the "kanakas" whose lives their coming had upended. In the jaunty dialogue Leahy crafted for *The Land That Time Forgot*:

> "What is going to happen to those thousands of nigs on the Bina Bina," mused Dwyer, "when we get out and spread our little story?"
>
> "Well, for one thing," I replied, "there will be a stampede of labor recruiters into that territory."
>
> "And what will happen to our little cannibal friends when they are brought out to see the wonders of civilization?"
>
> "The first thing that will happen to them," I said, "is that they will get malaria when brought down to the coast, and being mountain natives, they'll probably die like flies. A nice thing to think about, isn't it?"

It was not until 1931 that relations with the highlanders took an ominous turn. On his third expedition, Mick Leahy was joined by his brother Pat, while Dwyer went his own way. On the Langemar River, the party entered the homeland of the Kukukuku tribe (known today as the Angu), who were feared by their neighbors as a particularly warlike people. Ignorant of this fact, but on edge because one of their carriers had had arrows fired at him by natives hidden in the forest, Mick Leahy slept that first night with a revolver and a rifle close at hand.

He was awakened before dawn by one of the porters shouting in pidgin, "Massa! Massa! Kanaka killum me fella!" Leahy grabbed his revolver and crouched behind the tent, but could not find his flashlight. A shadowy figure loomed nearby. Assuming it was one of the porters, Leahy called out, "Where are the bastards?"

Leahy fired his gun at the same moment as the Kukukuku man

swung his stone club, landing a powerful blow to the head. Bleeding profusely, lapsing in and out of consciousness, Leahy crawled under the tent to hide, even as he was dimly aware of an all-out battle raging through camp. Pat Leahy caught arrows in his arm and chest, and several Waria men were also wounded. But guns prevailed over arrows and clubs. Once the Kukukuku had fled, the men counted six dead attackers in camp; how many others had been wounded but got away, the men could only guess.

In his book, Leahy recounts the battle in mock-heroic terms, reserving the highest praise for his brother, who yanked the arrows out of his body even as he kept firing his rifle: "Paddy is in physique and temperament the traditional fighting Irishman, and except for his concern over my smashed head, I think he thoroughly enjoyed himself that morning." But Mick Leahy was all too aware that the blow from the stone club had nearly killed him. Writing in 1937, he reckoned the toll: "I still have three distinct dents in my skull as a souvenir of that crack of the stone club, and have never since been able to hear anything with my left ear except a continual dull roaring."

According to Connolly and Anderson, the fight with the Kukukuku changed Leahy's attitude for good. "From that moment onwards, a ruthless determination seems to have settled upon him never to allow such a thing to happen again. It was kill or be killed, he told himself . . ."

The battle ended the 1931 expedition, as the Leahy brothers led a dispirited retreat to the coastal town of Lae. On subsequent journeys from 1932 to 1934, hostilities sometimes broke out over incidents no more weighty than the theft of an axe. Leahy's self-righteousness, expurgated from his book, emerges in the lines of his unpublished diary. Of one such conflict in 1932, he drily recorded, "Wiped off a few Ogofagu nigs who pinched an axe and then got too confident and opened up on us."

The demonstrations Leahy orchestrated to show off the power of the team's firearms—shooting through planks of wood set against the hillside, or executing a pig (filmed by Leahy and preserved in the Connolly and Anderson movie)—often failed to drive home the intended lesson. Half a century later, the documentarians recorded the natives' confusion. "We thought the gun was just for shooting pigs, and that it couldn't hurt men," said one man. "It never occurred to us that they would use the gun to shoot us," said another.

Leahy blamed soft-hearted bureaucrats in colonial offices for propagating an image of the highland native as a peaceful innocent. "Perhaps the so-called experts regarding primitive man's reactions were suffering from too much purely academic knowledge," he wrote. "Some of these experts had apparently never encountered a primitive savage in his natural element. . . . Such 'armchair administrators' can be found in any of the world's cities, sitting in their easy chairs, with a policeman on every other corner guarding their lives and property." Leahy fully expected the "kanakas" to absorb the white man's code of right and wrong, and to adjust their cultures accordingly. To the end of his life, he clung to his hard-won wisdom about "primitive" morality. "There is no law among these savages but the law of might, and no achievement considered more praiseworthy than a cunningly planned murder. To kill or be killed is to the wild kanaka a normal condition of his insecure life."

Leahy's diary comes the closest to reflecting the man's true beliefs and actions, and it is a loss to the history of New Guinea that it has never been published. According to Connolly and Anderson, between 1931 and 1934 those pages record the killing of no fewer than forty-one highlanders. Nor does the diary show much remorse for the victims of his incursions into their homeland. In the 1980s, Dan Leahy, the brother with whom Mick shared the most highland probes, still swore, "The only reason we had to kill people was simply, if we hadn't killed them, they would have killed us."

Leahy recognized that the biggest obstacle to mining in the high-lands was the backbreaking logistics of getting men and machinery to any stream he hoped to exploit—not to mention getting the gold to market. In March 1933 he hired a plane and a nervy pilot to fly over the upland valleys, so that he could reconnoiter the unmapped terrain. And only a month later, in the Wahgi valley, where he had at last made a promising strike, Leahy enlisted natives to help his team prepare a runway for a landing. Some of the footage of this extraordinary effort is preserved in the film *First Contact*. Paid in shells and beads, the locals use long poles to dislodge stones, or axes to cut out roots. Linked arm in arm, singing, they stamp and jump to flatten the ground. Leahy also filmed the reaction of the Wahgi people as the De Havilland Fox Moth glided to a landing on the new airstrip. Men, women, and children flee or fall to the ground.

"All the men and women held each other tightly and cried, 'Today will be the end of us all!'" recalled a witness half a century later. "The people lay flat on the ground and then ran off, keeping their heads as close as possible to the earth. Once home they killed their pigs and clung onto their brothers and cried for each other. . . . But after that crying and feasting, nothing happened. And the people said, 'That thing has instead brought us good things.'"

On one flight the plane brought in a gramophone. Leahy filmed the natives' reaction to this unfathomable device. "We heard its cry and thought it was a box full of ghosts," recalled one informant fifty years later. "We thought our dead ancestors were inside."

Since airplanes could bring in trade goods by the cartload, Leahy was able to flood the Wahgi valley with items coveted by the highlanders—especially kina shells. One arresting photo shows a crowd of natives gathered around a row of more than forty kina shells laid out for display on fern leaves. Rapture and incredulity seize the faces of the onlookers. Yet inevitably, the flood of once precious rarities devalued them as currency. That his own incursion was destabilizing a culture and an economy that it had taken centuries to establish does not seem to have greatly troubled Leahy. Awing the natives with airplanes and a gramophone was a means to an end.

A strange paradox emerges in the attitude of Mick Leahy to the "kanakas." He took his documenting of native ceremonies seriously, subscribing to correspondence courses in photography and writing. A kind of proto-anthropological curiosity lurks beneath the man's surface, and many passages in *The Land That Time Forgot* detail native customs and crafts and dress and weaponry. But that curiosity is constrained by a blind faith in the superiority of white civilization, which dictates his recurring complaints when the "savages" fail to learn the moral codes of their colonial betters. In the end, gold was what Leahy was after, and all too often the natives loom as a nuisance to be put up with on the way to yet another creek to be panned and tested. His life's goal of striking it rich slips away month by month, year by year.

In 1934 Mick and Dan Leahy set off from the Wahgi valley westward toward the border of Dutch territory (today's Irian Jaya). They passed through the homeland of yet another uncontacted tribe, the Enga. As Connolly and Anderson write:

> *The country was poorer, food was scarcer, and this made the people reluctant to supply the newcomers. But more importantly, the Enga people did not appear to welcome the new arrivals as returning ancestors or as powerful spirit beings to be feared.... The response was neither tearful welcome of the returning dead nor abject terror, but confusion.*

On June 25, the team camped in the village of Doi. Mick Leahy strolled up the hillside to photograph the roped-off cluster of tents pitched in a clearing (on sacred ground, though he did not realize that fact), surrounded by the usual throng of natives. Less than an hour later, the bloodiest encounter among all eleven of Leahy's highland expeditions erupted. As he recounted in *The Land That Time Forgot*:

> *I had just concluded the daily diary entry, ending with the remark that one of the men in the crowd appeared to be trying to stir up trouble, when the individual mentioned showed that my surmise had been correct. Holding in his hand the green branch of a tree, the peace* takis, *he took up his position on a rise of ground nearby and made a vigorous harangue to the crowd, ending by casting the* takis *to the ground and trampling it under foot. Our interpreter afterward told me that in this harangue he had told the people we were unarmed, and had urged them to kill us and seize our shells. . . . The orator ran to the nearest house and disappeared inside. I had been sitting on the foot of Danny's cot, and without rising, dropped my fountain pen and reached for my rifle.*
>
> *The orator ran out of the house bearing three spears, one in his right hand and two held in reserve in his left. The crowd opened a way for him as he charged straight for the tent, the spear in his right hand poised for throwing. When he was almost at the rope barrier, I fired, the impact of the high-powered bullet apparently overcoming the momentum of his rush, so that he seemed for a fraction of a second to stop dead still before toppling forward. The spear slithered from his outstretched hand almost to the entrance of the tent.*

That violent outburst immediately triggered a fusillade of rifle fire from the porters in Leahy's team. The Enga people fled into the bush. "For a horrible moment I thought the boys had lost their heads and were firing into the packed mass of unarmed natives in front of our tent, but saw immediately that none of the shots were taking effect," Leahy wrote in 1937.

This sanitized account records the killing of only a single Enga man, the rabble-rouser who ran down the slope brandishing his spear. Leahy devotes several paragraphs to his men's efforts to find the wounded hiding in the bush, to bring them back into camp, and to treat their injuries. He insists that "The kanakas then became quite friendly, assuring us, through the interpreter, that the orator who had made the speech had been entirely to blame for the attack."

Yet the "battle," which Leahy insists lasted "no more than half a minute," so disturbed him that he spent a sleepless night "debating whether the exploration of this cruel country was worth the cost." In the end his, soul-searching resolved itself in a reaffirmation of the colonial credo.

> I could not blame myself for the shooting that had occurred, knowing well that if we had not been able to defend ourselves, all of us would have been wiped out.... Such clashes could be avoided only if white men stayed out of the country altogether—in which case the natives would go right ahead killing each other off anyhow. Death by violence for ages had been the main natural check on population among these people. I decided finally that exploration and the establishment of white authority were worth whatever they might cost; only the strong hand of the white man's government could eventually bring peace.

Leahy's diary tells quite a different story. As he sat in his tent, he noted, "There are a few loud-mouthed bastards among the thousand or more at present around the roped off area who badly want a lesson." As the "orator" charged, Leahy emerged from his tent, raised his rifle and "put a soft-nosed bullet through his guts." The firing that immediately broke out among Leahy's "boys" was far from harmless. "A second shot had torn out the brains of the big mouth and splattered the ground in the vicinity with blood. And the utterly unexpected turning of the tables, completely demoralised them, and instead of what . . . was going to be an easy murder and looting, they carted away at least ten to fifteen corpses and assisted as many more who were wounded to their houses. This morning all quiet, all savvy firearms."

Half a century later, Connolly and Anderson visited Wabag, the town that now occupies the site of the Enga village of Doi, and interviewed the son of the man whose charge Leahy had stopped with the "soft-nosed bullet through his guts." The orator's name was Pingeta, and his son, Petro Pisine, reenacted the battle as if it had taken place the previous week. In the film *First Contact*, he points around him as he narrates the slaughter, his voice straining in anger and indignation. "Pingeta—my father—had his head blown to pieces. And then they shot people there—and over there . . . back there . . . and all around. When he shot that way Teatakan was killed. Ambon was killed over there and also Nambon. . . . It was Lo's mother who was killed over there. In this direction Kalakoa was killed. . . . This is not counting the many who were wounded."

———

Once more, the unfathomably complex collision between explorers and natives during first contact had wrought tragedy that reverberated through the generations to come. Yet the clash between Mick Leahy's parties and the highlanders of New Guinea ended up far short of genocide, or even of true conquest. By the 1930s, some of the Australian officials in charge of the government of this island colony actually had the natives' welfare at heart. Doctrines that curtailed the exploitation by the "labor recruiters" Leahy himself envisaged ameliorated the miseries that befell, for example, the Aztecs under Cortés or the Inca under Pizarro. The virtual enslavement of coastal New

Guinea peoples from the nineteenth century onward never took hold in the highlands.

One aspect of the encounter between the gold miners and the natives that escaped the pages of *The Land That Time Forgot* was the sexual relations that slowly developed between the intruders and the highlanders. It began with the Waria men, who were charmed by the beauty of bare-breasted innocents among the tribes they visited, and it was lubricated by the relatively casual attitude toward sex of the highland tribes. What today could well be regarded as bribery, coercion, and even rape sometimes resulted in lasting marriages, such as that of Ewunga, Leahy's trusted Waria assistant.

Mick Leahy himself indulged in couplings with highland women. In the 1980s, Connolly and Anderson interviewed several of these "paramours" in their old age. They speak in the film *First Contact*. "My people gave me to the strangers to get their wealth [shells]. I was just a young girl. My breasts were still small.... I was the first.... We were terrified. We cried mother! father! We thought they'd eat us. In fact they were kind to us. We had sex together, then we knew they were men.... Not spirits, just men."

Quite a few offspring resulted from these pairings. Mick Leahy fathered three sons who, despite the stigma of being branded as "half-breeds," ended up as wealthy coffee planters and plantation owners in their home valleys. According to Connolly and Anderson, their parentage was an open secret in the highlands, but Leahy, despite living the rest of his life in New Guinea, never acknowledged them. Disillusioned and reactionary, he spent his declining years venting his fury against the colonial government for its leniency and liberal reforms. Though he lived well enough in his old age, Leahy never got over the failure of his lifelong quest for the ultimate bonanza in gold.

Connolly and Anderson interviewed a man named Bob Fraser, who witnessed the accidental meeting of Mick Leahy and his mixed-race son in the coastal town of Lae. "Mick was very polite to him, but made no sign of recognition," said Fraser. "He knew who he was. Well, my respect for Mick fell through my boots. He had come down from his pedestal. He was just a bloke. I said to him afterward, 'Jesus Christ, Mick...!' and he said, 'Well, Christ! What can I do?'"

SIX

THE
UNDISCOVERED
EARTH

"What have you learned from all your travels?" It's a standard question that talk show hosts and Q & A journalists throw out, usually near the end of the session, to wrap up an interview with some grizzled veteran who has rambled across the globe. It's a lazy question, too, as it asks the subject to distill decades of conflicting experiences down to a fortune-cookie answer.

But all too often the beleaguered traveler comes back with a lazy answer: "That people all over the world are basically the same. They're just like us."

That pat reply, I suspect, stems from an egalitarian impulse. *The Maasai in East Africa, the Bedouins in the Near East, the Sami in Scandinavia may seem strange and look different, but beneath the skin they're all human.* Yet how insultingly reductionist that formula inevitably is.

Mick Leahy was blinkered in his dealings with the highlanders of New Guinea because he failed to recognize how diametrically opposed his own Aussie/colonial take on the world was from that of the Enga or the Chimbu. To the end of his life, he believed that if only the "kanakas" could be taught the white man's moral code, peace and justice would prevail.

What *I've* learned in my scattershot travels during the last fifty years is how profoundly different cultures are from one another, and what violence it does to a subjugated people to force them to live in the ways of their conquerors. Throughout history, tribes have embodied the sense of their own differentness in the very words they choose to name themselves. Inuit, Diné, San, and scores of other appellations translate as "the People" or "the True People." It is their enemies who call them "Eskimos," "Navajos," or "Bushmen." Some cultures build the sense of their separateness into their own languages, as they label all others "the Un-People."

"People all over the world are just the same" is a feeble-minded but kind-hearted stab at defusing the tensions that have fueled millennia of war, slavery, and oppression. When the Romans branded all the tribes that roamed the outskirts of their great empire "barbarians," they assigned themselves the righteous mandate of conquest. Inextricably bound up through the ages with the recognition of cultural differences are the dismal pageants of racism and xenophobia—currents that are alive and well in the United States of America in 2017.

To my mind, the only tenable stance to take in the face of a world teeming with "otherness" is an inflexible cultural relativism. That dictates that I part ways with my friend Judi Wineland on the issue of female genital mutilation among the Maasai. As barbaric as the practice seems to me, I believe that it is not our right to "educate" the Maasai (or any other people) to purge their culture of the practice of clitoridectomy.

Between 1989 and 1992, I crisscrossed the Southwest (including the states of Chihuahua and Sonora) as I researched a book about the last twenty-five years of the relentless war between the U.S. and Mexican governments and the Chiricahua Apache, the last tribe of American Indians to hold out against the nations that usurped their homelands. The principal leaders in that resistance—the heroes, if there were any, of my *Once They Moved Like the Wind*—were Cochise and Geronimo. The story of that epic contest was already an oft-told tale by the time I started writing, but to my mind, no previous book about the Apache wars paid more than token lip service to the Chiricahua side of the narrative.

Trying to get inside that point of view, however, proved formidably difficult. By 1990 the living memory of the conquest was still bathed in an apocalyptic bitterness. After Geronimo's final surrender in 1886, the Chiricahua were shipped en masse to concentration camps in Florida and Alabama, where they were held for eight years. In 1894, they were relocated to Fort Sill in the Indian Territory. There, still prisoners of war, they languished for another nineteen years. In 1913, when the Chiricahua were finally freed, the tribe had dwindled to 261 men, women, and children.

Thanks to that legacy, today's Chiricahua Apache have never bought into the commercial sideshow that obtains on other Indian reservations. There are precious few Apache gift shops or trading stands in Arizona, and even the reservations of other Apachean peoples, such as San Carlos and White Mountain in Arizona, or Mescalero and Jicarilla in New Mexico, do almost nothing to attract visitors. The sites of massacres by U.S. troops and vigilantes, such as Aravaipa Creek and Cibecue, bear few historical markers memorializing the tragedies.

As I learned again and again, I could not simply show up on today's reservations and hope to interview the descendants of Cochise and Geronimo and Juh and Victorio. For the Chiricahua point of view, I relied on the work of an extraordinary schoolteacher named Eve Ball, who after 1942 labored for decades on the Mescalero reservation near Ruidoso, New Mexico, to win the trust and record the stories of the descendants of the Chiricahua principals. Her books, *Indeh* and *In the Days of Victorio*, remain priceless primary documents, though Ball never tried to weave those testimonies into a historical chronicle.

Launching my own research forty years after Ball, I succeeded in interviewing the granddaughters of Geronimo and of his right-hand man, Naiche (Cochise's son), as well as of other elderly Chiricahua on the Mescalero reservation and at Fort Sill. From the start, I was struck by the intensity of the Apache feeling for their homeland, so I set myself the challenge of visiting every location where the pivotal events in the last twenty-five years of the resistance had transpired. In that quest, the deed I was proudest of was finding the mesa top deep in the Sierra Madre, near the border of Chihuahua and Sonora, where General George Crook had surprised Geronimo's band in 1883, turning the tide of the war for good. In more than a century since Crook's daring thrust, no Anglo, as far as I could learn, had ever rediscovered the site of the battle. To the Chiricahua, who had believed that the Stronghold in the Sierra Madre would forever serve as an impenetrable hideout in which they could live free, Crook's invasion dealt a profoundly demoralizing blow. My own journey to the site, guided only by an X on the sole surviving map from the campaign, bore confirmatory fruit when I found the very piles of stones—"breastworks"—the warriors had thrown up on the mesa to crouch behind as they fired on the bluecoats swarming up from the valley below.

The temptation for a revisionist historian of the Indian wars is to recast the struggle as a simplistic clash between wrong and right, as the triumph of manifest destiny over the sovereign integrity of native tribes. In 1970 Dee Brown produced a runaway bestseller predicated on that formula in *Bury My Heart at Wounded Knee*. I tried to resist the urge to romanticize the Apache way of life. For the men who fought with Cochise and Geronimo, the worst punishment they could suffer was to be locked up in a cell. After Kaytennae, one of Geronimo's fiercest warriors, endured a year and a half at Alcatraz, he was returned to his people shortly before the final surrender. To his jailors, Kaytennae had "become a white man and . . . an apostle of peace." To Geronimo and the other warriors still at large, Kaytennae had lost his mind, had been brainwashed into a mute, meek shadow of his former self.

A Chiricahua man would unfailingly choose death in battle over surrender and incarceration. He would even prefer to be tortured than to be locked up. In my empathic effort to comprehend another people's worldview, the most disturbing cultural trait with which I had to grapple was the Apache enthusiasm for torture.

The chronicles of the Anglo-American invasion of the Indian West are rife with lurid and sensational accounts of "atrocities" and "outrages" committed by "savages" against innocent homesteaders. But there is no point denying that torture of the cruelest kind played a central role in Apache culture. Well-documented testimony records that Cochise sometimes executed victims by hanging them head down over slow fires that inflicted agonizing deaths. Another chief, Eskiminzin, buried an American alive up to his neck and let the ants feast on his head. One of the most brutal treatments was to drag a victim behind a horse back and forth through prickly pear thickets until he expired.

Other historians seemed to have ducked the question of Apache torture altogether. Trying to fathom the practice, I ransacked the anthropological literature, but I found only a huge lacuna in the theoretical discussion of how torture served the moral and spiritual needs of indigenous peoples worldwide. Simple revenge failed to explain the phenomenon, as did the idea that extreme punishments were required to undo the evil of witches. In a chapter titled simply "Torture," I made a stab at my own explication, but I knew I had fallen short. Cultural relativism could take me only so far, and I was not willing to see such leaders as Cochise and Geronimo as congenital sadists. (My mother, who read everything I wrote, was so sickened by my short chapter on torture that she closed *Once They Moved Like the Wind* around page 45 and never finished the book.)

During the last twenty-five years of the relentless campaign against the Chiricahua, virtually no Anglo-Americans, whether army men like General Crook or territorial officials such as Governor Anson Safford, made the effort to suspend their own notions of civilization and see the world from the Chiricahua point of view. The great exception was a prospector turned stagecoach supervisor named Tom Jeffords. Baffled and distressed by having lost fourteen drivers to Cochise's raiders on the run between Santa Fe and Tucson, Jeffords "made up [my] mind that I wanted to see him." Sometime between 1867 and 1870, Jeffords walked alone into the Cochise Stronghold in the Dragoon Mountains. So impressed was the chief by the white man's bravery that instead of killing the interloper he sat down to talk. Somehow Jeffords had already acquired a smattering of the Apache tongue, and during a series of visits lasting to the day before Cochise's death in 1874, the tall, red-bearded American became the only white man to befriend the Apache leader. Among all the citizens of Arizona in his time, Jeffords was the only one who ever gained a deep understanding of the Chiricahua world.

Tom Jeffords lived on near Tucson for another forty years. In all that time, no historian bothered to pick his brain for the matchless comprehension of the Apache lifeway that he had absorbed. Only in the last year of his life, in 1914, did a pair of journalists sit down with the old man to produce cursory résumés of his career. Outside of the oral traditions of today's Chiricahua, who are loath to share their knowledge with outsiders, Cochise remains a shining enigma, the greatest of all Apache chiefs, but a man whom white Americans never understood.

———

The most powerful insight I gained from my research on the Apache was how inextricable a lifeway is from the landscape across which it flourishes. As it did with virtually every other Indian tribe in the West, the U.S. government imposed reservations on arbitrarily defined tracts of land (usually regions deemed worthless for mining or Anglo settlement), then reacted with dismay and outrage when the indigenes refused to relocate. For the Chiricahua, their homeland was inviolable, the only space in which the people could be free and happy. But what struck me again and again was how a specific place—the Ojo Caliente hot spring at the head of Cañada Alamosa, the granite domes of the Dragoon Mountains, the Stronghold above the Bavispe River deep in the Sierra Madre—brimmed for the Apache with an otherworldly numen that I could only dimly perceive.

In 2003, for *National Geographic*, I traveled to Guatemala, Mexico, and Belize to investigate an aspect of the culture of the Maya, both ancient and living, that scholars had woefully ignored. On previous trips, I had toured many of the great city-states that had anchored the civilization during its Classic period, from 250 to 900 AD. Some of them, such as Tikal, Uxmal, and Palenque, had been restored and turned into tourist destinations. Others, such as Calakmul and Dos Pilas, lay mostly buried under the trees and vines of the rain forest, their structures adumbrated by sprawling mounds of vegetation that only hinted at their erstwhile glory. Much of the Maya heartland, however, is made of limestone, and all across its domain caves and underground passages abound, many of them drowned in water.

The underworld was a supernatural realm that the ancient Maya called Xibalba—the Place of Fright. For the seven or eight million Maya living today, speakers of some thirty different languages, Xibalba remains a complex domain, the dwelling place of monstrous beings, but also the source of life-giving rain and corn and the home of the beloved dead.

A century and a half of archaeology, beginning with John Lloyd Stephens and Frederick Catherwood in the 1840s, rediscovered the pyramids and causeways and stelae of the city-states, which had consolidated as many as ninety thousand inhabitants apiece. But those rediscoverers remained all but ignorant of the Maya underworld. That neglect is epitomized in the story of Balankanche, a cave not far from lordly (and tourist-thronged) Chichén Itzá in Mexico's Yucatán. The cave had long been known and, it was thought, thoroughly explored; only a few potsherds scattered along the main passageway testified to an ancient Maya presence. One day in 1959, however, a Mexican tour guide noticed that a patch of wall looked unnatural. Scraping away the mud, he discovered a small portal sealed with clay. The guide chipped away the clay and crawled through a hole, emerging in a tunnel. A hundred yards on he came to a large chamber dominated by a column of limestone reaching from floor to ceiling. Scattered across the cave floor lay a dazzling assemblage of brightly painted clay vessels. Many were incense burners shaped as effigies of the rain god Tlaloc, whose grotesque, sneering face was molded in bas-relief on the clay itself.

Fifty-eight years later, Balankanche has been preserved as a shrine open to visitors on guided tours. The original Tlaloc effigy pots rest in situ on all sides of the limestone column. We know now that about a thousand years ago the local Maya performed elaborate rites in this secret lair so near the underworld—probably in a desperate petition for rain. But Tlaloc had failed the Maya, so they sealed shut the shrine—no doubt forever, they hoped, for they took pains to camouflage the portal. Yet a faint memory of the lost shrine has perhaps come down through the centuries in the name of the cave. Balankanche translates as "throne of the jaguar," but it can also mean "hidden throne."

In highland Belize I entered a more complex cave called Actun Tunichil Muknal, or the Cave of the Stone Sepulchre. The grotto had remained unknown for more than 1,100 years, before a small group of hard-core cavers had pushed its passageways. With photographer Stephen Alvarez and archaeologist Jaime Awe, I swam across the entrance pool, waded chest-deep against the current of a rushing stream, then climbed a steep and slippery rubble pile. Two hours in, we reached the spacious chamber at the heart of the cave. Two hundred ceramic pots lay scattered about, some arranged in natural niches as if placed in museum display cases. Only moments later, we gazed upon a human skeleton. "This is a human sacrifice," said Awe, who had discovered the remains of fourteen humans inside the cave. During the next several hours we hovered over one victim after another, including a pile of tiny bones, all that was left of an infant. The most startling skeleton was that of a twenty-year-old woman, sprawled in the position of her death, legs and arms akimbo. According to Awe, some priest had either slit her throat, cut her heart out, or disemboweled her. The skull, staring upward at eternity, seemed frozen in a silent scream.

Awe believed the skeletons were sacrifices to Chac, the principal Maya rain god (Tlalac being a deity borrowed from central Mexico). "Earlier the Maya had implored Chac near the entrances to the caves," said Awe. "But by the middle of the ninth century AD, something wasn't working. The rain never came. So the Maya went deeper and deeper into the caves, making more and more desperate petitions to Chac. This is what they left."

Even those prayers failed. Within fifty years the Classic civilization had collapsed. The center of Maya culture moved north to the Yucatán Peninsula, leaving the heartland, stretching from Copán to Palenque, empty and abandoned.

The Maya are far from the only people for whom caves embodied a world of transcendental mystery. In 1879, a man named Marcelino Sanz de Sautuola was digging up animal bones and prehistoric stone tools inside Altamira cave, near the town of Santander on the north coast of Spain. He had brought along his eight-year-old daughter Maria, who while he dug in the soil noticed paintings of bison on the ceiling of a side chamber. The next year, Sanz de Sautuola published a description of the cave art. Experts were quick to dismiss the paintings as a modern forgery, for the images looked far too well-drawn and sophisticated to be the work of Stone Age nomads.

By now, caves adorned with Paleolithic paintings have been discovered from the Urals to the Iberian Peninsula—some 340 of them in France and Spain alone. All of them date from before 11,000 BP (Before Present). The most famous is Lascaux in southern France, discovered in 1940 by four teenagers chasing a stray dog. The excellence of the paintings, often massively superimposed and rich in images of animals now extinct, such as the aurochs, the cave bear, and the mammoth, continues to astound and bewitch the public and archaeologists alike.

For more than a century, experts have debated the meaning of the Paleolithic cave art in grottos like Lascaux. For many years, a theory advanced by the Abbé Breuil held sway. The Abbé argued that the paintings were "hunting magic"—the depiction of prey in an effort to ensure the continued plenitude of the game the nomads hunted with spears and clubs. That theory was neatly demolished by studies that documented, for example, the scarcity of images of reindeer among the cave paintings, during a time when that animal supplied the great majority of the locals' diet. By 2017, the intentions of the artists working all across the regions where the caves are found remain an intractable mystery. Collectively those painters, in the words of journalist Judith Thurman, "invented a language of signs for which there will never be a Rosetta stone."

Having visited six or eight of the Paleolithic grottos in southern France, I was stunned to imagine the courage and skill the painters must have mustered simply to get to their ateliers to begin work. Often the chambers in which the art ranges across convoluted walls and ceilings lie far from the entrances. Sometimes the routes to these sanctums require difficult maneuvers, verging on technical caving. We know that to light their way, the intrepid artists carried nothing more reliable than pine torches, which quickly burn and sputter out. As they painted, they used primitive grease lamps made from animal fat. If your light goes out very far inside a subterranean cave, even today, you are in deep trouble. The risk involved in making the art, I concluded, was an intrinsic part of its power.

In 1994, in the Ardèche region of southern France, three amateurs whose weekends were devoted to searching for new underground passages made one of the great discoveries of the twentieth century. On a nondescript hillside close to a modern highway, near a natural arch called the Pont d'Arc, the three *spéléologues* stumbled upon a small opening in the ground. The hole "breathed," emitting a steady stream of cool air—a reliable sign that a sizeable cave lurked beneath the ground. The trio moved some rocks blocking the hole, then squeezed into a vertical shaft 30 feet deep, which they used a chain ladder to descend.

In the generous chambers that branched away from the foot of the entrance shaft, as they played their headlamps across the limestone walls, the cavers were astonished to discover a vast gallery of images. The Grotte Chauvet (named after the leader of the team) turned out to enclose a museum of Paleolithic art, the equal in variety and mastery of Lascaux. The 30-foot entrance shaft, the cavers concluded, was not the original entrance, which must have been blocked by a landslide, but rather a fortuitous shortcut to the inner sanctum carved by some other movement of the earth long after the painters had left their mark.

Within a week or two of the discovery, I was on a plane to France, determined to cover the story for *Men's Journal*. I knew beforehand that I would never be allowed inside the Grotte Chauvet. Lascaux had been nearly ruined by a black mold that encrusted the paintings, the fruit of the cumulative exhalations of thousands of visitors over the decades. The cave had been closed to the public in 1963. Since then, on ground not far from the real thing in the Dordogne, an artificial replica, called

Lascaux II, had attempted to slake the tourist appetite for prehistoric Picassos. So brilliantly executed was the "fake Lascaux" that, far from feeling like an amusement park, the replica made the hairs on my neck stand up when I visited it.

In the Ardèche, I strolled up the hillside through a vineyard to find the small hole in the ground, now covered with a locked steel grate, that Jean-Marie Chauvet and his two companions had slithered through in December 1994. Later, near the Pont d'Arc, I met the three *spéléologues*, who were still breathless as they recounted the find of a lifetime.

On my way to southern France, I had stopped in at the Musée de l'Homme in Paris. There I perused the timeline that summarized the experts' consensus about the invention and development of art in Europe. It all began with crude lumps of clay or stone, obese female fertility symbols, crafted around 30,000 BP. Only thousands of years later did the first painted images appear. They grew slowly in complexity and sophistication, climaxing around 17,000 years ago in the masterpieces of Lascaux.

Everyone assumed at first that the Chauvet paintings must be contemporary with Lascaux. Then the radiocarbon dates came back. The Chauvet art clustered around the unthinkably early date of 32,000 BP, and ranged as far as 4,000 years before that. Obsolete in an instant was the Musée de l'Homme's confident timeline, along with the collective wisdom of scores of textbooks about man in the Paleolithic Era.

I came away from the Ardèche bursting with admiration for the unfathomably old paintings hidden from human sight for some three hundred centuries, even though all I had seen (or would ever see) were photographs of that art, and with a new-found awe for pioneers who, long before humans learned how to plant seeds or fire clay pots, had risked their lives to imprint upon the underworld a record of their spiritual cosmos. If any men and women who ever lived deserved to be called explorers, it was those barefoot mystics carrying their pine torches into an undiscovered world too dark and sterile ever to inhabit, but the only place on earth sublime enough to bear the homage of the visions by which they lived.

————

During my lifetime, the highest and hardest mountains in the world have been tamed. Hillary and Tenzing reached the summit of Everest on my tenth birthday, May 29, 1953—a triumph that reverberated for me throughout my adolescence. Ten years later, in 1963, I participated in my first expedition, to the previously unclimbed Wickersham Wall on the north side of Mount McKinley (not yet known as Denali). By that year, in southern Patagonia, the highest peak, Fitz Roy, had been climbed, but a far more difficult mountain called Cerro Torre awaited its first ascent. In the Karakoram, although K2 had received a single ascent, such soaring thrusts of rock and ice as Trango Tower, the Ogre, and Mitre Peak were still untouched. In Alaska, where I would focus my ambitions for the next fifteen years, a pair of ranges that would eventually test some of the best climbers in the world—the Kichatna Spires and the Revelation Mountains—had not even been discovered, let alone explored, by mountaineers.

In Boulder, Colorado, in the late 1950s, I was regarded by my high school classmates as a geek because of my passion for the mountains. (The cool kids went skiing at Arapahoe Basin and Winter Park.) Nowadays, of course, Boulder is as *sportif* a town as can be found anywhere in the country, and rock climbers, who constitute a hefty percentage of the populace, wear their racks and chalk bags as insignia of the in-crowd.

Yet by now, virtually all of the most challenging mountains in the world have been climbed. In 1963, the sheer 2,700-foot face of El Capitan in Yosemite Valley had been climbed by only two routes (the Nose and the Salathé Wall). Today, there are more than seventy lines up that stern monolith, routes that weave in and out of one another or guard their autonomy only yards away from their neighbors.

Old-timers looking back on the playing fields of youth occasionally lament that a given range is "climbed out." The temptation to enshrine the years of one's prime as a golden age lies close at hand. If several hundred people—most of them clients on guided expeditions—can stand on the summit of Everest on a given day and snap selfies, it's hard not to regard big-range mountaineering as a travesty of what it meant to Hillary—or to Eric Shipton. Yet the climbing game remains in 2017 as vital in crucial respects as it was half a century ago. Consider the north ridge of 23,440-foot Latok I in the Karakoram—as pure and daunting a route as any peak in the world can boast. It was first attempted in 1978 by four of the finest American alpinists of the day—Michael Kennedy, Jim Donini, George Lowe, and Jeff Lowe. After twenty-six days, they got within 500 feet of the summit, only to be turned back by weather and a nearly fatal illness that struck Jeff Lowe in the team's highest camp. Almost forty years later, the north ridge has been assaulted by some twenty-five expeditions, still without success. None of the subsequent teams, in fact, has matched the 1978 high point.

There has always been, one would think, a close affinity between mountaineering and caving. The passion to reach the summit of an unclimbed peak has its mirror image in the challenge of exploring a subterranean grotto. A primary goal is to "push" a cave to the deepest point possible below the surface. Yet in my experience, few climbers show any interest in caving; many of them shudder in claustrophobic horror at the very prospect of crawling through tunnels and rappelling down vertical shafts in the pitch-black labyrinths that abound on every continent (except, as far as we know, Antarctica).

Caving today is far from chic. The public image of "spelunkers" (as serious cavers balk at being called) remains at least as geeky as my small coterie of climbing buddies was in Boulder in the late 1950s. Yet if ever an era of geographical exploration deserved to be called a golden age, for cavers that time is now.

Consider a simple question: What is the deepest cave in the United States? The startling answer is, no one knows. It is entirely possible that the deepest cave in our country has yet to be discovered. In the 1980s, most ardent American devotees of the subterranean world focused their efforts on pushing Lechuguilla, a grotto full of amazingly beautiful speleothems (ranging from stalactites and stalagmites to soda straws to calcite dams to cave pearls) not far from Carlsbad Caverns in southern New Mexico. In 1988, for a magazine assignment, I was guided on an eighteen-hour trip into Lechuguilla by Rick Bridges, one of the pioneers in its exploration. The cave's entrance, a nondescript hole in the ground on a hillside in the Guadalupe Mountains, had been known since 1914—for decades, it was mined for bat guano, a high-end fertilizer. But the verdict that the pit was "very small and somewhat disappointing" held sway until 1986, when Bridges and fellow zealots pried loose the dirt and stones clogging the entrance in pursuit of the elusive promise of a strong wind blowing out from the depths.

In August 1987, Lechuguilla was pushed to the depth of 1,058 feet, exceeding its famous neighbor by a scant 20 feet. Carlsbad Caverns, first explored by a local teenager around 1898, had been made a national monument in 1923 (it is now a national park). No terrain on earth can be more thoroughly trivialized by commercial development than a cave. The day before my initiation into Lechuguilla, I made the standard tourist visit to Carlsbad. It had taken five all-out pushes over three months to stretch Lechuguilla to a depth of 750 feet. In Carlsbad, I reached that depth in fifty-seven seconds, thanks to an elevator that whisks passengers to a once-pristine lower sanctum. Just outside the elevator doors, a gift shop-cum-snack bar offered relief from the rigors of the abyss.

During the week I visited the Guadalupes in 1988, the dedicated efforts of Bridges and his cronies extended the depth of Lechuguilla from 1,207 to 1,415 feet, earning it the laurel of the second-deepest known cavern in the U.S. The record-holder was Columbine Crawl, a cave in Wyoming's Teton Range that was discovered only in 1980. Compared to the relatively warm air and dazzling beauty of Lechuguilla, Bridges told me, Columbine was "a death hole, a horrible cave." Not long after my visit, cavers found new shafts and tunnels that extended Lechuguilla to 1,604 feet deep, beating Columbine Crawl by 53 feet. For almost two decades, Lechuguilla held the record.

Then in 2014, a determined caver named Jason Ballensky led a team on a two-day, 22-mile backpack into Montana's Bob Marshall Wilderness Area. Nine years earlier, Ballensky had discovered a small hole on the slopes of Turtlehead Mountain that hinted at huge spaces underground. He had been probing his discovery ever since, convinced that the new cave had major potential. Like Columbine Crawl, Tears of the Turtle, as Ballensky named his find, was scary and challenging even for experts, combining chilly temperatures with a plethora of vertical drops on which ropes had to be fixed. (The air inside a cave assumes an annual mean temperature of the terrain surrounding it. The Bob, as aficionados call it, is a high-altitude northern wilderness.)

On the 2014 thrust, Ballensky's team pushed the cave to a depth of 1,629 feet. Tears of the Turtle thus exceeded the vertical relief of Lechuguilla by a mere 25 feet. As of 2017, the cavern deep in the Montana outback retains the American record. Ballensky is certain that potential for further development lies among the remote seams and tunnels at the bottom of Tears of the Turtle. The 2014 push was stopped by a deposit of "quicksand-like mud" left by recurrent floods. "It's the sort of thing where we were worried about getting stuck in it and not getting out," Ballensky told a Missoula newspaper. The small band of cavers exploring the Bob is also convinced there are other entrances to

unknown caverns with vast potential waiting to be discovered on Turtlehead and other peaks in the back country.

Just how extraordinary the uncertain designation "deepest cave in
the United States" is can be gleaned by a comparison with mountaineering. Before Alaska was admitted to the Union in 1959, the highest
peak in the United States was Mount Whitney in California, at 14,505
feet above sea level. Whitney's supremacy had not been seriously
doubted since the beginning of the twentieth century. The first known
ascent (whether Native Americans had preceded Anglos to the summit
remains an open question) came in 1873, the deed of three fishermen
from the nearby town of Lone Pine. By its easiest route, Whitney is, in
climbers' dismissive parlance, a walk-up.

Mount McKinley, named by a Republican prospector in 1896, was
thought even then to be the highest peak in the Alaska Territory. That
Denali (the great mountain's official name since 2015) was also the
highest point on the continent, at 20,310 feet, was established before
the second decade of the twentieth century. First attempted in 1903,
Denali was successfully climbed by a party led by Archdeacon Hudson
Stuck in 1913. Nowadays, more than a thousand climbers attempt
Denali each year, nearly all of them opting for the easiest route, the
West Buttress, with a success rate slightly above 50 percent.

That Everest was the highest mountain in the world has not been
seriously doubted since the 1930s. But the likes of Jason Ballensky are
vigorously searching for caving's Mount Everest—or even for caving's
Denali. Yet as lively and passionate as the quest for deeper passages in
the U.S. waxes today, caves in this country are distinctly minor-league
by international standards. Tears of the Turtle ranks nowhere near the
roster of deepest underground systems in the world. A cave system in
Mexico has been pushed to a depth more than three times as great as
the pride of the Bob Marshall Wilderness Area. As of 2017, the most

profound abyss in the world is a cave system in the former Soviet republic of Georgia, stretching an unimaginable distance of 7,206 feet from
entrance to lowest sanctum. Yet even now, none of the experts will
claim that a deeper cave may not exist somewhere on earth, waiting to
be found.

Of these dizzying explorations among the chasms of the underworld, more below.

———

The distances cavers travel underground tend to be short compared to
treks of all kinds on the surface. In Actun Tunichil Muknal, the grotto
in Belize in which Jaime Awe guided me to the chamber containing the
remains of Maya sacrificial victims, it took us two hours to cover a
mere 800 yards. By the time we got there, that eerie refuge felt quite
remote from the entrance portal.

There are three main reasons why caving magnifies distance. The
first is that the going can be difficult and tiresome. In terms of pure
climbing challenges, no pitches tackled inside caverns such as Lechuguilla or Columbine Crawl approach the technical extremes of cutting-
edge rock climbs. In the larger underground passages, explorers can
sometimes hike for minutes at a time. But more often, the limestone
mazes carved by water over the eons reduce the visitor to crawling and
even slithering. Indeed, the trick to pushing a cave to new depths or
extents often depends on the efforts of veterans who inch and squeeze
their bodies through orifices that at first look impossible to breach.
Caving is not for the claustrophobic. Every caver's nightmare, in fact, is
getting stuck for good in some dead-end tube or slot that looked at first
as though it might "go." The horror story that still looms largest in the
general public's fearful image of subterranean exploration is the grim
demise of Floyd Collins inside Kentucky's Crystal Cave in 1925.
Although Collins was imprisoned in a crawlway only 55 feet below the

entrance, the frantic labors of an army of rescuers failed to extricate him from his death trap. It took him fourteen excruciating days to die of hypothermia and dehydration. (Robert Penn Warren wrote a novel, *The Cave*, based on Collins's plight and the media circus it spawned.)

The second reason that caves seem to stretch real distance stems from their complexity. For every "lead" that opens a route to new passages, there are dozens of tantalizing holes and crannies that go nowhere. Route-finding inside caves can be fiendishly complicated, and the penalties for screwing up can be dire. Experienced cavers carry marking tape to tag the many junctions where a pivotal choice of leads must be made.

Deep inside Lechuguilla, Rick Bridges led me and two relatively inexperienced cavers along a narrow and (to my mind) unpromising tunnel. All of a sudden we popped out of the tube and hoisted ourselves into a massive "room." As we played our headlamps across the distant walls of the chamber and stared up at the high ceiling, we could not suppress our cries of awe. Bridges let us revel in the moment, then said, "Okay, guys, which hole did we just come out of?" We stared down at our feet. The floor of the chamber was a massive talus pile of collapsed rocks. A hundred dark nooks among the stones within a few yards of where we stood adumbrated ninety-nine wild goose chases. Had the cavers who first discovered the great room not carefully taped their progress, the route leading back to the entrance pit in the Guadalupe Mountains might have taken hours or even days to rediscover.

Getting lost inside a cave, in short, is a real danger, one that can have fatal results.

A geologic quirk of underground topography intensifies the challenge of route-finding. Because there is little or no wind deep inside a cave, no variation of temperature with the seasons, no storms pummeling the landscape, erosion makes little impact on the terrain. Talus piles such as the one we emerged upon in Lechuguilla are far more unstable than their counterparts on mountain slopes. One must be very careful hiking across these chaoses, for huge stones can roll and shift under the lightest tread. Big slabs that a climber would guess are solidly lodged in place can pry loose under the careless grip of hand or foot.

The third reason that caves seem more gigantic than they really are has to do with sensory deprivation. A standard trick that veterans inflict on novices is to get them comfortably seated in some corner of the underworld, then ask them all to turn off their lights. If you think you've experienced true pitch darkness before, at that moment your synapses will undergo a radical recalibration.

The underground is devoid not only of light but for the most part of odor. After hours inside a cave, you may feel as though you've adjusted to the alienness of the place—until you pop at the end of the journey back into the "real" world. That act always delivers a strong emotional jolt. It's common to liken the experience to being reborn. A few years after my visit to Lechuguilla, my friend Jon Krakauer spent five days inside the labyrinth, as he accompanied scientists looking for the closest earthly facsimile to the landscape of Mars. Of his re-emergence from Lechuguilla after more than a hundred hours, Jon wrote:

> Sunlight washes over my chest and face. I inhale a greedy lungful of desert air, savoring the scent of juniper and sage. The colors that flood my light-starved retinas—the blue of the sky, a pale green drift of cactus, the creamy palette of the clouds—seem electric, surreal, almost overwhelming. An involuntary whoop of joy erupts from my throat. I feel as if I've just been released from prison.

Caves, then, are serious places. But consider for a moment how much more serious they become if they are filled with water.

The Yucatán is the fist that the bent arm of Mexico thrusts toward the Caribbean Sea. Long before Columbus, it was home to the Maya, especially after the collapse of the Classic Era civilization around the year 900. Such imposing congeries of pyramids and temples as Chichén Itzá anchored the still-thriving Maya world during the Post-Classic period. By now the Yucatán Peninsula has become a favorite tourist destination, as college kids on spring break flock to the nightclubs of Cancún and trendy Euros congregate in Playa del Carmen. Yet away from the northeast coast, in the rain forests of the interior, the terrain approaches the status of wilderness.

Most of the Yucatán is flat, and most of it is made up of a bedrock called karst, a kind of limestone that is easily dissolved by water. Normally hidden under a layer of soil and vegetation, the bedrock resembles an enormous lattice of stone riddled with holes. The annual rainfall in the Yucatán is a soggy 50-plus inches, and during the rainy season, from June through October, you can count on drizzles or downpours every day. Yet the paradox is that because of the karst, all that rainfall filters through soil and stone to pool underground. There are virtually no rivers flowing across the peninsula, and very few lakes. For the traveler in the rain forest, finding water to drink can be a daunting challenge.

The restored ruins of Chichén Itzá and Tulum, as well as of Cobá and Uxmal, seem to be orderly and civilized places, with trim grasses carpeting plazas and lanes, out of which, with geometrical rigor, soar the spectacularly decorated buildings. But if you venture off the tourist track to a minimally excavated site such as Calakmul, near the Guatemalan border, you are smitten by the monumental struggle the Maya must have waged with a smothering jungle to erect and maintain their city-states.

From the air, or from a cruise ship coasting the shore, the Yucatán looks like a tame landscape. Yet encountered on foot, beyond the roads and trails, it asserts its primeval fierceness. The Yucatán, in fact, has always struck me as one of the scariest landscapes on earth. On my own visit to Calakmul, I wandered through the trees tracing the vague lumps and ridges swarming with vines and roots that camouflaged the fallen glories of the past. In its heyday, in the seventh century AD, Calakmul was one of the greatest and most powerful of all the Maya centers, on a par with Tikal and Copán. I followed the faint impression of a causeway as it led away from the ruin—followed it for only a hundred yards or so before I lost it in the snarls of underbrush. When I turned back to get my bearings by sighting the main ruin, I saw only a blind frieze of leaves and branches. Suppressing a twinge of panic, I realized that I could easily get lost only a quarter mile away from the edge of civilization. Nothing but trees, no water, no glimpse of the sun, a bewildering flatness everywhere—here would have lurked a wilderness test of survival.

All through the untamed jungles of the Yucatán, occasional interruptions of the monotony burst to the surface in pools of crystalline water. They are called cenotes, poorly translated as "sinkholes." For the Post-Classic Maya, they were not only vital sources of water, but portals to Xibalba. At Chichén Itzá the tour guides take you to the famous cenote, where, they blandly inform you, the ancients sacrificed virgins to the gods. A cenote can range in size from a tiny lake down to less than a puddle. Because of the rain forest, thousands of cenotes have yet to be discovered by humans—or, at least, by humans in our modern age.

Yet the cenotes are not isolated from one another. Underground, underwater, the limestone opens into passages and cavities that spread in all directions. The whole of the Yucatán, in fact, amounts to a huge sponge cake of cave systems, virtually all of them filled with water. Some of the systems even connect with the sea. They remain, in the aggregate, one of the least well-explored places on earth.

The only way to discover these hidden sanctums is to cave dive. And cave diving, a "sport" still in its relative infancy, happens to be one of the most dangerous forms of exploration yet concocted. Cave divers must wed the complex crafts of scuba diving and caving. During the formative years of the endeavor, practitioners learned about the insidious perils of their exploit by trial and error, and an inordinate number of them died as a result of their mistakes. Even today cave diving remains extremely dangerous, and the death toll embraces not only novices but some of its most skilled devotees.

In an underwater cave, divers cannot depend on simply "tagging" their progress with tape or other markers. Instead they trail guidelines—nylon cords regularly tied off to natural features as they swim through tunnels and holes and traverse massive rooms. In theory, the diver need only follow his guideline back to the entrance pit. As they lay the line, divers try to avoid snagging it on what are known as line traps. If the cord becomes trapped under a ledge, and a diver cannot flip or jerk it loose, he faces the terrifying option of abandoning the guideline as he tries to find its continuation on the other side of the ledge under which it's jammed. Another hazard is the notorious silt-out. Not only the floors but the walls and ceilings of underwater caverns are often coated with a fine powdery sediment. The slightest disturbance can stir all that dormant silt into a local hurricane that takes many hours to settle out. A diver trapped in a silt-out is at least as blind as a mountaineer or pilot ensconced in a whiteout—or as blind as a dry caver who loses all his sources of light. It is virtually impossible to retrace one's journey underground without a guideline, by feel alone.

Add to these nightmare scenarios all the usual hazards of scuba diving—equipment failure, improper decompression on an ascent from deep water, the narcotic trance induced by "rapture of the deep"—and you can see why cave diving stacks up today as a pursuit as perilous as any form of terrestrial exploration. In 1994, inside a deep cenote in Mexico called Zacatón, forty-five-year-old Sheck Exley, widely regarded as the savviest and most experienced cave diver in the world (with twenty-nine years of service spanning more than four thousand dives), perished when he failed to resurface from a push intended to reach a near-record depth of 1,000 feet. The cause of Exley's demise remains a mystery more than twenty years later.

No region on earth promises a more complex network of underwater caves than the karst of the Yucatán. The first divers to explore the cenotes soon discovered that few of the crystalline pools were self-contained: instead, they branched in all directions, connecting to other cenotes and to mazes of watery passages with no outlet to the surface. The more they probed, the more these pioneers recognized how limitless the subterranean voyages they could perform might be. During the last twenty years, a small gang of adventurers has focused on exploring the cenotes of Yucatán. None of them is more passionate or articulate than Sam Meacham.

Fifty years old, Meacham has been cave diving for more than a quarter century. His interest in scuba diving led him to move from the U.S. to the Mexican state of Quintana Roo in 1994. This in turn led to his fascination—nearly an obsession—with Yucatán's cenotes and underground rivers. A pet peeve of this seasoned explorer is his quarrel with the general perception that cave divers are, in his words, "a bunch of cowboy adrenaline junkies out there rolling the dice, leaving it to chance, cheating death on every dive." Yes, he acknowledges, cave diving can be dangerous, but "the majority of fatalities . . . involve people who lack common sense, training, and the proper equipment. In the end, they made a horrible decision that ended their lives and, in many cases, the lives of others."

The hazards of cave diving, Meacham insists, can be controlled by proper training and judgment—not to mention an intangible skill he calls "situational awareness." Among the iron-clad rules he now follows is never to dive solo. At the same time, Meacham practices a "small team approach." As he explains, "The fewer cooks in the kitchen, the better. Suppose we have to hike three-quarters of a mile from the vehicle to the cenote. Each diver requires about 220 pounds of equipment. More people equals more gear equals more of a logistical headache. We may have a team of four or five people in the field that day, but only two of us are diving."

The inevitable risks of cave diving nonetheless threaten every venture. "You can't completely prevent silt-outs," he says, "but if you experience zero visibility, either from silt-out or from light failure, you keep your act together by ensuring that all the divers stay in contact with one another. Even in zero visibility, you can loop your thumb and forefinger around the guideline and follow it back to the entrance.

"Whole chunks of cave ceilings can collapse without warning," Meacham adds. "I've never been injured by falling rocks, but I've followed lines and found house-sized boulders collapsed on top of them. In those cases you need to know what your limits are and what you are comfortable with. Everyone in a team has the right to call the dive off at any time, no questions asked. Everyone's limits are different, and that is accepted going into the dive. If you are not comfortable being there, we shouldn't be there, period.

"There are venomous snakes hidden all through the rain forest, including pit vipers, rattlesnakes, and coral snakes. You have to be as careful as any other traveler in the jungle to stay on the lookout for them. We had a fer de lance in the water once just prior to a dive. As we were clearing brush around the cenote we must have spooked it into the water. Our Maya crew jumped into action and dispatched it pretty quickly.

"In some of the caves, especially near the coast where fresh water pumps into the Caribbean, the flow is so strong it's hard to fight your way into a new passage. On rare occasions, particularly in the coastal caves, there can be a flow reversal that reduces visibility and complicates our exit.

"Cave diving doesn't have to be a daredevil sport. The keys to safety are training, gear, and judgment. We are risk managers, not risk-takers."

In a kind of manifesto he wrote to answer cave diving's critics, Meacham vividly evokes the challenge of the endeavor.

> *We take our life support in with us and we are, for all intents and purposes, measuring time in breaths, not minutes. We are on constant alert, monitoring our gas supply and switching through tanks and scooters as the dive progresses, monitoring our depth, monitoring our decompression obligations, assessing our environment and the other members of our team and ourselves for the slightest sign of anything out of the ordinary.*
>
> *On top of that, we are task-loaded to the hilt, constantly equalizing our air spaces to compensate for changes in pressure, holding a light in one hand, adjusting our buoyancy, running the exploration line, surveying, observing, running a scooter ... all with, in some cases, hundreds of pounds of gear strapped to us.*

In the same manifesto, Meacham makes an eloquent case for exploring the cenotes as one of the last and most rewarding arenas of geographical discovery left on earth.

> *Certainly, it is the physical beauty of the caves that is the prime attraction. I can say that I am an explorer in the twenty-first century and that is a kick. Caving presents human beings with some of the last frontiers of physical exploration on the planet. And here in Quintana Roo, we are not just planting a flag on some lone mountaintop and then flying home. We live here, we are part of our community.... Mountaineers can see the mountain they have to climb, study it, and prepare accordingly. When cave divers pitch into an unexplored cenote, they have no idea what they are going to find at the bottom.*

As they probe the underwater mazes beneath the karst bedrock of the Yucatán, Meacham and his companions demonstrate the mind-boggling complexity of those networks of tunnels and slots and amphitheaters. One of those networks, called Sistema Ox Bel Ha, has been pushed to a total of 167.9 miles of surveyed passageway, with no end in sight. At the moment, the system stands as the longest known underwater cave in the world. No fewer than 143 different cenotes offer entryways from the surface to this aqueous fairyland.

The embarrassment of riches that stirs the blood of Meacham's clan is bodied forth in the dazzling variety of complexes so far discovered. In Quintana Roo alone, eighty-two underwater systems have so far been partially explored, most of them not far from the tourist destination of Tulum. As with dry caves such as Lechuguilla, the most unpromising entrance pits can give way to majestic hidden domains. Ox Bel Ha, Mayan for "Three Paths of Water," was first explored only in 1998, in large part because the most accessible cenotes leading to the system were, in the words of one explorer, "small, complex, and unattractive tunnels."

In 2014, a team of divers made an astounding discovery in a pit called Hoyo Negro, part of the Sistema Sac Actun, a close rival to Ox Bel Ha for the longest known underwater cave. More than 130 feet down inside the cenote—a depth at which no sunlight relieves the darkness, and from which staged decompression must be practiced on the way back to the surface—the team found a collection of odd-looking bones. Many of them belonged to megafauna that are now extinct, including saber-toothed tigers, giant ground sloths, and a gomphothere, a relative of the mastodon dated to around 40,000 BP. The pièce de résistance of the dive, however, was the nearly complete skeleton of a human. Before collecting any of the remains, the team carefully documented their find in situ.

Subsequent analysis proved that the skeleton was that of a woman fifteen or sixteen years old who had stood only four feet ten inches tall. A sophisticated meld of carbon dating with uranium–thorium dating established the age of the skeleton at between 12,000 and 13,000 BP. The Hoyo Negro woman, nicknamed Naia by the team, emerges as one of the oldest skeletons discovered in the Americas, as well as the most complete skeleton yet found in the New World of any human older than 12,000 BP. DNA found in one of Naia's wisdom teeth identifies her as belonging to a haplogroup of humans of Asian origin found only in the Americas—further corroboration of the old hypothesis of a Bering land bridge exodus followed by rapid dispersal southward across North and South America.

Divers and researchers think the pit was once a dry cave that functioned as a natural trap into which animals blundered over the millennia. Naia may have been a young woman out looking for water, who was either killed by a fall or could not escape from the chasm into which she had tumbled.

The fundamental allure of cave diving for Meacham centers on his passion for exploration. "There is the thrill of going where no one has ever before gone," he says, "but more than anything I'm motivated by the idea that we are slowly putting the pieces of an enormous jigsaw puzzle together, one for which we do not have the box-top picture. Every hike in the jungle and every dive into a cenote helps put that picture more into focus." In the past, to discover new cenotes, Meacham and his partners simply hiked through the rain forest looking for pools of water. By now, however, he has developed a high-tech procedure involving analysis of satellite photos. As he explains, "We operate from the simple hypothesis that during the annual dry season the vegetation surrounding cenotes will be more lush than the surrounding jungle, because it has year-round access to water. By taking satellite imagery from 1984, one of the driest dry seasons on record, and applying a filter that accentuates moisture content in vegetation, we've been able to find a number of new cenote entrances in the Ox Bel Ha system."

Once such a prospect has been identified, divers must hike overland, guided by GPS readings, to the telltale spot. More often than not, the cenote proves to be little more than a dead-end pool. But there's always the tantalizing promise of finding the portal to another Ox Bel Ha. So far Meacham and his colleagues have been able to handle the complicated logistics of transporting tons of equipment to remote base camps. Using vehicles, horses, and manpower, they have leapfrogged their way from cenote to cenote in an elaborate game of connecting the dots. But fresh challenges remain—among them, exploring cenotes too remote to reach overland. "We might fly in to these sites and hope there's a clearing big enough to land a chopper," he muses. "If not, we might even rappel out of the helicopter to reach the ground."

For the small bands of diehards who have devoted their careers to exploring the cenotes, being "an explorer in the twenty-first century" is all a man (or woman) could ask for. "Cave diving in the Yucatán," Meacham claims, "is the most sublime, surreal, and calming thing that I have ever experienced in a life that is rich with experiences."

The whims of geology are all but unfathomable. According to John Middleton and Tony Waltham, in *The Underground Atlas* (1986), some 15 percent of the contiguous United States (excluding Alaska and Hawaii) is underbedded by the kind of rock that lends itself to caves: limestone, dolomite, marble, and gypsum. On September 9, 1972, cavers made the crawl that connected two massive systems in Kentucky, Mammoth and Flint Ridge. Forty-five years later, Mammoth–Flint remains by far the longest known cave complex in the world, with some 405 miles of explored passages. The second-longest system barely adds up to half the extent of this gargantuan labyrinth.

Yet, as detailed above, the U.S. is strangely deficient in really deep caves, where vertical relief is measured by the gulf between the highest and lowest nooks and crannies of a grotto that humans have physically explored. Montana's Tears of the Turtle, the current record-holder, weighs in at 1,629 feet.

The country of France covers less than one-twelfth the area of the contiguous U.S. (248,000 square miles versus 3,119,000), yet France abounds in wild limestone landscapes that challenge the vertical skills and endurance of the best cavers in the world. One of them is the Gouffre Berger, in the Vercors region near Grenoble. ("Gouffre" is a quaint borrowing from the Greek *kolpos*, meaning "gulf, pit, abyss," but also a mother's breast.) Discovered in 1953, within only three years the Berger was pushed to a depth that won it the distinction of the first cave plumbed anywhere in the world whose depth exceeded 1,000 meters, or 3,281 feet. It's also a remarkably beautiful piece of underground real estate. Middleton and Waltham claim that the Berger is "commonly regarded as the finest caving trip in the world."

I've climbed and hiked in the Vercors, and one day, curious about the demimonde beneath its grassy surface, I sauntered up to the entrance of another cave that ranked not far behind the Berger. I was stunned by how nondescript that dark hole at the foot of a soaring cliff looked. By the beam of my headlamp, I saw that I could worm my way along a downward-sloping ramp for 20 or 30 feet, and I breathed the dank air pouring out from the depths. But the notion that a whole world of tunnels, tubes, chimneys, and rooms beckoned beyond that gloomy portal was hard to fathom.

In the 1960s, an ambitious club of cavers based in Lyon started prowling across another pristine massif, that of the Haute Provence some 80 miles northeast of Grenoble. In the *commune* of Samoëns, not far from the chic ski resort of Morzine, these adventurers pushed through dense thickets of trees and bushes looking for holes in the ground breathing wind. In 1964 they stumbled upon an entrance that they soon realized led to a massive underground maze. They named their cavern the Gouffre Jean-Bernard. The club appropriated the first names of two good friends who only the year before had died in a nightmarish scenario, one that all cavers dread. Underground, you have no way of knowing what the weather is doing on the surface. That day, in another cave called the Foussoubie, in the Ardèche, Jean Dupont and Bernard Raffy were oblivious to a storm that drenched the hills above. Their fate arrived in the form of a flash flood surging down the passageways of the Foussoubie. They were swept away by a tide so powerful that their comrades never found their bodies.

By 1981, Jean-Bernard had been pushed to 4,740 feet below the surface, making it the deepest known cave in the world. Ten years earlier, a shepherd tending his sheep on a tangled hillside not far from Jean-Bernard discovered another strange hole in the ground. For decades ardent cavers probed this system's complexities, naming the new grotto the Gouffre Mirolda, as they incorporated the first letters of the names of three more companions (Michel, Roland, and Daniel) who had likewise perished in an underground flash flood, this time in the Vercors. In January 2003, explorers extended Mirolda to a remarkable 5,684 feet, elevating it to number one status worldwide. It was a distinction the French cave would retain for a mere eighteen months.

Caving has never inspired the kinds of coordinated national campaigns that seized Himalayan mountaineering in the 1950s, when all-star teams from France, Switzerland, Italy, Germany, Austria, Great Britain, and the United States competed to claim the first ascents of the fourteen highest mountains in the world. But cavers are prone to a kindred passion fueled by nationalistic impulses. In particular, the French corner on the world's deepest cavern, which long predated the pushing of the Gouffre Berger past 1,000 meters, stuck in the craw of several generations of America's best cavers.

In 1965 several of these zealots discovered a huge limestone plateau in the northern part of the Mexican state of Oaxaca. Within only three years they had plumbed the passageways of the Sistema Huautla to an impressive 2,007 feet—almost 400 feet deeper than Tears of the Turtle would attain in setting the U.S. record forty-six years later. Every caver who ventured into the wilds of Oaxaca agreed that Huautla had unlimited potential.

During the next decade and a half, the quest for the deepest pit in North America was propelled by a close-knit band of enthusiasts based in Austin, Texas. They called themselves the Kirkwood Cowboys, after the road on which most of them lived in cheap housing, and jocularly referred to one another as "pit hippies." By the 1960s, American mountaineering had gone mainstream, attracting generous sponsorship and public attention. The 1963 American Everest expedition, on which Jim Whittaker became the first U.S.-born climber to reach the summit, was supported by 185 donors, including NASA, the National Science Foundation, and the National Geographic Society. Its budget was $430,000— the equivalent today of $3,500,000. During the same years, the best cavers in America scrounged expedition funds by working menial jobs, and drove in beat-up trucks from Texas to Oaxaca on bone-jarring two-day jaunts.

By the late 1970s, the exploration of Huautla had ground to a halt 2,750 feet below the surface, when the cavers ran smack into a huge sump—a pool of water that had collected in a long tunnel whose farther reaches could only be guessed at. As one of the Kirkwood Cowboys was fond of remarking, "A sump is God's way of telling you the cave ends there." One of the pit hippies, however, refused to give up. Bill Stone was a twenty-six-year-old working on his Ph.D. in engineering at the University of Texas. Six feet four inches tall, with a formidable physique, Stone was animated by a feral intensity that stood out even within the intense community of Kirkwood cavers. In March 1979, supported by two companions, Stone lugged scuba diving gear down to the San Agustin Sump, as the team had named the apparent dead-end pool. He was not the first caver to try to penetrate a sump with scuba gear (the French had made similar thrusts), but cave diving itself was still in its infancy, during an era in which an alarming number of its practitioners had come to gruesome ends in underground lakes far more accessible than San Agustin.

Because the sump might require tight swims through narrow passages, Stone hauled "pony bottles" into Huautla—side-mounted air canisters he would drag along, in lieu of the back-mounted tanks usually employed in scuba diving. And because he was wary of a possible underground current that might sweep him toward a deadly waterfall, he tied into a rope that his buddies would feed out as he swam into the darkness. The agreed-upon signal that he had reached his limit would be three sharp tugs on the line. Stone counted on his teammates to pull him back to the chamber where they waited on the edge of the sump.

This dramatic episode is recounted in two excellent books that cover the exploration of Huautla: *Beyond the Deep* (2002), by Stone, diving partner Barbara am Ende, and journalist Monte Paulsen, and James Tabor's *Blind Descent* (2010). In the sump, things seemed to go wrong from the start. Because he carried no diving weights, Stone floated up to the ceiling of the spooky tunnel, and, lacking fins for his feet, he could not propel himself along effectively by swimming alone. Instead, he was reduced to crawling upside down against the corrugated ceiling.

The air Stone lugged in his pony bottles allowed for a dive of at most thirty minutes. When he had used up a third of the air in his tanks, he realized it was time to turn back. But before reversing course, he flipped over to get a hard look through the crystalline water at the void that lay beyond. Then he tugged three times on the line.

Nothing happened. As it turned out, there was so much rope drag underwater that Stone's two teammates never felt the tug. They simply sat and waited for the signal, increasingly agitated about the elapsed time. Meanwhile, Stone frantically tried to reverse his ceiling crawl. He started to panic, gasping for breath as his lungs sucked in the precious air at far too fast a rate. And then his scurrying stirred up the sediment coating the walls and ceilings of the tube. All at once, he was floating blind in a silt-out.

Remarkably, Stone fought down the panic and started a methodical crawl in the direction from which he hoped he'd come. And then the rope drew tight. According to *Beyond the Deep*, Stone's partners decided it was time to haul him in. "We figured, hell, he's been down there too long anyways," one of them later said. "And so we started pulling."

By the time Stone resurfaced to join his belayers, the air in his last tank was down to 300 pounds per square inch—enough for three deep breaths. Despite his terrifying journey, Stone was ecstatic. At his farthest penetration, when he flipped over to gaze at the view beyond, what he saw mesmerized him. "The water was so pure," he reported, "that the twin beams from [my] dim electric headlamps pierced down into the deep blue canyon and faded to black before revealing any hint of a bottom. [I'd] never seen anything like it." Now he blurted out to his teammates, "Man, you wouldn't believe it. That canyon is headed straight for the center of the earth."

Stone's was not the last close call cavers would undergo on the Huautla Plateau. But to his dismay, his daring thrust failed to win over the more conservative veterans among the Kirkwood Cowboys. In their view, the San Agustin Sump remained an impenetrable obstacle. On a second expedition in 1980, the cavers focused instead on a nearby pit called Li Nita. That, too, seemed to dead-end in a sump. Once more, Stone hauled scuba gear into the abyss. This time he got through the sump and emerged in a massive dry canyon. A hunch that had driven him into Li Nita now caused Stone to drop his gear and scramble onward. Within minutes, he found what he was looking for: a survey mark scrawled in charcoal on the wall. Stone had linked Li Nita and San Agustin. And because the entrance to the former cave lay at a higher altitude, in one bold stroke Stone had stretched the Huautla system to a total depth of 4,002 feet.

At that moment, Huautla became the third deepest known cavern in the world. At last, North American caving was playing in the big leagues so long dominated by the French. And who knew where the farthest reaches of Huautla ended?

The San Agustin Sump, which lay below the Li Nita connection, still loomed as a formidable obstacle. It became Bill Stone's obsession. But the decade after his breakthrough linkage with Li Nita in 1980 unfurled as a series of expensive and exhausting failures. By 1988, Stone had led or participated in a dozen expeditions to the Huautla Plateau, without any of them denting the depth barrier of just over 4,000 feet.

Convinced that diving was not only the key to Huautla but perhaps to all the deepest caves in the world, Stone apprenticed with the master, Sheck Exley. Meanwhile, a born inventor, he spent months developing a radical new rig that he called a rebreather. Through state-of-the-art technology, Stone figured out a way to convert exhaled carbon dioxide into fresh, reusable air, even in the middle of a dive. But Stone's teammates found the new apparatus complex and unwieldy. Almost none of them really trusted the rig. Stone became a lone believer crying out in the wilderness.

In 1986, another pair of cavers, Carol Vesely and Bill Farr, hiked across the trailless Huautla Plateau searching for other cave entrances. Several hours into the forest, they stumbled upon a huge sinkhole. It formed a ramp that Vesely and Farr followed downhill until it abruptly ended in a cliff. But across the void, an opening in the hillside loomed. In James Tabor's vivid description, "It looked like a giant black mouth with ragged teeth, several stories high and wide enough to hold two Greyhound buses parked end to end."

In that moment, the two cavers discovered a system that would rival Huautla in promise. They called it Chevé. During the next three decades, Chevé would be pushed deeper and deeper, but the kinds of obstacles that had thwarted progress in Huautla stymied the best efforts of a legion of explorers. Stone himself would come to believe that Chevé had the potential to set records. The chief reason for his enthusiasm was the startling result of an experiment that sounds as if it came out of a high-school science lab.

One way to determine the true extent of a cave system is to put a luminous dye into the water near the entrance, then wait hours or even days to see if the dye shows up in a current flowing out of a hillside miles away and thousands of feet lower. If so, the experiment proves the connection. In Chevé such a dye tracing produced a dazzling result. The colored water emerged, as its partisans had hoped, in a resurgence that lay a mind-boggling 8,354 feet lower. Cavers, however, are purists. Chevé didn't count as the deepest cave in the world unless human beings could physically perform the connection.

With the kinds of challenges that Huautla and Chevé posed, American caving became a more serious business than ever before. To get to the farthest reaches of a known passageway, teams had to spend days at a time underground. Inevitably, a logistical pyramid of supplies, not unlike the buildup of a Himalayan mountaineering expedition in the 1950s, had to be thrown at the problem. That buildup demanded the coordinated efforts of teams of cavers, most of whom served in the inglorious role of porters, to position a pair or trio of experts to push the system to new lengths and depths.

It is worth pointing out the peculiar constraints that caving imposes on its pioneers, and that keep it "purer" as a means of exploration than above-ground exploits such as mountaineering and polar exploration. Airplanes and helicopters, of course, are useless in caving, except in rare cases to gain access to a remote entrance. If a person is seriously injured very far below the surface, saving his or her life requires a herculean and perilous effort by rescuers who must bodily carry and shuttle the victim to safety. Nor do radios work underground. Throughout most of caving's current golden age, communication from the depths to the surface took place only by virtue of personal contact, as one teammate made the arduous trek back out to relay news of progress below. In recent years, cavers have laid telephone wires from entrances to the farthest passages, but so far the efficacy of such systems has proved uncertain. In general, in caving, there are no shortcuts to safety, no hopes of calling in a rescue, no substitute for the time-honored skills of crawling, slithering, climbing, and rappelling.

Despite the blossoming promise of the two great Mexican cave systems after 1986, the Huautla Plateau began to seem a cursed place. In 1991, a moderately experienced caver inside Chevé set up his rig to rappel a 65-foot shaft. Somehow he failed to attach his rappel device to the rope. He leaned back and plunged into space. Despite a desperate effort to grab the rope with his hands, he was dead on impact with the talus pile below. Despairing of retrieving his body, his teammates buried him in the pit. A full year later other cavers, using a complex system of pulleys and ropes, were able to hoist his body to the surface.

Meanwhile, Bill Stone kept tinkering with his rebreather. The advantages of the new rig were immense. As Jim Tabor explains, "A rebreather uses chemicals to 'scrub' carbon dioxide from a diver's exhaled breath, which it recycles over and over, producing dramatically longer dive times. . . . A single standard scuba tank gives about twenty minutes of dive time at 100 feet. A rebreather can provide twenty *hours*—at least."

By 1987, Chevé had been pushed to 3,406 feet. But at that depth Stone's team ran smack into a massive talus pile that blocked all access beyond. Cavers were willing to move rocks to enlarge passages, though the use of dynamite, once a staple of underground exploration, had been relegated to the limbo of overkill. But the breakdown pile in Chevé was far too daunting to dig through. Bitterly disappointed, Stone turned his back on Chevé . . . for the time being.

The focus returned to Huautla. In 1994, Stone organized the most ambitious assault yet on the complex system. Partway through the expedition, divers finally cracked the San Agustin Sump, only to discover a whole series of sumps interspersed with dry "airbells" beyond. Despite such progress, delays and setbacks sapped the team's morale. Then a sudden tragedy shook the expedition to its core. Ian Rolland, an experienced Brit who was a sergeant in the Royal Air Force, failed to return from a dive through two sumps separated by an airbell. It was Stone who found and retrieved Rolland's body, in a formidable feat of solo diving and hauling. What killed the veteran was a mystery, and diabetes was suspected to have contributed to the man's demise. But the grim event triggered a wholesale mutiny within the team. Bill Farr, who had co-discovered Chevé, announced, "There aren't going to be any more dives. This expedition is over." Stone disagreed, and tried to rally the troops with an appeal to their exploratory pride. "Three or four hundred years ago," he said (according to Tabor), "ships would often lose fifty percent of their crew in the course of a voyage. The difference between us and them is that our society now places so much importance on life."

Stone's intransigence, along with his determination to push Huautla at all costs, only further fractured the demoralized team. A caricature of their leader as a heartless fanatic and egomaniac circulated among the ranks. The upshot was that only Stone and his girlfriend, Barbara am Ende, along with a very small supporting crew, still had the nerve and will to try to push Huautla through the dangerous series of sumps that stretched beyond the San Agustin watershed.

I met Bill Stone at a conference organized by NASA in the late 1990s. Its declared agenda was to give the country's astronauts the benefit of the insights adventurers such as ourselves might offer about the future of exploration. The astronauts were privately scornful of us mavericks and misfits, but even so the back-and-forth proved stimulating. I cornered Stone to ask him about Huautla and Chevé. As he rhapsodized about the unknown realms he still hoped to discover, I basked in the full force of the man's intense volition. It was easy to see how his 1994 teammates had been first cowed, then alienated, by Stone's unswerving pursuit of the Holy Grail of world caving. But I caught myself as I realized, *This is the kind of brilliant zealot that Columbus must have seemed to his shipmates, or Shackleton to his comrades—a man to be feared but followed.*

The stupendous drama of Stone and am Ende's six-day push of Huautla into uncharted terrain forms the narrative centerpiece of their book, *Beyond the Deep*. By the end of the 1994 expedition, using the rebreather, they had solved seven further sumps and all kinds of convoluted slots and tunnels. They had extended Huautla to a relief of 4,839 feet, certifying it as the third-deepest in the world. Still the record holder, the Gouffre Jean-Bernard plunges only 287 feet deeper. At their farthest penetration, Stone and am Ende reached the edge of yet another subterranean pit filled with water. It looked like a tougher challenge than the San Agustin pool. They named it the Mother of All Sumps.

———

During the years that Stone's teams were pushing Chevé and Huautla hard, and French cavers were exploring the farthest nooks of the Vercors and Haute Provence, another band of devotees was quietly investigating a plateau far from France, even farther from Mexico. The Arabika Massif is a limestone sub-range of the Caucasus Mountains, located in the former Soviet republic of Georgia, close to the northeastern shore of the Black Sea. The presence of caves across the massif was known as early as the first decades of the twentieth century, but the consensus of the experts was that the region lacked the potential for really deep pits.

One of the Arabika caves, named Krubera after Alexander Kruber, an early scientist intrigued by the geology of the region, seemed even less promising than its neighbors. For twenty years after cavers tried to push it in 1963, Krubera yielded a depth of only 290 feet, where a squeeze too tight for human passage seemed to write a *finis* to the system. The more zealous explorers turned elsewhere—in particular to a cave called Kalsi, which they plumbed to a depth of 3,328 feet, making it not only the first cave in the Soviet Union to exceed 1,000 meters but also the deepest cave yet discovered in that sprawling federation of republics.

So matters stood until one man, Alexander Klimchouk, had second thoughts. A geologist by profession, Klimchouk put dye into the entrance streams of several Arabika caves. When the luminous water later sprang from hillsides almost at the level of the Black Sea, Krubera gained a new cachet. James Tabor structures the narrative of his enthralling book *Blind Descent* around the characters and passions of the two leaders of their disparate campaigns, Bill Stone and Alexander Klimchouk. The Ukrainian geologist differs strikingly from his American rival not only in physical presence (five foot eight, with an unprepossessing build) but in temperament. "Stone is a classic Type A—," writes Tabor, "brusque, impatient, rushing. Klimchouk, or 'Father Klim,' as younger cavers sometimes call him, is mild-mannered, soft-spoken, polite to the point of courtliness, deliberate in thought and motion."

The contrast between Krubera and Huautla, as well, could not be more dramatic. Krubera lies at a latitude of 43° N, fully 1,800 miles north of the Huautla Plateau. As a result, it is a cold cave, in which water immersion poses the immediate threat of hypothermia. Krubera is also relentlessly vertical, while both Chevé and Huautla stand out for the branching complexity of their gently inclined passages. In Tabor's words, Krubera unfolds as "pitch after pitch connected by short passages called 'meanders.' While non-cavers would be terrorized by the yawning pits, one of which is 500 feet deep, experienced explorers look forward to their thrilling rappels, if not to their grinding ascents. They uniformly despise, however, 'the fucking meanders,' as they are most frequently called."

Klimchouk's great insight, which opened up Krubera, was to investigate what he called "windows"—small portals in the walls of shafts—rather than try to force his way through such putative dead ends as boulder chokes and sumps. Such an approach required great patience and endurance. In caves such as Krubera, according to Tabor, "Of hundreds of leads, 95 percent went nowhere; 4 percent yielded more depth and distance; only 1 percent produced substantial breakthroughs."

The teams that worked in Krubera were dominated by Ukrainians, many of them from an ambitious club based in Kiev. The organization they brought to the challenge of Krubera was both more massive and more cohesive than Stone's often fragmented group efforts in Mexico. And once the vital windows were discovered and pushed, Krubera just seemed to go and go. In 2000, a team stretched it to a depth of 4,600 feet, at which it began to rival the deepest pits in Europe. And in January 2001, another Ukrainian team forced passages all the way down to 5,609 feet below the surface. Suddenly Krubera was the deepest cave in the world—the first grotto outside western Europe ever to claim that honor.

The Georgian supremacy was short-lived, as in January 2003 a team in France extended the Gouffre Mirolda to 5,685 feet—a mere 74 feet deeper than Krubera. Klimchouk and his comrades, now fortified by some of the best cavers in post-Soviet Russia, redoubled their efforts, and in 2004 those efforts bore fruit. The team that now assaulted Krubera comprised fifty-six cavers from seven different countries. Their gear amounted to 10,000 pounds of supplies, which included two miles of rope. And they strung a telephone line into the abyss to facilitate communication between the surface and the depths.

Diving through sumps and rappelling past waterfalls, an advance guard reached a depth of 6,307 feet. Krubera had regained first place. And since 2004, the cave has never looked back. Only two months after the record-setting push, another team lowered the cave to a vertical relief of 6,822 feet (2,080 meters). Krubera thus became the first known cave to break the magical barrier of 2,000 meters. Thirteen years later, it is still the only cave in the world exceeding that number. In 2017, the Krubera record stands at 7,206 feet—more than a thousand feet deeper than its nearest rival, another Georgian cave called Sarma. As of this writing, Huautla ranks eighth in the world, with a depth of 5,068 feet. Chevé lags slightly behind its Oaxacan neighbor, at 4,869.

Yet even now, none of the best cavers in the world—not even Alexander Klimchouk—will declare unequivocally that the Krubera labyrinth they have discovered is the deepest in the world. Who knows what prodigies of karst lurk unsuspected in the highland jungles of New Guinea, on the remote plateaus of western China? The Everest of caving may still lie out there, undiscovered, in some limestone wilderness where few humans have ever ventured.

———

In this book, I have dwelt on the ways in which exploration and adventure have been adulterated by the machinery of communication—cell and sat phones, radio, Internet—and by the rescue capability of airplanes and helicopters. Caving, almost uniquely, has been transformed virtually not at all by such modern inventions. Bill Stone and Barbara am Ende, feeling their way through the sumps beyond San Agustin, were almost as alone in 1994 as Douglas Mawson on his desperate solo jaunt back to base camp in 1913 in Antarctica. There is no fear at present that the grottos of the world, or even a single plateau like Arabika or Huautla, are in danger of being "caved out." The driving geniuses of the underworld, the Bill Stones and Alexendar Klimchouks, have the visionary passion that stamped George Leigh Mallory on Everest, Roald Amundsen on his way to the South Pole. They also share a strong competitive streak. Even now, Stone is not willing to cede second-place status to his Ukrainian rival. The Chevé resurgence, promising more than 8,000 feet of depth, gnaws away at him. So in 2015 he announced yet another assault on Chevé, tentatively scheduled for 2017, when he would be sixty-four years old.

If any exploratory endeavor nowadays truly confronts regions of the earth that are still undiscovered, it is caving. No one knows where a new passageway in Chevé or Krubera goes until men and women actually explore it. There are no aerial photos, no maps except the ones cavers draw as they survey onward.

Record depth is only the most ardently sought benchmark of the underground. Every cave, in all its twisting passages, abounds in mysteries. Deep inside Lechuguilla on my guided tour, in the twelfth or thirteenth hour, as we sat on a limestone shelf taking a breather, Rick Bridges pointed to an orifice gaping 10 yards away. "This whole section of the cave was discovered only yesterday," he said. "You want to have a look down that chute? Nobody's been in it yet."

I jumped to my feet and started off. The bending tunnel lay swathed in deep drifts of gypsum powder. With every step, I left footprints. Bound by Bridges's injunction to push only 50 or 60 yards, I nonetheless passed out of his sight. I was gripped by a frenzy I had first tasted on the north face of Denali in 1963. *In the whole human history of the world*, my brain sang, *no one has ever been here before. I am the first.*

If I could start life over as an explorer, in 2017 rather than 1960, I think I might become a caver rather than a climber. But in my seventy-fourth year, with a cancer I cannot cure circumscribing every whim or ambition I might throw at the world, I can only dream of subterranean discovery. Still, it was dreamers who unlocked Huautla, who found the key to Krubera...

SEVEN

THE FUTURE
of ADVENTURE

According to the *Online Etymological Dictionary*, a resource compiled from several authoritative lexicons including the *Oxford English Dictionary*, the word "aventuren" first appears in English around the year 1300, as a verb meaning "to risk the loss of something." That original meaning catches the essence of what adventure means to me. Not just "risk," but "the loss of something." The adventurers celebrated in this book all risked their very lives to achieve goals, however arcane, that the rest of the world deemed too hazardous to pursue. Without danger, adventure is reduced to a mere sport.

The word "adventure" was used sparingly before the nineteenth century. Since 1800, the term (usually as a noun) has grown in popularity even as its meaning has been cheapened. Today, "the adventure of a lifetime" is a phrase shamelessly applied to everything from a tour of the Caribbean by cruise ship to taking a year to study abroad.

The text of the King James Bible runs to 789,626 words. Among them, "adventure" appears only twice, in senses quite alien to our modern take on the word. Thus, in Deuteronomy 28:56, one of the cursed fates the Lord will mete out to nonbelievers is the corruption of a seemingly virtuous woman who "would not adventure to set the sole of her foot upon the ground for delicateness and tenderness, her eye shall be evil toward the husband of her bosom, and toward her son, and toward her daughter."

Throughout Richard Hakluyt's Renaissance accounts of the great voyages of Britain's boldest explorers, "adventurer" is deployed in a way that turns on its head our notion of what was at stake. For Hakluyt, the adventurers were the businessmen at home who financed the voyages, stalwarts of such enterprises as the British East India Company. It has been estimated that on any sixteenth-century voyage from Europe to the New World, the fatality rate was one in three. But in the Elizabethan mind, vagabonds who signed up for the expedition were mere crew, unskilled laborers. In Hakluyt's world, what stood to be lost was money, not human lives. It was the financiers who took the risk.

I doubt that the mariners who sailed with Odysseus on the voyage from Troy back to Ithaca conceived of their journey as an adventure. The trials they endured—threading the needle between Scylla and Charybdis, escaping the cave of Polyphemus, resisting the song of the beautiful Sirens—were obstacles to overcome, challenges thrown up by the gods in all their Olympian perversity. No one in Homeric Greece would have deliberately sought out such ordeals, since ordinary life was perilous enough. Yet the epic poem, among the earliest forms literature took on in the Western world, was conceived as a celebration of the deeds of an extraordinary man, told in heroic verse, i.e., dactylic hexameter. Ironically, "having an epic" has become climbing slang for getting into serious trouble on an ascent that ought to have been straightforward.

Vilhjalmur Stefansson, the Canadian Arctic explorer and ethnologist, liked to claim that adventure was what happened when you screwed up. A sound explorer, in his view, pulled off his expeditions exactly as planned, with no tawdry melodramas spawned by avoidable mistakes. Yet the curmudgeonly Stefansson was belied by his own record, as during the disastrous voyage of the *Karluk* from 1913–16.

When the ship was frozen into sea ice north of Point Barrow, Stefansson and five companions left the vessel, ostensibly to hunt for game to sustain the crew. Those remaining with the ship suspected that Stefansson had simply abandoned them, and indeed, the hunting party never returned to the *Karluk*, which sank in January 1914. Of the twenty-four men and one woman left with the ship, eleven died in various ways before Captain Robert Bartlett led a handful of teammates on a desperate march to Siberia to set a rescue in motion. Stefansson never took full responsibility for his crucial role in the fiasco, which unfolded as part of his own grand scheme of scientific research in the Arctic.

To push the question in another direction, one might argue that adventure is the luxury of a modern world, or at least of that part of the world affluent enough to escape routine threats of starvation, disease, or ethnic oppression, in which ordinary life has become secure enough to take for granted. In that world, we seek out adventure, rather than having it thrust upon us as it was for Odysseus.

When I took up mountain climbing as a teenager in Boulder in the late 1950s, I was following no mandate to serve my country or my kin, no vision of a way to improve the lives of others, not even a sense that here lay a path to a sustainable vocation. As much as anything, I started climbing because I was bored. Even hiking in the Colorado Rockies had grown humdrum. Yet within only two years, climbing became the most important thing in my life. I never doubted that it was worth the risk.

Some years later, in graduate school at the University of Denver, I still shaped each year around the next summer's expedition to Alaska. The beginning of the fall term each September loomed as shattering anticlimax. Studying poetry at DU, I started playing with the most demanding verse forms, such as the villanelle and the sestina. Free verse seemed too easy, too undisciplined. It was, as Frost had memorably said, playing tennis without a net. It was hiking up the dreary trail on Mount Audubon rather than attacking the east face of Longs Peak.

At age twenty-three or twenty-four, I wrote a rondeau—a tight, twelve-line poem in iambic tetrameter in which the first phrase repeats at the end of both stanzas—that, I realize looking back, encapsulated my youthful angst about being an adventurer born too late.

We drove all night to reach the shore.
There was a time when men would sail
All night to reach the land, and fail;
And only hunger could restore
The vision they had seen before.
Along a paved, familiar trail
    We drove all night.

What were all of us looking for?
The truth of some persistent tale?
A golden city, or the Grail?
Because we could believe no more,
    We drove all night.

Yet during those years, I gloried in the embarrassment of riches that the mountains of Alaska poured into my lap. Whole ranges that climbers had never approached! Soaring spires of granite that had never felt the touch of human hand! If I had stopped to reflect, I might have told myself, *No, you weren't born too late. Born at the perfect time. Pity the generations to come.*

Looking back at age seventy-three on my career as a mountaineer, I have to resist the temptation to deplore the current state of adventure as a tattered scrap of the abundance in which I reveled in my prime. In 2007, I wrote an essay for *Alpinist* titled "The Epigoni," in which I did just that. My thesis was a brash put-down of the current scene. "It hit me," I wrote, "that the young climbers of the day . . . were what the Greeks called *epigoni*: the born-too-late, the hangers-on, the feeble imitators of the heroic alpinists of a more healthy age. At their worst, they were spoiled kids fighting over the leftovers."

I wrote the piece tongue-in-cheek, or so I thought. Little did I realize that it might give some of the best climbers of the younger generation serious, self-doubting pause—until I came across a piece published in *Appalachia* in 2014 titled "Epigoni, Revisited." That deft essay was the work of Michael Wejchert, the son of my longtime climbing buddy Chris Wejchert. The year before, Michael and two partners had attempted the south face of Alaska's Mount Deborah, on the east ridge of which Don Jensen and I had been defeated during a forty-two-day two-man expedition in 1964. I had written my second book, *Deborah: A Wilderness Narrative*, about that protracted, nightmarish failure.

Then twenty-six years old, Michael consulted with me in Cambridge before his own expedition. But I only glimpsed the fact that *Deborah* had been an inspirational text for him as a teenager, and that now he harbored the dark suspicion that the modern technology his team was throwing at the mountain might run the risk of cheapening their experience. I had no inkling, in fact, that he had read my *Alpinist* putdown, "The Epigoni."

Michael and his buddies flew by bush plane in to the West Fork Glacier, whereas Don and I had backpacked in from the Denali Highway. They carried a sat phone and planned to make a film of their exploit. Alas, a freakishly cold April—the coldest in Alaska since 1923—flattened their attempt before it even got started. In minus 40-degree temperatures, they never came to grips with the south face. Back at base camp, they called their pilot, who picked them up. They had spent only two weeks in the Hayes Range, compared to Don's and my six.

In *Appalachia*, Michael recounted the decision to give up.

I realize the mountain doesn't care who we are, why we're here, or what we've brought. My frozen fingers unzip four layers and finally fumble with the camera lens. I manage 30 seconds of shaky footage almost automatically: Elliot below the mountain, swinging his feet like a football punter to stay warm. I don't need the film to remember the moment though: We two grown men doing jumping jacks miles from anywhere, beneath a hunk of granite nobody really cares about, pistons of humanity bobbing down, fighting for enough warmth to stay alive. The climbing ceases to matter, and the movie, too. Sometimes, surviving is enough.

When Michael got back to his home in New Hampshire, I consoled him over the phone. His attempt, I thought, had had the same kind of boldness about it that Don and I had been proud of in 1964. Only when I read the *Appalachia* essay did I realize that he had glumly consigned his attempt to the marginalia of the *epigoni* whom I had so cavalierly dismissed. The good thing is that the defeat on Deborah slowed Michael down not at all. He has returned to Alaska on two more ambitious expeditions, and is planning another in the future. At age thirty, Michael Wejchert is one of America's strongest and most visionary mountaineers.

Michael's plucky example reset my curmudgeonly compass. I no longer worry that the skills and technology of the current band of alpinists relegate the deeds of my own generation to the limbo of "pretty good for its time." I am surprised and pleased, in fact, that the hotshots of today express admiration for the climbs we made in the 1960s and 1970s. That some of our ascents have earned the label of "classic," let alone "breakthrough," fills me with pride. Climbers in general have a decent sense of history—as professional athletes do not. The great majority of major league baseball's current stars have little or no idea who Willie Mays was, or Hank Aaron. But the typical twenty-five-year-old making his mark in Yosemite in 2017 reveres and honors Royal Robbins or Lynn Hill.

The media, of course, focus inordinately on Everest, or on the Seven Summits. But all over the globe young adventurers set their sights on ranges that remain almost as unexplored as the Kichatnas and Revelations were for me and my teammates in the late 1960s. It matters little that the peaks they covet are officially unnamed—that neglect only redoubles their value. If I were twenty-five myself, and setting out now in quest of new worlds to conquer, I'd head, like the most imaginative of today's mountaineers, for the fjords on the east coast of Greenland, or the massifs of western China, or the enclaves of wilderness in Alaska that still, despite the campaigns of my own generation and the next, have escaped assault by piton and ice axe. I've seen the photos. I know what's there.

As I argued in the previous chapters, some forms of terrestrial exploration are only now luxuriating in the discovery of unknown worlds. Chief among them are caving and cave diving. And the descent of wild rivers that earlier kayakers and rafters judged unrunnable stirs the blood of a small legion of daring young paddlers. Nor must an explorer today be an expert in some arcane discipline that takes years of training and an arsenal of specialized gear to master. In 2001, two veteran American mountaineers, Mark Richey and Mark Wilford, climbed a little-known peak in the Karakoram called Yamandaka. After three bivouacs and several snowstorms, the men decided that descending the same side of the mountain as the face they had climbed would be too dangerous. As Richey told me years later:

> To the south, there appeared to be an easy descent to a broad meadow. Although we had no map or knowledge of the area, we decided to go that way. We spent the night in the meadow but noticed something strange—no sign of grazing and the wild animals we

encountered seemed almost tame, like they had never seen humans. It turned out that this glacier meadow was isolated by a steep cirque and a torrent-filled canyon. We later learned that no humans, not even local herders, had ever visited this place. Our only choice was go back up and over the mountain and reverse our route or take our chances with the unknown canyon below. We chose the latter.

That choice almost cost the two men their lives. Only a series of desperate rappels through waterfalls, followed by an irreversible traverse to escape the canyon, delivered them to safety. Back at base camp, they learned that their teammates had given them up for dead, and had built a small shrine in their memory.

A similar experience, though not so perilous, befell a team of adventurers trying to explore a jungle plateau in Honduras in 2015. Inspired by an old legend of a lost Ciudad Blanca, or White City, and galvanized by new lidar (ground-penetrating radar) images obtained by airplane that revealed the outlines of a massive complex of buildings buried under dense tangles of trees and roots, the team helicoptered into a clearing in the rain forest. Their remarkable story is blithely told in Douglas Preston's *Lost City of the Monkey God* (2017). On the ground, the searchers at once noticed something strange about the wildlife. One of the men was an ex-soldier in the British Special Air Service named Andrew Wood. In Preston's telling:

Woody said he had spent a large part of his life in jungles all over the world, from Asia and Africa to South and Central America. He said he had never been in one like this, so apparently untouched. As he was setting up camp, before we arrived, a quail came right up to him, pecking in the dirt. And a wild pig also wandered through, unconcerned by the presence of humans. The spider monkeys, he said, were another sign of an uninhabited area, as they normally flee at

the first sight of humans, unless they are in a protected zone. He con-
cluded, "I don't think the animals here have ever seen people before."

In this case, the corner of the wilderness the team explored was not a place where no humans had ever been. But it had been lost to human ken for many centuries after the still mysterious founders of the civilization that built the lost city—evidently contemporary with the Classic Maya to the west and north—had disappeared.

During all my expeditions to Alaska, I've often climbed on ridges and walls that I knew had never before been touched by human hands. But I've never entered a wilderness where the animals themselves seemed to have no awareness of the threat of man the intruder. (I would value such an encounter as one of the magical experiences in my life.) Yet as these two examples prove, in the twenty-first century you can still find a meadow in Pakistan, a rain forest in Honduras, where *Homo sapiens* has never set foot, or set foot so long ago that the ecology itself has swallowed any echo of his passing.

In terms of the future of adventure, the ultimate frontier is outer space. As the son of an astronomer, I daydreamed throughout my childhood about flying in a rocket ship to distant galaxies. Even a quick jaunt to Alpha Centauri, the nearest star in our own Milky Way, would have gladdened my restive spirit; or for that matter, a year or two to hike among the red buttes and craters of Mars. From age thirteen to fifteen I read virtually nothing but science fiction. But even in my juvenile world of wish-fulfillment, I knew deep down that humans would never get to Andromeda, let alone to the galaxies on the other edge of the universe that were fleeing from us at close to the speed of light. And I knew that the cosmonaut heroes of Isaac Asimov and Robert Heinlein and A.E. van Vogt owed more to Tom Mix and Roy Rogers than to the reality of the first men who might set foot on the moon or Mars.

In the 1960s, I felt only a lukewarm enthusiasm for the space program that culminated with the moon landing in 1969. John Glenn and Buzz Aldrin were no heroes of mine. I shared my father's admiration for their courage and technical skill and willingness to die in the service of exploration. But they seemed to lack (necessarily, given the demands of space) the fundamental traits of independence and hardiness and athletic prowess that made Hermann Buhl and Lionel Terray the paragons I dreamed of emulating, or, for that matter, John Wesley Powell and Sir Richard Burton. Strapped into their Apollo rockets, the astronauts seemed to me sentient automatons whose every decision was made by programmers in Houston, and whose bouncing jogs on the lunar surface required less nerve or stamina than a ramble in the Lake District.

Half a century later, I cling to my skepticism about space. The greatest mysteries of all lie hidden among the stars, the strangest of all unknown worlds, and I hang on every new revelation that scientists can wring from the cosmos. But the discoveries out there will be made by telescopes such as the Hubble and the James Webb, by theoreticians cogitating at CERN and JPL. The exploration of space, alas, will have little to do with adventure as we know it, or at least as I wish to celebrate it in this book, and everything to do with machines and laboratories and brilliant men and women laboring over computers and scribbling with pencils on pads. Einstein was the Columbus of space.

In a previous chapter I saluted the deeds of Sam Meacham and his band of cave divers probing the cenotes of Yucatán. But I did not address the wilderness that remains by far the greatest unknown region on earth. That is the deep sea depths. After all, 71 percent of the surface of our planet is covered by oceans. The divers who first seriously explored the underwater wonderland were true adventurers. No one has written more rhapsodically about the undiscovered earth than Jacques Cousteau, and William Beebe made his expeditions by bathysphere sound as exciting as Lewis and Clark's exploration of the West. Within the last forty years the discovery of bizarre creatures thriving near hydrothermal vents in total darkness far below the surface—tube worms, shrimp with eyes in their backs, and the like, as well as all kinds of strange microorganisms—has revolutionized the most basic theories of the origins of life on earth.

The Challenger Deep in the Mariana Trench near the island of Guam is the lowest known point on the underwater surface of the globe, at 36,070 feet beneath the surface. It was visited by two daring men, Jacques Piccard and Don Walsh, in 1960, by means of a contraption called a bathyscaphe that protected them from a crushing pressure of eight tons per square inch. Those two pioneers were able to spend only twenty minutes on their inverted "summit," and silt stirred up by the device prevented them from taking any photos. In 2012 James Cameron, director of the film *Titanic*, piloted a submersible to the same location, where he managed to collect samples and shoot footage in 3–D.

Here, and among all the rest of the unknown places in the ocean depths, lies a frontier as challenging as the polar regions loomed in the 1880s, or the Himalaya half a century before that. The discoveries that lie ahead of us in those unfathomably remote regions promise to be as profound as the ones that probes will find on the moons of Saturn or beneath the Red Spot on Jupiter. But my skepticism about the role of adventure in outer space extends to the ocean depths. The great breakthroughs are likely to come not in the visits of aquanauts such as Piccard and Cameron, but thanks to the deployment of unmanned submersibles capable of shooting film and gathering specimens. There will be no room, I fear, for deep-sea John Wesley Powells in the twenty-first and twenty-second centuries. I hope I'm wrong—but more than one scientist has already voiced the same idea.

The fear that there are no more undiscovered worlds to explore is an age-old bugaboo for restless adventurers. Wilfrid Noyce was one of the leading British mountaineers of his day, as well as an eloquent writer. On the 1953 Everest expedition, he played a crucial supporting role in the well-coordinated effort that thrust Tenzing and Hillary to the summit. His memoir of that campaign, *South Col*, is a far more interesting book than Sir John Hunt's official account, *The Ascent of Everest*. In 1957, with David Cox, Noyce made what is credited as the first ascent of Machhapuchare, one of the most striking peaks in the Himalaya, though the two men stopped 150 feet short of the summit out of respect for the local belief that the mountain was sacred. (It has long been closed to climbers for that reason.)

In *The Springs of Adventure*, a quirky personal survey of discovery and exploration worldwide, Noyce wrote in 1958, "All the really obvious points on the earth's surface having been reached, people . . . go out privately, in which case the lone sailor and explorer, caver and diver, hail each other as fellow lunatics in a sane world (or vice versa) . . ." The success of Everest five years earlier seemed to Noyce to herald the end of an era. "Now that the greatest giants have fallen, public interest has on the whole waned, and it needs public interest to fan competition. The climbers themselves sink back into a welcome obscurity."

How cloudy Noyce's crystal ball turned out to be! Since 1958, mountaineering has exploded in popularity, claiming the attention of a public once indifferent to or unaware of any challenges other than Everest. Today, even formerly arcane facets of the climbing world such as bouldering inspire international competition and motivate men and women to devote their lives to perfecting their arts. In October 2016, a Finn named Nalle Hukkataival succeeded in climbing a bouldering route less than 25 feet long. Hukkataival spent four years on Burden of Dreams, as he named his "project," in the course of 4,000 attempts, before everything came together on a single magical go. He claimed the world's first V17, upping the grade rating for bouldering by a single digit. Climbers all over the world, almost none of whom had ever seen the boulder, let alone attempted it, tipped their caps.

The forms that adventure takes are so manifold that sometimes a whole new discipline must be invented to embrace them. Although thousands of years ago daredevils must have jumped into underground lakes, holding their breaths as they tried to see what lay below and beyond, cave diving as a serious pursuit in quest of unexplored regions is less than eighty years old, and it did not become a highly skilled endeavor until the 1970s.

Years ago I had a conversation that has lodged in my imagination ever since, when I chatted with John Kramer, one of Sobek's founding whitewater rafters and the strongest hand on our unsuccessful attempt to descend the Tua/Purari River in New Guinea in 1983. In a few places on earth Kramer had seen major streams churning with rapids disappear into limestone caves. For my benefit, Kramer speculated about the future of a new kind of adventure—whitewater kayaking underground. The very notion gave me the willies. How would you save yourself, I wondered, from unforeseeable death traps such as a sudden waterfall, or a rapid that squeezed down to a chute that the current filled like a water hose? Pitons hammered into the walls, ropes to lower the boat cautiously toward the void ahead? In the face of some apocalyptic impasse, could you use ascenders to climb the rope back to safety against the raging current?

The ancient Greeks imagined underground rivers as loci of the ultimate. The Styx, the Acheron, the Lethe carried men toward the afterworld. Coleridge, in "Kubla Khan," saw one such torrent in an opium-induced dream, "Where Alph, the sacred river, ran / Through caverns measureless to man / Down to a sunless sea."

The John Kramers of some future generation may actually set out on journeys through such landscapes of the unthinkable . . . and emerge to tell their tales.

———

By February 2017, thanks to regular doses of Pembrolizumab, the still experimental immunotherapy drug, my body had settled into what felt like a shaky truce with cancer. Several CT scans over the months since September had revealed that the deadly nodules in my lungs had grown not at all. Nor had they shrunk, however. Some mechanism within the cells that combat invasive threats deep inside one's tissues had won a temporary armistice. I was still dependent on the feeding tube taped to the hole in my stomach, though I had reduced the cans of oozy supplement from six to two per day. I had learned to swallow all over again, though it had been a year and a half since I had felt even the faintest pangs of hunger. Eating was a tedious daily chore, an exercise regimen rather than a pleasure. Rotating through the same insipid menu of soups, soft pasta, eggs, yogurt, and smoothies, I struggled to ingest 2,200 calories a day. I knew that I would never again eat a cheeseburger, and because radiation had killed my saliva glands and left my mouth hypersensitive to sharp tastes, I doubted whether I could ever reacquaint my palate with wine, which I had savored throughout my adult life. The hormonal dysfunction called SIADH was still at work, forcing me to limit the liquids I drank and to bolster my sodium with salt tablets crushed and dissolved and flushed down the feeding tube.

Gradually after September I had gained strength, though I was nowhere close to matching the fitness of the previous May, before the metastasized cancer had torn me down. I could walk or hike for about a mile and a half, but no farther. Trips to the climbing gym were grim reminders of the feebleness I had to accept, as even a 5.6 route pushed me to the limit and left me gasping for breath and on the verge of throwing up. (The previous May I was climbing 5.9.) But for six straight months I had not had to be hospitalized—the longest stretch free from incarceration in the antiseptic wards of Brigham and Women's that I had enjoyed since I first noticed the lump on my lymph node in June 2015.

Amidst all this erosion of my powers, a blessing lay in the fact that my mental faculties seemed undimmed. My memory was as sharp as ever; the scraps of poetry that had lodged decades earlier in my brain responded promptly to each summons; and I was reading more voraciously than ever. Best of all, I kept writing, even though neuropathy in my right arm had robbed me of the laborious one-finger pecking technique with which I had delivered all my books and articles to the keyboards of the typewriter and computer. Now I write longhand on yellow legal pads, then dictate my scribblings to Sharon, who tirelessly types them up. And though every session leaves me exhausted, I count the hours spent in our living room trading ideas and stories with my closest friends—the endless riffs that climbers spin about bivouacs and bergschrunds, the boundless flights of fantasy wrung out of literature and music—as among the happiest in my housebound life.

Each morning I arise with the hopeful formula several friends have sent me like *billets doux* imprinted on my mind: "Every day is a gift." But all too often, by nightfall, the Puritan superego that stands in the wings of my psyche scolds, *Another whole day wasted.* The cruelest reminders of what I have lost come to me in my dreams. Once fatigue puts my superego to sleep, my id takes charge. I am striking out batters again on the sandlot, or tossing perfect spirals on the touch football field. I am camped out on a high ridge watching the Perseid meteor shower. I am hiking down a canyon I have never seen before, and around the next bend I spot petroglyphs. I take the lead on the seventeenth pitch and solve the headwall that leads to the summit. Then I awake, and know that the gift of another day on earth promises no adventure more stirring than a five-block walk through the streets of Watertown.

Often now, in unbidden moments, a surge of grief washes over me, as I recognize that I will never hike Bowdie Canyon on the Dark Canyon Plateau, that I will not climb the routes in the Dolomites that were on my tick list, that I may never travel (as I was sure I would) to South Africa or Thailand or Mongolia. But if there is recompense in that loss, it is the mandate the gift of each day thrusts upon me to assess what my life was all about. After all, no matter how soon I die, I've had at least seventy-three years on earth. Schubert, Mozart, and Keats were given less than half that span to pour their visions into eternity.

I think of myself—of my vocation—not chiefly as a writer, or a climber, or even a husband or a friend, but as an adventurer. This book represents my effort to get at the core of the elusive phenomenon we call adventure, both past and future, both in the lives of explorers and in the wayward paths along which my own wanderlust has propelled me.

The temptation, especially for us Puritans, is to divine some higher purpose served by all those journeys into the wilderness, those vagabond rambles that at the time seemed pure fun or, as they grew sterner, pure compulsion. Climbers have long subscribed to a weirdly self-congratulatory distillation of the meaning of ascent. The mold was set by Mallory who, bridling against the metaphor of mountaineering as conquest, penned his second-most enduring apothegm in an essay published in the *Alpine Journal* in 1918: "Have we vanquished an enemy? None but ourselves."

This quasi-mystical affirmation evolved over subsequent decades into the claim that the reward for flirting with death in the pursuit of summits was the discovery of self. Reinhold Messner, one of the greatest mountaineers in history, was particularly addicted to this formula. He climbed at the most extreme level, Messner swore in book after book, in order to dig deep into his own soul to find out who and what he really was. He came back from his ordeals on Nanga Parbat and Everest with the inestimable treasure of self-understanding. The trouble is that Messner never goes on to define the self that he went to such desperate lengths to excavate. The reader is left wondering, *Is that all? Is the Messnerian core simply the driven, rivalrous, haughty egomaniac that sprawls across page after page?*

I remain deeply skeptical about the facile proposition that through the trials of extreme adventure we learn bedrock truths about ourselves. Climbing, along with other forays into wild places, has given me the most piercing transports of joy I have ever felt. But when I came home and tried to settle back into the petty pace from day to day, I would have been at a loss to articulate what I had learned about myself—or about any other important matter. Perhaps joy itself is the reward. Mallory said as much, in a less well-known quote about the purpose of ascent: "What we get from this adventure is just sheer joy. And joy is, after all, the end of life."

And yet . . . Joy for its own sake is a selfish thing. What does it have to do with others? What good does it do in the world?

The notion that adventure leads to the discovery of self is closely allied to the lazy but commonplace bromide that travel broadens the mind, that journeys to other lands open our eyes to the richness and diversity of the human condition. I'm skeptical, too, of this pious recipe. In my experience, travel often reinforces prejudice and xenophobia. In the eighteenth century, some of the best British poets, essayists, and novelists advanced the notion, heretical to our own Pelagian age, that travel left a man, in Pope's phrase, "in endless error hurled." The classic text is Swift's *Gulliver's Travels*. That masterpiece only pretends to be the adventure story that its transmogrification into a children's book posits. In Swift's deeply pessismistic satire, Lemuel Gulliver is a fool, a voyager whose limitless adaptability seduces him over and over again into confusion. In Lilliput and Brobdingnag, in Laputa and the land of the Houyhnhnms, after his initial shock Gulliver adjusts to the crazy worlds into which he has blundered. When he returns to England, he has lost his moral compass. It is no coincidence that Swift gave his anti-hero a name cognate with "gullible."

If I have ever found an endeavor that led me to a better understanding of myself, it was not adventure but psychotherapy. Over the decades, I've spent serious time in the offices of half a dozen shrinks. I signed on because I was unhappy, or because I felt caught in some aimless drift. Several of the therapists to whom I poured out my troubles were in the end helpless to assuage my condition; one or two were a complete waste of time. But two of them made a difference. In the armchair or on the couch, as I recited stories that were buried in my past, they guided me, slowly and fitfully, toward something new. It wasn't a cure for unhappiness. It was the next best thing—or perhaps a better thing: a comprehension of why, at the deepest level, I behaved as I did, why I kept heading down the same dead-end paths, why I banged my aching head against the unyielding walls of reality. Somewhere, I think, Freud argues that that outcome is the aim of psychoanalysis. His great contribution to humankind, in my view, was the discovery of the unconscious.

But back to adventure. There is little point, I think, in trying to unearth an overarching purpose in our madness. We go off again and again on our voyages in quest of the undiscovered world because we can't help it. We cannot claim that it does anybody besides ourselves any good. We are all, as Lionel Terray put it in the title of his autobiography, "conquistadors of the useless." Yet we share our outcast state with other pursuits that are equally useless but equally wonderful. As W. H. Auden wrote in "In Memory of W. B. Yeats," "For poetry makes nothing happen."

I take heart from the ironic answers two of my heroes offered to the implicit question, "What is the value of adventure?" In 1946, bursting with impatience to launch a new expedition after the grim hiatus of World War II, Bill Tilman sensed the disapproval of his peers. In *Two Mountains and a River,* he wrote:

In the late war ... anyone was free to indulge in careless talk about the new and better world which would emerge refined, as they put it, from the crucible of war. ... My survey of the war-shattered world in the autumn of 1945 was directed naturally to the Himalaya, to the ways and means of getting there, and to the chances of finding like-minded survivors with the same extravagant ideas. So loud was the din raised by the planners of the new world that it was hardly possible for me to avoid absorbing something of the spirit of the times, so that I did feel some slight uneasiness at attempting to do once more what I wanted to do. But I argued as Falstaff did about stealing, it was my vocation.

A dozen years earlier, Eric Shipton struggled with his conscience on the eve of the expedition with Tilman that opened up the hidden valley through which the ascent of Nanda Devi would be accomplished. In *Upon That Mountain*, he recalled:

Then the thought occurred to me, "Why not spend the rest of my life doing this sort of thing? ... It was a disturbing idea, one which caused me much heartsearching and many sleepless nights. ...

I do not know how long I fought the temptation. I certainly suffered qualms of conscience, but they were due more to the mere prospect of such exquisite self-indulgence than to fear of the consequences of abandoning the search for an assured future, provision for old age and other worldly ambitions. I had always rather deplored the notion that one must sacrifice the active years of one's life to the dignity and comfort of old age. ... So the decision was taken, albeit with a faint heart.

Whatever the costs of spending half a life in adventure, I have few regrets about all the time and energy and passion I squandered trying to figure out how to get from the base of some mountain to the top. But cancer forces another kind of reassessment. What great adventures did I fail to pursue because of the demands of humdrum daily existence? What challenges did I shirk?

From 1981 onward, I made my living as a freelance writer. One of the delights of my trade was the opportunity to plunge into the esoteric worlds of other people's passions. Because they were only too glad to have some magazine pay attention to the labors to which they devoted their lives, but of which the general public remained indifferent or unaware, those experts usually welcomed my intrusion. But if the chance to tag along on other folks' high-octane journeys into the unknown and the unsolved was often a delight, it could also engender a deep frustration. If the subject of a magazine assignment captivated me, I read everything I could about it, interviewed everyone who would talk to me, and often went into the field to watch it happen. For several weeks, or even several months, that world engrossed me. Vicariously I took on the challenges that kept the experts awake at night. Then I wrote the article—and after that it was time to move on to something else. The rupture of tearing myself away from the universe I had so briefly visited could be painful. And too often it damaged my self-esteem, as I wondered if I was, after all, a professional dilettante.

My one-day trip into Lechuguilla embodied just such a heady immersion and rude withdrawal. It was not that I wished to become a caver, but I could see why nothing mattered more to Rick Bridges than finding a new passage in what might be the deepest cave in the United States. I could feel in my nerve endings why exploring the underground fulfilled the dreams of its fanatics as mountaineering had mine. Likewise, my brief journey into the Mato Grosso stunned me with the complexity of the culture of a tiny tribe of unassimilated, marginalized people in Brazil. Ten days with the Suyá was enough for me, but I could see why Tony Seeger had devoted his life to comprehending and championing the tribe's cause.

For *Atlantic*, I dived into the frenetic world of the epigraphers who were cracking the code of Maya hieroglyphics. For *Smithsonian*, I trundled through the deserts of Yemen in 100-degree heat to hunt for stelae marking the frankincense trail that stitched together the Near East two thousand years ago. For *Life*, I searched with Percy Trezise for lost panels of Aboriginal rock art in Queensland. Also for *Smithsonian*, I climbed to the ruined castles left by the Cathars in southwest France who defied the Albigensian Crusade in the thirteenth century, and mused upon the standing stones and passage graves from Avebury to the Orkneys that linger as the inexplicable testament of Neolithic Britons to posterity.

For *National Geographic Adventure,* I interviewed the German photographer Carsten Peter, who dared to get closer to active volcanoes than any sane person should in order to capture the fury of the earth's molten core exploding through its placid crust. I asked Peter what scared him most. His answer surprised me: "Teenage border guards in Africa high on drugs carrying Kalashnikovs." Sometimes I got so involved with my assignment that I lost all touch with what my readers needed to know. For *National Geographic,* I spent four months spread across a year crisscrossing central Europe talking to archaeologists who specialized in the Copper Age, when Ötzi, the Iceman found intact melting out of a glacier on the Austria–Italy border, had lived. Toward the end of my travails, I was chatting with my editor in his office in Washington, DC. "You know," I said, "the wheel was invented in the Copper Age. But what's really fascinating is that the French archaeologists think that the first carts had two wheels, while the Swiss insist they had four." The man gave me a withering look. Then he said, "I don't think our readers give a goddamn whether the carts had two wheels or four." *But wait*, I started to plead, before perspective snapped me back to earth.

If dabbling in the worlds that others think matter more than anything else in life is both the bane and the glory of the freelance life, what all those encounters gave me was a glimpse of the endless richness of adventure. I came away from each immersion filled with admiration for the men and women who counted the days before one more expedition into the heart of their mysteries. In another life, I could have spent years trying to fathom what the runes on the hieroglyphic staircase unearthed just yesterday at Dos Pilas really said, or figuring out how the bluestones at Stonehenge were hauled 200 miles from southwest Wales, or trying to find the deepest cave on earth.

Even when I've spent years on a subject for a book, rather than a magazine article, the fear that I've only scratched the surface bedevils me. In 1997, I came across a forgotten story of an episode in Arctic Svalbard (Spitsbergen) that I decided at once was the most astounding true survival tale I'd ever come across. Its heroes were four Russian walrus hunters who were shipwrecked off the uninhabited island of Edgeøya in 1743. I spent years ransacking libraries from Harvard to London to Paris, then weeks in Russia searching for lost primary sources, ending with a trip to the sailors' remote home town of Mezen, which no American had ever before visited. Most of the time, the journey spawned by the insatiable itch of the old story felt more like a wild goose chase than a proper quest.

At the end of my research, with three companions, I spent thirteen days on Halfmoon Island, just off the coast of Edgeøya, where I believed the walrus hunters had fetched up, as I searched for clues to their ordeal. All four of us agreed: Edgeøya was the most godforsaken place in which we'd ever spent time. Yet when I wrote *Four Against the Arctic*, I was haunted by the knowledge that I had only peeled away the outer skin of the enigma.

The men from Mezen had been cast into their fate carrying only the clothes on their backs, a handful of tools and gear, and 20 pounds of flour for food. They had survived not just for thirteen days, not for a few months, not just through the iron cold and darkness of a single winter, but for six years and three months. Nothing I had ever done, not even the climbs in Alaska of which I was proudest, could compare to that achievement.

———

An illness that may well prove fatal nudges one into this sort of appraisal. And more than other diseases, cancer scares people—not only its victims, but the bystanders who hold their hands, even as they say to themselves, *Thank God it isn't me.* The most empathic of comforters cannot resist the temptation to soften the stark reality of cancer. A few months into my treatment, I was a dinner guest at the home of one of my best friends, a woman who would have dropped whatever she was doing to rush me to the emergency room or just given me a hug whenever I was feeling sorry for myself.

As I picked at the food that was so hard to swallow, she said, "We all get a chance to ride along with you on this journey you've undertaken."

I knew she meant her words as staunch support, but I was in a grouchy mood. "It isn't a journey," I snapped.

She took a long sip of wine. "What is it, then?"

I searched for the right word. "It's an assault."

Language means too much to me, perhaps. In my pedantry, I was cruelly fending off my dear friend's love. But death was in my thoughts. If only the course of a terminal illness should unfold as a journey! Instead, it is something else, something more frightening, something that tears apart one's dignity, loss by tiny loss. Yet even our greatest poets cast the spiral toward death as a journey. For Shakespeare, it is a

voyage into "that undiscovered country from whose bourn / No travel-
ler returns." For Tennyson: "And may there be no moaning of the bar, /
When I put out to sea."

Even before I got sick, another metaphor about cancer set my teeth
on edge, one that is so pervasive in our culture that it emerges in obitu-
aries like a default setting: "So-and-so died after a long and courageous
battle against cancer." For some reason, that trope clings uniquely to
cancer. We do not read about long battles against Alzheimer's, or hepa-
titis C, or diabetes. What's so pernicious about the metaphor is that it
implies that if one had only fought harder, one might have (in John
Wayne's memorable phrase) "licked the Big C." If twenty months of cancer have taught me anything, it's that will is powerless against the blind
proliferation of devouring cells. By casting the course of the illness as a
battle between the self and an invader, our culture implicitly blames
the patient who dies rather than recovers. In her brilliant polemic *Illness as Metaphor* (a book I fear too few oncologists have read), Susan
Sontag nails this point: "Cancer is the 'killer' disease; people who have
cancer are 'cancer victims.' Ostensibly, the illness is the culprit. But it is
also the cancer patient who is made culpable."

The insidious truth about metastasized cancer is that no matter
what kind of temporary stay the best care and the cleverest drugs can
effect, the malady lurks in the body. And sooner or later it comes back.
When it does, it usually appears in a more virulent guise. Of course, we
must all die, and few are the endings that arrive as the ones we would
script for an exit from this world.

What does adventure have to do with all this? For me, the days when
I was afoot in the wilderness, headed toward some uncertain goal, were
the ones when I felt most alive, furthest from death, even when mortality
hovered over my shoulder, as it did on the most dangerous of my climbs.
During those days, the precious spark of existence hummed in my fin-

gertips. Though it may be a romantic delusion, I'd like to think that what we call the zest for adventure lies dormant in all human beings, numbed by the creature comforts of home and the tedium of the job. I'd like to believe that wanderlust is encoded in our DNA, the legacy of the countless eons we spent as nomadic hunter-gatherers, when life itself depended on finding out what lay beyond the horizon, in the next valley over or on the other side of the high hill—so infinitely longer a span than the mere eleven millennia since our ancestors first turned to agriculture and tried to live in dwellings for more than a few weeks at a time. If my romantic notion has any merit, then it would recast "adventure" not as some exploit we choose to pursue, but as the response to an instinct embedded in our genes. It would help me understand why it's so hard to articulate what drove me to adventure and what it gave me in the end.

Consider the monarch butterfly, which rides thermals and wind currents to travel over 2,500 miles from its winter habitat in Mexico to summer destinations as far away as Canada—a journey unthinkable for modern humans unaided by motor vehicles. The butterfly sets out on its epic pilgrimage not by choice, but in response to a genetic injunction as basic as the need for sun and food—an injunction so precise that the fourth generation of monarchs returns to the same oyamel fir trees in Mexico from which its ancestors fled, where it begins the cycle anew. This in a creature whose life span covers at most eight months.

Or consider the gray whale, whose annual migration takes it over 12,000 miles round-trip between its birthing grounds off Baja California and its feeding grounds in Alaska's Beaufort Sea. We know now that whales are intelligent animals, and that they communicate with one another through eerie vocalized cries, some at frequencies lower than the human ear can detect. But what are they saying? Not, I think, "Let's go have an adventure."

I take comfort in the fact that even the greatest explorers have been notoriously poor at explaining why they set off on their quests. Mallory's famous quip about Everest, "Because it's there," may be as good an answer as any.

No one ever wrote about adventure more eloquently than Antoine de Saint-Exupéry. *Wind, Sand and Stars* is an elegy to aviation in the age when flying still depended as much on the nerve and pluck of the pilot as mountaineering or caving does on the skills of its adherents today. His account of his crash landing on a remote plateau in North Africa, and the desperate trek to safety performed by his mechanic Prévot and himself, is as stirring a tale of survival as anyone ever committed to print. A loner by instinct, Saint-Exupéry nevertheless found in the comradeship of the sky the ultimate rationale for risking his life to fly the mail to distant outposts in Africa and South America. In a passage eulogizing his friend Jean Mermoz, who had disappeared in an attempt to fly across the Andes in a malfunctioning airplane, Saint-Exupéry wrote:

> *Old friends cannot be created out of hand. Nothing can match the treasure of common memories, of quarrels and reconciliations and generous emotions....*
>
> *We forget that there is no hope of joy except in human relations. If I summon up those memories that have left me with an enduring savor, if I draw up the balance sheet of the hours in my life that have truly counted, surely I find only those that no wealth could have procured me. True riches cannot be bought. One cannot buy the friendship of a Mermoz, of a companion to whom one is bound forever by ordeals suffered in common. There is no buying the night flight with its hundred thousand stars, its serenity, its few hours of sovereignty. It is not money that can procure for us that new vision of the world won through hardship ...*

Across the fifty-five years during which I pursued adventure in one form or another, companionship of the sort that Saint-Exupéry extols has been the deepest reward, deeper even than, or rather inextricable from, the glory of a first ascent. At the age of nineteen, I formed the first bond with a partner whose kindred passion seemed to transform the act of inching our way up a mountain wall into a transcendent quest. Don Jensen and I met as sophomores at Harvard, and on our first expedition, to Denali's Wickersham Wall in 1963, we shared the rope whenever we could. That blithe success, on top of winter first ascents in the Colorado Rockies, filled Don and me with the youthful conviction that we were invincible, that no mountain could defeat us.

To test our perfect partnership, in 1964 Don and I tackled a smaller but far more difficult challenge, Mount Deborah by its unclimbed east ridge. Instead of rounding up a party of seven, as we had on Denali, we chose, against our mentors' stern advice, to plunge into the Hayes Range as a team of two.

Deborah defeated us 2,000 feet below the summit. During the course of our forty-two-day failure, locked in grim silence next to each other in the too-small tent, roped together on every step we took across three unexplored glaciers, we slowly grew to hate each other. The very sound of Don's chewing as our rations dwindled sent me into a wordless fury, and he signaled his contempt for my days of weakness by shouldering his load and plodding onward. At last a 60-foot crevasse fall that nearly killed Don wrote the end to our misadventure. Yet even in the abyss of that dark dead end, he wanted to go on. It was I who declared the halt and escape that I thought would save our lives.

We parted that summer as enemies. But our bruised feelings slowly healed, and by the next summer we had organized yet another expedition, to Mount Huntington's west face. There we climbed better together than ever, and when we reached the summit on the thirty-fourth day, the finest climb of our youthful careers seemed to restore, if only for the moment, the dream of invincibility that Deborah had shattered.

Yet in the end, Don and I were too different from each other. After Huntington, we drifted apart. Eight years later, in 1973, out of the blue, I learned that Don had been killed on a wet road in Scotland when a truck hit his bicycle. I wept inconsolably, mourning not only his disappearance from the world, but the loss of the illusion of invincibility that had first bound us together. Forty-four years after his death, I mourn Don still.

On Huntington, I cemented the second partnership that seemed to partake of near perfection, in Matt Hale, one year younger than Don and I at Harvard. Shy and deferential, Matt shone in the brilliance of his technical skill on rock. Two years after Huntington, we paired again on the longest expedition of our careers, to the untrodden range we named the Revelation Mountains. Among the six of us, Matt was the strongest climber. When, on the forty-ninth day of the expedition, he and I turned back only 750 feet below the summit of the Angel, the most beautiful of the peaks surrounding our base camp, after four previous attempts by our team on its south ridge, we stained our souls for life with the steepest pang we would ever suffer of *Oh, what might have been!*

Matt is still, in 2017, one of my closest friends in the world. During the decades after the Revelations, we climbed together all over the Lower 48, as well as in France and Italy, and we shared all kinds of other adventures ranging from Mali to Kashmir and Ladakh. In my beloved Southwest, Matt became the steady companion of one jaunt after another in search of prehistoric ruins and rock art.

At Hampshire College, where I started teaching in 1970, I met two other of my longest-tenured cronies in adventure, in the persons of Ed Ward, whom I bumped into by chance at a local crag, and Jon Krakauer, who showed up in 1972 as an impressionable student in the third year of the college's existence. Ed and Jon soon became inseparable partners on the rope, not only with me but with each other. On the two finest climbs of my life after Huntington, the first ascents of Shot Tower in the Brooks Range in 1971 and of the southeast face of Mount Dickey in the Ruth Gorge in 1974, Ed was the driving force. On my one expedition with Jon, to the Tombstone Range in the Yukon in 1975, our friendship was sealed in a single terrifying moment, when, as he tried to push the last pitch up a 1,000-foot wall, on sketchy ground with no protection, a foothold broke and he fell through space. All that attached us to the world was my hanging belay. As Jon flew past me, I hunkered against the rock, screaming to myself, *Hold on!* The belay did its job, though I ended up with a mangled left hand, Jon with bad bruises but no broken bones. Only 50 feet short of the summit, we had to back off the whole wall, setting up one exhausted rappel after another. That moment in the Yukon dusk remains the closest call Jon has undergone in the mountains.

Only a few years later, he and I became comrades in writing, after I persuaded him to give up pounding nails to support his climbing habit and try crafting articles and books for a living instead.

Long after Jon and I became friends, I formed the last of my enduring partnerships in adventure, when I talked Greg Child, who had moved to Utah in the late 1990s, into coming along with me on a hike down a canyon on Cedar Mesa full of Anasazi wonders. I had known Greg casually for years, as we shared the occasional beer at meetings of the American Alpine Club. I was in awe of him as a climber, for I knew that this Aussie genius, fourteen years my junior, had an all-around record matched by no climber of his generation: cutting-edge firsts as a teenager in the Blue Mountains, new routes on El Capitan in Yosemite, big-wall breakthroughs on Baffin Island and in Alaska, and daring triumphs in the Karakoram and the Himalaya on such cynosures as Shivling, Gasherbrum IV, and K2. The Anasazi bug bit Greg as keenly as it had me. During the last fifteen years, Greg has been my partner on my happiest excursions into the lost world of the Old Ones, on which his talent as a climber and his gimlet eye for the faintest of fugitive traces have delivered us to sites no one else has visited in at least seven hundred years.

As of 2017, Matt, Ed, Jon, Greg, and I still climb together, no matter how modest our outings, and the camaraderie and cajolery that ricochet among us remind me every time of Saint-Exupéry's "new vision of the world won through hardship." The forging of friendships too deep for words is almost never the reason we set off into the wilderness to probe the unknown. But in the end, it is what glows in memory.

In October 2016, Sharon and I celebrated our forty-ninth wedding anniversary. It was a gray, chilly late autumn day, and, limited by my fatigue, we contented ourselves with a pokey drive along back roads to some of the colonial towns north and west of Boston—Carlisle, Littleton, Groton, and the like. In Concord we hiked a short piece of the trail memorializing the ragtag American army's holding off the Redcoats in 1775, the trail of Emerson's "shot heard round the world." We asked a stranger to use our camera to shoot a couple of pictures of ourselves, one of which I liked enough to print up and frame in a small mount that now stands perched on our living room cabinet—an image that captures my emaciated feebleness but also the happiness of that day.

We met in a creative writing class at the University of Denver in 1966, during my first year of graduate school and Sharon's last as an undergrad. We got married only a year and a half later, at ages twenty-four and twenty-three—too young, perhaps, but we knew we were in love in a way neither of us had felt before. Our wedding day came only two months after I had emerged from the Revelation Range, still throbbing with the joys and terrors of the longest expedition I would ever go on, and one of the three or four most intense. Already I was planning another venture among unclimbed mountains in the Far North for the coming summer.

After five straight years of coming to grips with the challenges of the Alaska Range, in all its glaciated and storm-tossed glory, I had set my sights on the Brooks Range, at latitude 67 a good 60 miles north of the Arctic Circle, but an outback I knew to be far gentler than the environs of Denali or Deborah or the Kichatna Spires. Sharon had spent little time in the outdoors before she met me, but I dragged her along on hikes up 13ers in Colorado's Front Range and tied her in for beginner climbs on the Flatirons in hopes she would take to the magic of ascent. Nothing came easily for her, and she never tamed the primal fear of the void that yawned beneath her boot soles. But she was game.

In the summer of 1966, only weeks after we had met, I talked Sharon into spending the summer with me in Anchorage, where I had snagged a job teaching English on an air force base, a lucrative penance that would allow me to head off to the Kichatnas in September. We rented a squalid one-room shack in a dingy suburb of Spenard. Sharon got a job as a sales clerk in the sewing department of J. C. Penney. Neither of us had ever cohabited with a lover before, and the claustrophobic intimacy of those months took its toll, but we survived that summer and the school year that followed. Then, throughout August 1967, while I was out of touch in the Revelation Range, Sharon endured a lonely month on a pioneer homestead in Homer, Alaska. Under the mistaken notion that she was a welcome guest, she holed up in a barn, subsisting on white bread and Coca-Cola, while the dysfunctional family that took her in like a stray cat acted out their deep-rooted craziness all around her.

Undaunted, Sharon came along on my two expeditions to the Brooks Range in 1968 and 1969. From the start, the rigors of those month-long campaigns, which I had advertised as easy-going larks, tested her nerve and stamina to the breaking point. The first summer, we landed with two teammates who were serious climbers on a gravel bar near the headwaters of the Noatak River, then backpacked for three days and 25 miles up nameless valleys and across an ancient Inupiat pass to base camp under unclimbed Mount Igikpak, the highest summit in the western Brooks Range. For Sharon, the trek was an unrelieved ordeal—a 45-pound load, hordes of mosquitoes, tundra tussocks that threatened to sprain her ankles with every wobbly step. And she was terrified of bears, though we carried a 30.06 rifle with which we had both fired a couple of practice rounds back in Denver. Indeed, as we deduced from fresh scat the next morning, a bear had walked right through our camp on the pass as we slept, and the next morning we spotted a massive grizzly browsing among the bushes just across the stream that led to base camp.

Still, Sharon settled in to the empty magnificence of the Brooks Range. We had our halcyon off-days, when she and I went off to fish for trout in a pocket lake, or sunbathed on tundra shelves, or filled our bowls with ripe blueberries plucked from thickets close to camp. But then, as the three of us climbers set off to figure out a way to get up Igikpak, Sharon sat alone in our tent, the loaded rifle laid across her lap, trying to read and not count the minutes, listening for the thud of paws on the ground, while we were gone for two days before coming back bursting with summit pride.

Likewise the next summer in the Arrigetch Peaks, when my comrades and I claimed the first ascents of Ariel and Caliban and the Albatross while Sharon hunkered alone in camp. In August 1969, there were no mosquitoes, because freakish early snowstorms ruled the month, so Sharon wrapped herself in our double sleeping bag as she waited and wondered what to do if we didn't come back. We ended that expedition with a float trip down the Alatna River, and during those lazy days, sharing a Klepper kayak with me, she lapsed into a reverie that made up for the anxious vigils of the previous weeks.

After Sharon came into my life, the untroubled commitment that carried me into expeditions became more complicated. At the end of our summer spent in the boxy shack in Spenard, she flew back to Colorado as I flew in to an unnamed glacier in the Kichatnas. By now, Sharon knew enough about Alaskan mountains, and enough about me, to gauge how risky any climbing expedition was. Back at DU, soldiering through classes in Shakespeare and the English novel, she worried about me. And in our base camp igloo on the glacier, I worried about her worrying. We had no radio, no phone, no way to get in touch to tell her, *Don't be afraid—everything is all right.* The invisible threads that stretched 3,000 miles between us mired me in a new ambivalence. On Denali, Deborah, and Huntington, nothing going on in the outside world had disturbed my dreams. There, the universe had reduced to the mountain and the men I had paired with to solve its puzzles.

In 1966, a pattern that would persist throughout our married life emerged. "Be careful," Sharon always whispered as we kissed goodbye, but I carried that pledge of love with me into every new adventure like a stone in my pack. Even through the decades after I stopped climbing in Alaska, that strange tension warped the bond between us. *If only she wouldn't worry,* I often said to myself, knowing not only that she could not help it, but that in an odd way her concern gave me an anchor.

When I began to write for a living, I would head off to Mali or Brazil or New Guinea, Svalbard or Ethiopia or China, often for as long as a month at a stretch. It was a blessing that in those days it was impossible to phone home from a Dogon village or an uninhabited island in the Barents Sea, for however welcome some burst of contact might have proved, it would have diluted my resolve and only redoubled Sharon's anxiety. Among younger adventurers in our more connected times, I've seen how the sat phone and the radio can undercut the headlong flight of a mission into the unknown, or vex the one who waits at home with the intermittent pain of separation.

We decided early on not to have children. I was sure that kids would further attenuate the single-minded zeal I needed to pursue my phantoms, and I knew that a writer who traveled more than two hundred days a year would have made a negligent parent. Though Sharon was not so sure at first about childlessness, as her career as a psychoanalyst began to flourish, she learned to cherish her independence as keenly as I did mine.

You cannot be married for forty-nine years without going through rocky stretches, and we had our share of those, our bitter quarrels, our temptations to flee. But we never came close to divorce, chiefly because, I think, we never ceased to respect and admire each other. Sharon's worries when I was incommunicado were normal, not neurotic. As for me, I never quite realized how much I depended on her, how much I counted on her being there, until my own freedom was irrevocably threatened.

The onset of cancer in June 2015 changed the dynamic between us profoundly. Under the onslaught of chemotherapy and radiation, I grew too weak to drive or shop or cook. When my exercise was limited to a halting walk of a single block, Sharon took my arm and helped me sit on some neighborhood wall to catch my breath. On bad mornings, I needed help getting out of bed or getting dressed. When I vomited into the toilet, she held my shoulders and wiped my mouth afterward. Several times I fainted at home, once keeling over backward in the bathroom, cracking my back and head against marble sills and walls. Sharon came running and got me slowly back on my feet. A hundred times she drove me to Dana–Farber or Brigham and Women's, and sat through the waiting room ennui and the sessions with men and women in white coats, asking the sharp questions I was too confused to articulate. On the two or three occasions when a doctor botched my treatment, she batted away their obfuscations and took them relentlessly to task.

The worst times of all came during my hospitalizations, seven or eight of them all told. Drugged up with intravenous feeds and painkillers, I sometimes lost track of where I was, or why. But hour after hour, day after day, Sharon was there, sleeping on a cot or in an armchair beside my bed to see me through another night in hell. My nadir came in October 2015, at the end of my last radiation zapping, when I contracted aspiration pneumonia and came close to death. I lay immobile, in so much pain despite the morphine drip that in rare semi-lucid moments I thought, *It wouldn't be so bad to give up now and die. It would be a relief.* But always Sharon was there, the anguish on her face, her hand stroking my brow, her lips bending near for a kiss. For her alone, I had to live.

I believe that the ordeal of my cancer, which continues even now, actually took a greater toll on Sharon than it did on me. She effectively gave up her practice as a psychoanalyst to take care of the invalid I had become. I was not the only one who saw her caring as nothing short of heroic—out of her earshot, some of my closest friends told me, "I hope you know how lucky you are to have her with you." Often I wondered if I could have done the same for her, and the guilty answer wormed to the surface: *Of course not. You're too selfish.*

So often during the decades of our marriage, I had felt Sharon's fears for my safety, whenever I ran off toward the exotic promise of yet another adventure, as a drag on my freedom, a yearning for intimacy between us that I feared like a barbed wire threatening to fence in my spirit. But now, post-cancer, I recognize that I craved that island of safety as longingly as she did, that as much as I thought I needed to flee from the oasis of domestic tranquility, its absence had left a hole in my life. Love in its purest form had always terrified me. Was it too late now to look for it?

In July 1970, in the third year of our marriage, Sharon and I shared the only expedition I ever concocted for just the two of us. A month before, I had graduated from the University of Denver with my PhD in English, while Sharon secured her MA in the same discipline. I had landed a teaching job in Amherst, Massachusetts, at Hampshire College, an "experimental" school that would open its doors the next September. It was a hectic sprint to the finish line for both of us, but also the crossing of a new threshold half a continent away in New England.

In early June, I skipped the DU graduation and set off at once for my eighth Alaskan expedition. On a spur-of-the-moment whim, Hank Abrons, my former teammate from Denali, and I decided to head for the Kichatnas, where four years earlier our team of five had made the first ascent of that small but spectacular range's highest peak. On a two-man expedition planned for only twenty days, Hank and I hoped to bag the second highest summit, a graceful pyramid called Middle Triple Peak, which I had admired in 1966.

Hank and I were out of shape, however, and weeks of storm loaded even the gentlest ridges with treacherous plumes and cornices of snow through which it was impossible to dig to reach the solid granite beneath. Not only did we never set foot on Middle Triple (whose first ascent would fall to a pair of brilliant alpinists six years later), but we failed on the smaller, easier peak we chose as a consolation prize. As we hiked out to Rainy Pass Lodge, I felt stung by the first unequivocal failure among my eight Alaskan quests for new routes and first ascents.

A few days later, I met Sharon in Anchorage before we took a commercial flight to Dillingham, a fishing port on Bristol Bay in western Alaska. The objective of our two-person jaunt was the Tikchik Lakes, in a swath of wilderness I had discovered not from the air but via a perusal of the maps. The Tikchik–Wood River system, unique in Alaska, was a set of eight major lakes, all of them long and skinny and aligned east–

west, stacked back to back like firewood, ranging from 10 to 80 miles north of Dillingham. The eastern ends of the lakes sprawled out into the taiga lowlands, but the western ends headed in cirques carved out of an unexplored massif of peaks ranging up to 5,000 feet in height. Only one of the peaks, Mount Konarut, had an official name.

My plan was to focus on the two most northern lakes, called Chauekuktuli and Nuyakuk, which were linked on their eastern ends by a stream that flowed from the former into the latter. We would land by float plane at the head of Chauekuktuli, then paddle during eighteen leisurely days the lengths of both lakes, covering a mere 67 miles, toward a pickup on the west end of Nuyakuk. We would have time to poke into the countless arms and bays of both lakes, as well, I hoped, as climb some of the peaks that loomed in the west. We might even hike across a low pass to the northernmost lake of the Wood River chain.

Yet as we flew in with a local pilot on July 5, I was in a sour mood, still castigating myself for Hank's and my feckless performance in the Kichatnas, and hoping to bag some unnamed summits to assuage the previous month's failure. The craft we would use to conduct our journey was the two-man Klepper kayak I had bought the year before, in which we had floated happily down the Alatna River at the end of our Brooks Range excursion the previous August. The Klepper was a collapsible boat made of a lightweight wooden frame and a canvas-and-rubber shell with inflatable side tubes. It was ideal for wilderness voyages, since you could pack it up and check it as airline baggage or for portages from one stream to another, but pretty much worthless in even easy whitewater, as Sharon and I had learned the hard way in June 1969. Infatuated by my new toy, I had talked Sharon into putting in on the Colorado River upstream from Moab, Utah. A few miles along, we hit a wave sideways and flipped. Saved by the life jackets we had bought the previous week, we wasted all our strength trying crawl on top of the kayak, which rotated like a barrel under our desperate thrashings, as we were swept another mile through more rapids before eddying out. Sharon swallowed a lot of water and thought she was going to drown.

That I aspired to travel at all in a kayak, since water scared me and I had never learned to swim, could be chalked up to counter-phobic obstinacy. But I also thought that since Sharon would never be comfortable as my climbing partner, we might find a wilderness idyll we could share in a boat. I went into our journey expecting a laid-back vacation, a "no-push, no-suffs trip," as I called it in my diary. But for me Alaska was inseparable from ambition. I also planned a several-day circuit away from the head of Chauekuktuli, as we climbed the peaks above its western end and maybe even bagged Konarut, which for all I knew awaited its first ascent. The names of the lakes were Yupik Eskimo, so I also hoped to find vestiges left by ancient hunters on the shores and slopes, as we had near base camp below Igikpak.

We set up our three-week supply of food in a cache covered with a plastic tarp, and headed the next morning for the heights. At once we ran into all but impenetrable alder thickets, some of the worst I had ever tried to bash through in Alaska, and the mosquitoes were relentless. Within hours, Sharon was in tears. We retreated, used the Klepper to move camp, and made a second start the next day, up a slash in the hillside where avalanches had torn loose most of the bushes.

In the end, we accomplished only a timid three-day loop among the foothills above Chauekuktuli, reaching a single summit on which we stacked rocks to claim the first ascent. Our only map was a 1:250,000 quad, four miles to the inch. As I crowed in my diary, "The map is so bad nothing gibes. Altitudes are meaningless. The cirque above us doesn't even show, and the peaks can't be determined. It's really neat, in a way." I never saw Konarut, or if I did, I didn't know it.

But Sharon was unhappy. On our first day, we came across bear scat so fresh it was still steaming. She hardly slept that night, thinking about bears and worrying about our cache, which we had safeguarded only by scattering ammonia pellets around the tarp. Throughout the trip, Sharon would agonize day and night about bears, and once we were launched on the lakes, she lived in fear of waves blown up by the wind that might capsize our Klepper. All of the quarrels we had during our eighteen days on the Tikchiks were about bears, and caches, and dangerous waves. I pooh-poohed her fears and tried to rationalize away the risks that I claimed were imaginary.

In retrospect, all these years later, I recognize how cruel was my cavalier dismissal of Sharon's qualms. And I grant now that she was right about the dangers. Depending on ammonia pellets to keep bears (or other critters) away from our food cache was a haphazard bargain at best, though in 1970 there were few other options. The hefty canisters that are now required for food storage in places like Gates of the Arctic National Park (which encloses my beloved Arrigetch Peaks) had yet to be invented, and on the west end of Chauekuktuli there were no trees from which to hang our supplies. On our Igikpak expedition in 1968, we had left a food cache in a neighboring valley. A week later, when we retrieved it, we discovered that a bear had found our goodies and commenced to gorge on our candy bars and raisin bran. By sheer good luck, one of the animal's first bites gouged a hole in a can of compressed butane. The burst of super-cooled stove fuel point-blank in the face had evidently sent the bear into headlong flight.

Having hiked past half a dozen grizzlies browsing among the lowland bushes on my previous expeditions without provoking a charge, and having twice before had bears walk right through camp as we slept, I had grown blasé about the threats posed by *Ursus horribilis*. On Igikpak and in the Arrigetch, we had toted a 30.06 through a month of wanderings without ever having to load and aim it, let alone fire. Yet other climbers in the Far North had had to shoot bears that invaded their base camps, and I was aware of those rare events when bears had killed unwary hikers in the Alaska wilderness. So serene was I in my overconfidence, however, that I had not even brought a pistol to the Tikchik Lakes.

Later in the trip, as we boated down Chauekuktuli and Nuyakuk, the waves whipped up by steady winds gave me pause, and several times I acceded to Sharon's fears and stayed put in camp rather than launching out against the whitecaps. But our arguments were always one-sided, Sharon pleading for caution against my sanguine assessment, "It doesn't look so bad out there." I should have learned from our spill on the Colorado just how unstable the Klepper was when buffeted by waves, and though I was a novice paddler I floated in the Tikchiks on the surface of my ignorance. Many years later, in Patagonia, a world-class mountaineer and kayaker, Doug Tompkins, founder of The North Face and Esprit, had his kayak overturn in high winds on a lake that would normally have been child's play for him. He died of hypothermia before his mates could rescue him.

Had Sharon and I flipped the Klepper on Chauekuktuli or Nuyakuk, we might not have perished at once, but if we had lost our boat or even just the gear and food we had stored fore and aft, we would have faced a desperate fight to survive. We had no radio, and sat phone use in the wilderness was still decades in the future.

I had hoped that the weather in the Tikchiks would partake of the benign pattern that obtained in the Brooks Range, but alas, the storms we waited out were all too reminiscent of the gales and blizzards of the Alaska Range. A week into our trip, we were marooned by three days of wind and nonstop rain a few degrees above freezing. We lay in our double sleeping bag, reading the few books we had brought as slowly as we could, scrounging for topics for conversation. The driftwood branches scattered along the lakeshore were so thoroughly soaked we couldn't keep a campfire going. I had gone into our Tikchik trip expecting a relaxing lark in a landscape much tamer than the glacial immensities of Denali and Deborah, but now I was awed by the raw grandeur of our surroundings. "It's a wild, often gloomy place," I confessed to my diary on July 9, "and the two of us seem very alone in it." And on July 15: "I can't rid myself of the sense of size and emptiness and 'Alaskan-ness' of the place."

Day by day, we grew accustomed to the strangeness of our wilderness, and by midway through our 67-mile journey, we found whole hours of tranquil delight to counterbalance the gloom. Birds were everywhere: flocks of ducks and geese skittering along the lake's surface, hawks and eagles soaring high above us as they rode thermals, the plaintive cries of gulls and terns and loons wafting from dark cliffs we floated past. On calm days the lake turned into a glassy mirror, reflecting the distant hillsides in inverted duplicate images. When the sun came out, we threw off our jackets and paddled in T-shirts. Each morning as we climbed into the Klepper, we clasped hands, and Sharon leaned back from her front seat to give me a good-luck kiss. During the first days our arms had ached from paddling, but now we were fit, and our swiveling strokes blended in a thoughtless choreography. Since we had seen no bears during the first twelve days, Sharon began to relax.

On July 17, we neared the western end of Lake Nuyakuk, five days ahead of our scheduled float-plane pickup. A pair of coves, called Portage Arm and Mirror Bay, nestled beneath the nameless peaks beyond. We could spend the remaining time leisurely exploring those sheltered mini-lakes. I had lost my peak-bagging ambitions: instead, I was content to poke among the miniature surprises that lay nearer at hand.

And then we found the perfect campsite. Half a mile inside Portage Arm, we came upon a small island just offshore. We pulled the Klepper out of the water to check the place out. Only a few yards back we found a clearing in the bushes swathed in a lush carpet of tundra. We pitched our tent there and sprawled inside. The tundra beneath the floor felt like a limitless mattress of down. Just outside the tent, instead of a sandy shore, a geologic quirk called greenstone pillows shelved into the water, sensuously curved like waves caught in mid-splash. Not far away, we found enough dry alder and willow branches for a week's worth of campfires.

We spent our last five days on the island. Because we were separated from the coast of Portage Arm, Sharon felt completely safe for the first time during the whole expedition. (Bears can swim, of course, but why would they bother?) On the warmest day of all, we took off our clothes and basked on the greenstone pillows. Then we tiptoed over to the tundra cushion beside the tent, where we made love, our skin bare to the sky and sun, our souls in harmony with our temporary universe—and with each other.

I reread my Tikchik diary recently. It left me disappointed—all the talk of miles paddled, of topography unraveled, of rations and weather and schedules calibrated. Why had I not paused for a single day to reflect, to try to place our eighteen-day trip in context? By the end, it became the idyll I had hoped it would be. Why did I not try to weigh just how that brief escape from our normal lives fit into the uncertain journey Sharon and I had pledged to make through life together?

Years later, at a time when Sharon still dreamed of a career as a writer, she put a poem on paper that plumbed the murky depths of our time in Alaska in a way I never could. It ends with a rueful reminiscence of those days on Chauekuktuli and Nuyakuk:

> Between your loves and mine
> that summer on the Tikchik lakes
> we found a small island
> the size of a wilderness
> which made you happy
> and me safe
> Remember the anniversaries we had
> the glacial distance through the maze

black rain for days the small
fires on rock where I read
you were a wonder then
dreaming a route the lakes to the sea

What if we had needed it
I would have thought we were dead
you would have thought alive
even now the difference rivers
between us the trivial drift of summer
until we flood when it thunders.

———

Every couple that weathers the vicissitudes of a life together, that resists the temptation to chuck it in and start over, must confront the prospect of a last act to the play that fate weaves around its long trajectory. Barring a catastrophic accident—a car crash, a house burning down, an avalanche scouring the face of a mountain—one partner will in all likelihood die before the other. It is a denouement impossible to prepare for. I saw it happen to my mother, who lived on for seventeen years after my father died in 1990.

Throughout the decades of our marriage, Sharon and I never really talked about the scenario that seemed to lie so far in the future. But during the last year and a half, we have not been able to keep it far from our minds for very long. Still, we have scarcely discussed it, as if keeping our fears unarticulated might push the event further into the fog of the future.

Given, however, all the depredations that cancer has wreaked upon my body, and given the normal course of metastasis, I am pretty certain that I will die before she does. Illness drastically narrows one's imaginative scope. During the depths of my worst tribulations, when I lay in a hospital bed clinging to life, I could barely think beyond the pain and confusion. The world outside me shrank and dimmed; all I cared about was taking the next breath. Though death might be happening to me, it seemed an abstract matter: a pity, no doubt, and a nuisance, but not a turn of events over which I had much control.

During the last several months of even keel since my last medical crisis, however, I have turned my thoughts toward ultimate things. Yet it seems hard to reach beyond the threads of fantasy that float through my mind. As human beings, perhaps uniquely among the creatures on earth, we know that we are going to die. In an ideal world, we would claim the privilege of writing the script that trails toward the final page. Instead, thanks to doctors and hospitals and the desperate hope for another chance, the end usually arrives as an insensate spiral into coma, or in the smother of morphine dulling the sharp edge of pain. We are left all but powerless to orchestrate our last moments among the living.

For one who does not believe in God, prayer is a waste of time. In its place, I have only hope, or wish.

What I wish for, then, in that last conscious moment before the darkness closes in forever, is not the shining memory of some summit underfoot that I was the first to reach, not the gleam of yet another undiscovered land on the horizon, but the touch of Sharon's fingers as she clasps my hand in hers, unwilling to let go.

Note on Sources

CHAPTER 1: FARTHEST NORTH

Fridtjof Nansen's classic expedition narrative, *Farthest North,* first published in 1897, is available in an excellent Modern Library paperback edition (New York: 1999). Roland Huntford's biography, *Nansen: The Explorer as Hero* (London: 1997), offers valuable information about the later careers of both Nansen and Johansen.

CHAPTER 2: BLANK ON THE MAP

Eric Shipton's account of the 1937 reconnaissance of the Karakoram, *Blank on the Map,* is available in the omnibus *Eric Shipton: The Six Mountain-Travel Books* (Seattle: 1985). Jim Perrin, in *Shipton and Tilman: The Great Decade of Himalayan Exploration* (London: 2013), imparts details of the long and complex relationship between the two great explorers that their own writings do not cover. Ang Tharkay's *Sherpa: The Memoir of Ang Tharkay* (Seattle: 2016) presents a publishing enigma. The book was originally dictated in English to a mysterious go-between named Basil P. Norton, but no trace of an original English edition can be found. First published in French as *Mémoires d'un Sherpa* (Paris: 1954), the book was retranslated into English only in 2016 by Mountaineers Books.

Shipton's beguiling memoir, *That Untravelled World,* which first appeared in 1969, has likewise been reprinted by Mountaineers Books (Seattle: 2015).

CHAPTER 3: PREHISTORIC 5.10

Marjorie Nicolson's *Mountain Gloom and Mountain Glory* (Ithaca, NY: 1959) is the classic exposition of the revolution in the Western aesthetic of nature wrought by the Romantic era. Antoine de Ville's *procès-verbal* about the 1492 ascent of Mount Aiguille is reprinted in W. A. B. Coolidge's *Josias Simler et les Origines de l'Alpinisme* (Grenoble: 1904). Peter Hansen's *The Summits of Modern Man* (Cambridge, MA: 2013) contains the dubious claim that shepherds regularly climbed Mount Aiguille in the sixteenth century.

A good overview of the two-decade effort by the Dutch archaeological team to analyze the culture of the Tellem of Mali can be found in Rogier Bedaux's "Tellem: Reconnaissance Archéologique d'une Culture de l'Ouest Africain au Moyen Age," in *Journal de la Société des Africanistes* (Paris: 1972), 103–85. My own account of a month in Mali investigating the Tellem achievement appears in *Escape Routes* (Seattle: 1997). Keith Muscutt's *Warriors of the Clouds* (Albuquerque, NM: 1998) offers a good overview of the Chachopoya. Tony Howard's "The Bedouin: Hunting Routes of Rum" is available online at http://www.nomadstravel.co.uk/files/8514/1856/8483/Bedouin_Hunting_Routes_of_Rum_by_Tony_Howard.pdf.

CHAPTER 4: FIRST DESCENT

Richard Bangs's moving essay "First Bend on the Baro" is reprinted in Cameron O'Connor and John Lazenby, eds., *First Descents: In Search of Wild Rivers* (Birmingham, AL: 1989). My own "Rafting with the BBC" appears in *Moments of Doubt* (Seattle: 1986). Bangs's account of the Tekeze expedition centers his memoir, *The Last River* (San Francisco: 2001). My own "First Down the Tekeze" is reprinted in *Escape Routes* (Seattle: 1997).

Ben Stookesberry's river-running exploits are detailed on his Facebook site, at https://www.facebook.com/redonkulous2u.

CHAPTER 5: FIRST CONTACT

The film *First Contact* was released in 1983 in Australia. Bob Connolly and Robin Anderson's book, *First Contact*, which includes much detail not covered in the film, was published in the United States by Viking Penguin (New York: 1987). *The Land that Time Forgot*, by Michael Leahy and Maurice Crain (New York: 1937), gives Leahy's own (expurgated) account of his adventures in the New Guinea highlands.

My interview with photographer Michael Friedel appeared in *American Photo*, September/October 1990. My account of the last twenty-five years of the Chiricahua Apache wars against the Mexican and American governments, *Once They Moved Like the Wind*, was published by Simon & Schuster (New York: 1993).

CHAPTER 6: THE UNDISCOVERED EARTH

A good introduction to the painted Paleolithic caves in Spain and France can be found in Gregory Curtis's *The Cave Painters* (New York: 2006). Cenote expert Sam Meacham's website, which contains his philosophy of exploration, is at www.meachamdiving.com.

James Tabor's excellent chronicle about the quest for the world's deepest cave is *Blind Descent* (New York: 2010). Bill Stone and Barbara am Ende narrate their own efforts to push the Huautla and Chevé cave systems in *Beyond the Deep* (New York: 2002).

Michael Wejchert's account of his attempt on the south face of Mount Deborah in Alaska, "Epigoni, Revisited," appeared in *Appalachia*, winter/spring 2014.

A c k n o w l e d g m e n t s

By the time I started work on this book, cancer had left me so weak that I knew even the most routine kinds of research would prove exhausting or impossible. For weeks at a time, visits to the Harvard libraries, whose scholarly treasure I had mined for decades, were beyond my powers. I love doing research, and never before had I hired an assistant to help me hunt down texts and testimonies hidden among the stacks and archives. Now I needed to.

In Madeline Miller, I struck 24-carat gold. Why a Harvard postdoc in earth and planetary sciences at the start of her brilliant career might find it worth her while to unearth a fifteenth-century legal document in French or interview a cave diver in backwoods Mexico via a scratchy telephone connection baffles me to this day, yet Madeline not only aced these tasks but came up with leads and lore I would never have discovered on my own. It helped that she is a climber, scuba diver, and adventurer in her own right. That she's become my friend is a blessing I could not have anticipated.

Several experts in their fields aided me with their insights and opinions. In particular, I am grateful to old pals Richard Bangs and Judi Wineland for their elucidation of river-running triumphs and Maasai

enigmas, respectively, and to new acquaintance Sam Meacham for
making the unthinkably scary business of exploring Yucatán's cenotes
comprehensible to a scribbler who's never learned to swim.

The companions who shared my own adventures in the wilderness
during the last sixty years, from childhood through 2017, are too numerous to salute here. I hope the glow of satisfaction and excitement still
warms their souls as it does mine. From my new vantage point of the
physical handicaps cancer has wrought, I cherish those exploits more
keenly than ever. Thanks to all of those friends for lacing up their boots
to join me.

Two of them, Matt Hale and Ed Ward, read my book in draft. Their
comments helped me steer the course on which I had set out with only
a balky compass and a sketchy map.

This is the fifteenth book for which Stuart Krichevsky has served as
my agent. No partner of any kind has been more valuable to my writing
career during the last seventeen years. Stuart is that marvelous rarity—
an agent who still loves books, no matter how many wrangles he's
undergone in the ceaseless struggle to bring them to print. He's also a
witty fellow with a sense of humor that would have made Buster Keaton
smile. Whenever a new idea for a book swims into my ken, a single voice
in my head—half stern superego, half hearty cheerleader—delivers a
Krichevskian verdict long before I talk to the man himself. Over the
years, Stuart has filled his office with super-competent colleagues and
assistants. My occasional interactions with those folks have always left
me impressed with their diligence and judgment.

When I got sick in the summer of 2015, one of my darkest premoni-
tions sprouted from the insecurity all writers nurse like stubborn
weeds. I thought, *No publisher is going to take a chance on an author who
may be dying of cancer.* The fear was acute enough that I briefly pondered staying mum about my condition. To the contrary, in Star Law-

rence at W. W. Norton & Company, I have an editor who voiced his faith in my continued work as a writer. I am delighted to be embarking on my fourth book with a man of such compassion and integrity, who behaves as though he were unaware of his status as a publishing legend.

At Norton, Sarah Bolling and Laura Usselman deftly managed all the checks and balances that go into turning a manuscript into a book. And Allegra Huston, on her third go-round with me, proved again to be a model of perception and restraint, as her copyediting improved my prose on page after page, while she never quarreled with my arguments even at their crankiest.

That I was able to finish the job of writing this book depended month after month on the skills of doctors and nurses who not only kept me alive but for the most part compos mentis. The experts at Dana–Farber Cancer Institute in Boston who took charge of my case wrung from me thankfulness that often brought me to tears. Foremost among these savants was my primary oncologist, Dr. Guilherme Rabinowits, a man of great wisdom conjoined with deep empathy.

For my wife of forty-nine years, Sharon Roberts, nothing I say here can adequately express my gratitude and love. In order to take care of me after July 2015, Sharon effectively curtailed her flourishing career as a psychoanalyst. When neuropathy in my right hand and arm made typing on a word processor too arduous, I resorted to writing longhand. Then I dictated my chapters to Sharon as she typed them up, paying heed to every diacritical mark and parenthetical aside. What a strange way for her to read my book! It was as if she were listening to the audio version even as she offered suggestions how to make it better.

Far deeper than my debt to her skills as my amanuensis is the knowledge that I simply could not have survived the last twenty-two months without Sharon. In the hospital during my many incarcerations, and even at home in Watertown, there were many dark nights of both soul and body. Whatever source fills the wellsprings of love and commitment, Sharon's seems limitless.

I hope that in this book, particularly in the last chapter, I have returned a small portion of her love, even as I voice my admiration for her as a person. And I pledge what months and years I have left on earth to sharing the intricate wonder of existence with her.

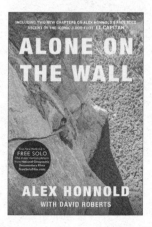
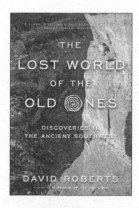
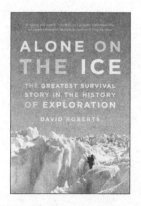